The Good Drone

While the military use of drones has been the subject of much scrutiny, the use of drones for humanitarian purposes has so far received little attention. As the starting point for this study, it is argued that the prospect of using drones for humanitarian and other life-saving activities has produced an alternative discourse on drones, dedicated to developing and publicizing the endless possibilities that drones have for "doing good." Furthermore, it is suggested that the Good Drone narrative has been appropriated back into the drone warfare discourse, as a strategy to make war "more human."

This book explores the role of the Good Drone as an organizing narrative for political projects, technology development and humanitarian action. Its contribution to the debate is to take stock of the multiple logics and rationales according to which drones are "good," with a primary objective to initiate a critical conversation about the political currency of "good." This study recognizes the many possibilities for the use of drones and takes these possibilities seriously by critically examining the difference the drones' functionalities can make, but also what difference the presence of drones themselves – as unmanned and flying objects – makes. Discussed and analyzed are the implications for the drone industry, user communities, and the areas of crisis where drones are deployed.

Kristin Bergtora Sandvik is Associate Professor at the Department of Criminology and Sociology of Law at the University of Oslo, and Senior Researcher at the Peace Research Institute Oslo (PRIO). She holds a doctorate from Harvard Law School.

Maria Gabrielsen Jumbert is Senior Researcher at PRIO and the Director of the Norwegian Centre for Humanitarian Studies. She holds a PhD from the Institut d'Etudes Politiques, SciencesPo Paris.

Emerging technologies, ethics and international affairs
Series editors:
Jai C. Galliott, *The University of New South Wales, Australia*
Avery Plaw, *University of Massachusetts, USA*
Katina Michael, *University of Wollongong, Australia*

This series examines the crucial ethical, legal and public policy questions arising from or exacerbated by the design, development and eventual adoption of new technologies across all related fields, from education and engineering to medicine and military affairs.

The books revolve around two key themes:

* Moral issues in research, engineering and design.
* Ethical, legal and political/policy issues in the use and regulation of technology.

This series encourages submission of cutting-edge research monographs and edited collections with a particular focus on forward-looking ideas concerning innovative or as yet undeveloped technologies. While there is an expectation that authors will be well grounded in philosophy, law or political science, consideration will be given to future-orientated works that cross these disciplinary boundaries. The interdisciplinary nature of the series editorial team offers the best possible examination of works that address the "ethical, legal and social" implications of emerging technologies.

Forthcoming titles:

Drones and Responsibility
Legal, Philosophical and Socio-Technical Perspectives on
Remotely Controlled Weapons
Edited by Ezio Di Nucci and Filippo Santoni de Sio

Super Soldiers
The Ethical, Legal and Social Implications
Edited by Jai Galliott and Mianna Lotz

Social Robots
Boundaries, Potential, Challenges
Edited by Marco Nørskov

The Good Drone

Edited by Kristin Bergtora Sandvik and Maria Gabrielsen Jumbert

Routledge
Taylor & Francis Group

LONDON AND NEW YORK

First published 2017
by Routledge
2 Park Square, Milton Park, Abingdon, Oxon OX14 4RN

and by Routledge
711 Third Avenue, New York, NY 10017

Routledge is an imprint of the Taylor & Francis Group, an informa business

British Library Cataloguing in Publication Data
A catalogue record for this book is available from the British Library

Library of Congress Cataloguing in Publication Data
Names: Sandvik, Kristin Bergtora, editor of compilation. |
Jumbert, Maria Gabrielsen, editor of compilation.
Title: The Good Drone / edited by Kristin Bergtora Sandvik and
Maria Gabrielsen Jumbert.
Description: New York, NY : Routledge, [2016] |
Includes bibliographical references and index.
Identifiers: LCCN 2016003282 | ISBN 9781472451118 (hardback) |
ISBN 9781315553405 (ebook)
Subjects: LCSH: Drone aircraft. | Drone aircraft–Moral and ethical aspects.
Classification: LCC UG1242.D7 G66 2016 | DDC 358.4/14–dc23
LC record available at http://lccn.loc.gov/2016003282

ISBN: 9781472451118 (hbk)
ISBN: 9781315553405 (ebk)

Typeset in Times New Roman
by Out of House Publishing

Printed and bound by CPI Group (UK) Ltd, Croydon, CR0 4YY

Contents

Notes on contributors   vii

Acknowledgments   x

Introduction: what does it take to be good?   1
MARIA GABRIELSEN JUMBERT AND
KRISTIN BERGTORA SANDVIK

1   Targeted "killer drones" and the humanitarian
    discourse: on a liaison   26
    SUSANNE KRASMANN

2   Lifting the fog of war? Opportunities and challenges of
    drones in UN peace operations   45
    JOHN KARLSRUD AND FREDERIK ROSÉN

3   Poison pill or cure-all: drones and the protection
    of civilians   65
    KRISTOFFER LIDÉN AND KRISTIN BERGTORA SANDVIK

4   Creating the EU drone: control, sorting, and search and
    rescue at sea   89
    MARIA GABRIELSEN JUMBERT

5   The public order drone: proliferation and disorder in
    civil airspace   109
    KRISTIN BERGTORA SANDVIK

6 A revolution in agricultural affairs: dronoculture, precision, capital 129

BRAD BOLMAN

7 Wings for wildlife: the use of conservation drones, challenges and opportunities 153

SERGE WICH, LORNA SCOTT AND LIAN PIN KOH

8 Drone/body: the drone's power to sense and construct emergencies 168

MAREILE KAUFMANN

Index 195

Contributors

Kristin Bergtora Sandvik is an Associate Professor at the Department of Criminology and Sociology of Law at the University of Oslo, and a Senior Researcher at the Peace Research Institute Oslo (PRIO), where she also coordinates the research group on humanitarianism. She holds an SJD from Harvard Law School (2008). She has published widely on the normalization of drones and on humanitarian technology, and her work has appeared in inter alia *Millennium, Third World Quarterly, International Review of the Red Cross*, and *BEHEMOTH*.

Maria Gabrielsen Jumbert is a Senior Researcher at PRIO and the Director of the Norwegian Centre for Humanitarian Studies. She holds a PhD from the Institut d'Etudes Politiques, SciencesPo Paris (2010). Her work focuses on how new information and surveillance technologies produce security and humanitarian practices, especially as related to human mobility. Her work has appeared in inter alia in the *Journal of Modern African Studies, Third World Quarterly*, the *International Review of the Red Cross* and the *Review of International Studies*.

Brad Bolman is a researcher in the History of Science at Harvard University. His work focuses on the connections between military, scientific and technical transformations of the natural world and new transnational exchanges produced by economic globalization. His current project is a manuscript that traces the development of scientific pigs in the twentieth and twenty-first centuries.

John Karlsrud is Senior Research Fellow and Manager for the Training for Peace programme at the Norwegian Institute of International Affairs, and External Associate at the Centre for the Study of Globalisation and Regionalisation, University of Warwick, where he also earned his PhD (2014). He has been a Fulbright Fellow at the Centre on International Cooperation, NYU and is a World Social Science Fellow on big data and peacebuilding in urban environments. John works on peacekeeping, peacebuilding and humanitarian issues and is interested in how big data and new technology can be used to improve action in these areas. He has published articles with, for example, *Disasters, Global Governance, International*

Review of the Red Cross and *Third World Quarterly*, and has forthcoming books with Routledge and Zed Books.

Mareile Kaufmann is a Senior Researcher at PRIO and holds a PhD from Hamburg University (2016). From a perspective of political philosophy and critical theory she explores the influence of security technology and the digital on society at large. At PRIO, she coordinates the Security Research Group and is a primary researcher in several Norwegian and EU-funded projects. Her work has appeared in *Media, Culture & Society* and *Environment & Planning D*.

Susanne Krasmann is a Professor of Sociology at the Institute for Criminological Research, University of Hamburg. Her main research areas are Law and Security, Critical Security Studies, Epistemologies of Control, Vulnerability & Political Theory and Poststructuralist Perspectives (in particular: Governmentality, Affect Theory, Regimes of Visibility). She has published with Routledge, Suhrkamp and Campus Publishers, and with international journals such as *Leiden Journal of International Law*, *Punishment & Society*, *Surveillance & Society* and *Theoretical Criminology*.

Kristoffer Lidén is a Senior Researcher at PRIO, where he coordinates the Research group on Law and Ethics, as well as the Research school on Peace and Conflict. He specializes in the ethics and political philosophy of peacebuilding, humanitarianism and security. He has published on the ethics of liberal peacebuilding, global governance, post-colonialism and international law. Lidén holds a PhD in Philosophy (2014) and an MA in Peace and Conflict Studies from the University of Oslo.

Lian Pin Koh is Associate Professor and Chair of Applied Ecology & Conservation at the University of Adelaide. He helped establish, and serves as Director of, the university's Unmanned Research Aircraft Facility, and is Deputy Director of the Conservation Science and Technology Program. In addition to his university duties, he is also Founding Director of ConservationDrones.org (a US-based non-profit) and Regional Technical Advisor for Conservation International. He also serves as Editor-in-Chief of Cogent Environmental Science, Editor of Biological Conservation and Editor of Scientific Reports (Nature Publishing Group).

Frederik Rosén is a Senior Researcher at the Danish Institute for International Studies. He is the director of the NATO Science for Peace and Security Program on cultural property protection in NATO-led military operations. He has published widely on international security, security technologies and peacebuilding in journals such as *Journal of Conflict and Security Law, Stability: International Journal of Security and Development, African Security*, and *Journal of Intervention and Statebuilding*. He holds a PhD from the Roskilde University (2011).

Lorna Scott is a freelance researcher. She has a BSc in Zoology from Liverpool John Moores University. Her area of interest is the conservation of great apes and their habitats, with a particular focus on the use of GIS technology.

Serge Wich is a Professor in primate biology at Liverpool John Moores University (Liverpool, UK) and in 2014 he joined the UvA as honorary professor for the conservation of the great apes. His research focuses on primate behavioral ecology, tropical rain forest ecology and conservation of primates and their habitats with a special focus on the Sumatran orangutan. He is involved in research at various fieldsites of wild and reintroduced orangutans, as well as in island-wide surveys and analyses of orangutan distribution and density and the impact of land use changes on their populations. Together with Dr. Lian Pin Koh he founded ConservationDrones.org and uses drones for conservation applications.

Acknowledgments

The origins of this volume lie in a workshop at the Peace Research Institute Oslo (PRIO) in 2013, where we gathered scholars working on different uses of drones for "good" purposes, and explored the similar dynamics, the different rationales behind, and how they relate to the use of drones for war purposes. As originally intended, the present volume focuses on a binary between the drone wars and emerging civilian uses. As time has passed, we have come to see the use of drones in war, humanitarian crises and in the "everyday" as mutually constituted. We hope that the volume will be a timely contribution to a growing debate on the reliance on drones as a policy tool, as well as the use of drones in civil airspace.

PRIO, the Norwegian Ministry for Defence and the Norwegian Research Council have funded part of the work for this book. We are very appreciative of their support.

We are grateful to good colleagues at PRIO, and its Director Kristian Berg Harpviken, for support and inspiring conversations and critical questions. We are also thankful to colleagues at NUPI, UAVIATORS, MSF Belgium, MSF Norway and the Norwegian Red Cross, with which we have had many good and productive conversations through a series of collaborations and common workshops. We are also grateful to J. Peter Burgess, Mark Duffield, Daniel Gilman, Derek Gregory, Ben Hayes, Tonje Hessen Schei, Kjetil M. Larsen, Tobias Mahler, Patrick Meier, Catherina Pino, Paul Scharre, Peter Singer, Astrid Suhrke, Gavin Sullivan and many others for inspiring conversations.

We are also very thankful to our contacts at Ashgate Publishing, where this series was first located, before becoming part of Routledge Publishing: Jai Galliot, Amanda Buxton, Kirstin Howgate and Brenda Sharp, who have believed in this project from the beginning and provided invaluable support throughout.

Introduction

What does it take to be good?

*Maria Gabrielsen Jumbert and
Kristin Bergtora Sandvik*

As the use of drones has proliferated in civil airspace throughout the world, the word *drone* has ceased to be synonymous with the targeted killings of the "war on terror." Instead, the media and the blogosphere are rife with reports on beneficial new applications for drones – for everything from peacekeeping to humanitarian relief, search and rescue, border control, and environmental and wildlife protection. We appear to be witnessing the ascendancy of a new concept: that of "the good drone." This volume investigates that ascendancy by exploring the increasing use of drones for humanitarian, commercial, and other civilian purposes, as well as the attendant discourses on how and why drones are "good."

While the military use of drones, and the associated ethical and legal problems, has been the subject of significant academic scrutiny,[1] the more recent, nonmilitary uses have so far received little scholarly attention;[2] in particular, there has been no critical examination of the "good drone." The goal of this volume is to address gaps in the existing literature by engaging a multidisciplinary group of policymakers, practitioners, activists, and academics in a critical conversation about new fields in which drones are being deployed – or imagined as potential game changers.

We believe that this is an important moment to have such a conversation. Most current discussions of drone use focus on the industry's struggle for access to civil airspace, where the emphasis is on privacy, safety, and the industry's maturity and motivations. As drone use proliferates, however, the debate will move beyond the question of access, and the focus of discussion will shift – possibly scattering into separate subfields that address specific concerns. The contributors to this volume, who represent such putative subfields, have been asked to identify and reflect on the ethical, legal, and political implications of drone proliferation.

We recognize the many possibilities afforded by drones, and we want to take these seriously by critically examining their genuine potential. At the same time, we want to explore the broader implications of the ubiquitous presence of unmanned flying objects. For example, while drone advocates focus on the transformative potential of drones as an instrument of social change, there has been little discussion of the fact that access to civil airspace entails a certain distribution of public resources, nor of the ways in which this new vantage point from above will affect power relations and modes of governance.

In our view, the good drone is attractive as a politics of the possible, combining a utopian vision of technology with imaginings about possible future functions. To explore the material and discursive creation of the good drone – that is, to better understand what it takes for a drone to be good, or to be seen as good – we examine the good drone as an organizing narrative not only for technological development but for political projects, governance practices, and social mobilization. To this end, we consider the terrain of the good drone as it is imagined, legally constituted, and deployed in three partially overlapping spaces: the global battlespace, the humanitarian emergency zone, and everyday politics in industrialized Western democracies. The volume also explores drone use in relation to the distribution of resources (including space) and access to technology, and with regard to still broader issues, including who gets to see whom, and who and what gets protection.

A key contribution of this volume is to unpack the differing conceptions of "good," from subjective moral criteria to the evocation of objective standards for what is ethically, legally, politically, or commercially desirable. The goal is to take stock of the logics and rationales according to which drones are "good," in order to initiate a critical conversation about the political currency of "good." To this end, the volume covers a broad range of thematic areas and academic perspectives, with a particular focus on how narratives of "good" are constituted.

The volume draws on the drone literature in the fields of science and technology studies, international law, critical security studies, international relations, political philosophy, and criminology. Each chapter integrates key theoretical concepts from these disciplines with empirical insights from the contributors' field of research, and the multidisciplinary approach provides the grounding for a comprehensive, crosscutting exploration of the issues raised.

In particular, we hope to develop a critical framework that will support efforts to identify and disentangle the many dimensions of the good drone, including its implications both as a theoretical concept and as a set of practices. To that end, the contributions illuminate the problem of the good drone in two ways: first, by carving out new conceptions of war; crisis and security; and resilience, preparedness, and response that the drone allows for (Kaufmann; Krasmann; Lidén and Sandvik, this volume); second, by offering empirically rooted explorations of the narrative of the good drone in various contexts, from the promotion of drones for public order and law enforcement to the use of drones in peacekeeping, migration monitoring, agriculture, and conservation (Sandvik; Karlsrud and Rosén; Jumbert; and Wich et al., this volume). Relying on conceptual tool kits from a range of academic disciplines, the contributions offer diverse and normative understandings of what drones are and can do, and where the limits of their promise lie.

Although *drone* has gained increasing currency as the term for a range of unmanned aerial platforms performing a wide array of tasks, the word has a controversial history – reflected in the insistence, on the part of both the military and the drone industry, that other terms should be used, including UAV (unmanned aerial vehicle), RPA (remotely piloted aircraft), and RPV (remotely piloted vehicle). Drones are used by military units for targeted killing and ISR (intelligence, surveillance, reconnaissance). To comply with more robust mandates that allow for greater use of force, UN peacekeeping relies increasingly on the use of drones. Humanitarian actors use drones for demining, population management, and crisis mapping, and are also experimenting with drone use for relief drops and medical logistics.

In civil airspace, government actors – including first responders such as firefighters, search-and-rescue crews, and police – are exploring the use of drones to increase the safety and effectiveness of their work. Civil society actors – including environmentalists, conservationists, cultural-heritage advocates, human-rights activists, and social-movement organizers – have great hopes for what drones can capture and document from above, in support of struggles for sustainability, cultural survival, and social justice. The press sees drones as potential game changers, because they offer the possibility of new vantage points – including those of "citizen drone" journalists – and thus access to new information. Finally, great expectations surround the commercial use of drones for package delivery, precision farming, and optimizing exploration and productivity in the gas, oil, mining, and maritime industries.

While the volume focuses primarily on deployments by North American and European actors (whether at home, in their borderlands, or in foreign interventions or peacekeeping missions), we believe that the insights offered here can help illuminate the implications of drone use elsewhere. Especially in light of lagging regulations regarding airspace, privacy, and data protection in many countries, the proliferation of drones across Latin America, Africa, and Asia is in need of critical investigation. So far, however, little scholarly attention has been given to drone use by non-Western actors, or to the experiences of those who find themselves living under the drone stare.

This chapter consists of four main parts: Section 1 explores what is fundamentally new about drones and how they are used today, and places the volume in the context of the broader scholarly landscape. Section 2 presents the volume's principal lines of inquiry: What does a good drone see, and what are the politics of the good drone stare? How does the good drone blur the boundaries between military and civilian uses? What kinds of trade-offs are imagined by the various actors who have a stake in drone use? Section 3 presents a conceptual framework for understanding what is "good" about the good drone. Among other topics, the section considers the ways in which the good drone is defined as one that is "not bad"; examines background discourses relating to global governance, public order, neoliberal principles of efficiency and effectiveness, global interconnectivity, and the war on terror;

and discusses emerging themes in the drone discourse, including the use of the term *drone* itself, the industry's increasing emphasis on the controllable drone, and the understanding of civil airspace as a public good. Section 4 provides an overview of the individual chapters.

The good drone: "newness," technological optimism, and technological fantasies

Proclamations of a "revolution in military affairs" are a constant feature of military technological development; equally constant is the skeptical retort that "nothing is new under the sun." Drones in themselves are nothing new. Although the idea of unmanned military airpower is much older, unmanned airplanes were first developed in the early 1900s. The origins of today's drone technology can be traced back to the First and Second World Wars, but it was during the Vietnam War (1955–1975) that the US Army engaged in the first systematic deployment of drones for military reconnaissance. Israel was a pioneer in the commercial use of drones, and the Israeli air force began using drones for surveillance in the 1980s. Japanese farmers began using drones for agriculture in the 1990s (Bolman, Chapter 6).[3]

Hellfire missiles were successfully mounted on the Predator drone in 2001 – and, by the end of that decade, the ethics and the humanitarian cost of the US "drone wars" had begun to garner significant international attention (Stanford Law School Human Rights and Conflict Resolution Clinic and NYU School of Law Global Justice Clinic 2012; Center for Civilians in Conflict and Columbia Law School 2012; Amnesty International 2012). As the global war on terror wound down and military procurement dwindled, manufacturers of military drones began to search for new drone clients and new drone tasks. The drone industry's ensuing push to open US and European civil airspace to drones (by 2015 and 2016, respectively) has provoked broad public debate, sparked by an imagined future in which drones hover above our daily lives, recording every detail, to the detriment of both privacy and security (FAA 2013; Dolan and Thompson 2013).

While military airpower and unmanned aerial platforms are not new, either in concept or practice, the good drone is new in a number of senses: first with respect to its applications; second with respect to the cultural narratives spun around its potential for doing good; and third with respect to the hardware and software that make up its body (Kaufmann, Chapter 8). In particular, new software and hardware have enabled "newness" in the form of enhanced performance: today's largest surveillance drones can not only cover vast areas but can surpass satellites, for example, in the provision of detailed, real-time images. Also new is the remoteness from which the good drone can be operated, and the resulting connections thereby created between distant geographical locations, which open up new definitions of space and time. Finally, drones promise not only better performance of civilian and military tasks but new practices and services, from "drone art" and pizza delivery to the emergence of new interest groups (e.g. hobbyist organizations like DIY Drones and UAViators, the global humanitarian UAV network). These practices and services, in turn, are engendering new commercial, social, and regulatory landscapes.

Political, media, and academic debates about drones have been characterized by two main approaches: technological determinism and constructivism. In the deterministic view, the drone's potential and pitfalls are inherent within the drone itself. For critics of targeted killings, for example, drones are the essence of the problem; and for those whom we would categorize as technological utopianists, drones have inherent and infinite possibilities: they are the ultimate game changers. In the constructivist view, drones and the issues they raise are socially constructed, and defined by politics, law, and ethics (Adey, Whitehead, and Williams 2011; Gregory 2011a; Holmqvist 2013). Although constructivists view drones as manifestations of existing power relations, they are also interested in how drone use can reshape social relations and understandings.

This volume, as a whole, attempts to chart a path between determinism and constructivism. In this chapter, our focus is on how drones generate new political settlements and constitute forms of institutional power. We take as our starting point the view that technology is neither neutral nor passively adopted by society; instead, society and technology are mutually constitutive. As Krasmann argues (in this volume), the good drone not only activates ethical and legal concerns but also shapes them. The good drone is more than an idea, and its social significance is not reducible to its functions. Thus, the construction of technology is subject to political contestation, as well as to the realities of professionalism, finance, and politics.

As evidenced by the ongoing drone wars, UAV technology enables a specific set of political and military rationales and projects that must be investigated, not for their often-alleged "newness" but for the power they represent (Herrera 2003; Fritsch 2011; McCarthy 2013; Bijker and Law 1992). The integration of a new technology is not a linear process, and its outcome cannot be predetermined: technology needs to be understood in the broader social, political, legal, and security contexts in which it is developed and put to use (Kroener and Neyland 2012). In other words, "good" and "bad" drones are not predestined to be so: good drones can be used in bad ways, and bad drones can be used in good ones.

We regard the good drone as part of a broader trend toward technological optimism – more specifically, toward technological fantasies (Sandvik et al. 2014). The good drone reflects two particular dimensions of technological optimism: the first imagines a world of future possibilities, and the second promises that the risks and uncertainties of the future can be mastered in the present. Building on theoretical insights from constructivism, securitization theory has shown how, through so-called speech acts, complex political issues can be lifted out of the political realm to justify tough, extraordinary security measures (Buzan, Wæver, and de Wilde 1998; Wæver 1993).

We hold that the narrative of the good drone has had a similar effect: by providing technology as an answer to specific political problems, it creates a set of "issues." Several contributions to this volume discuss the drone as a materialized form of securitization, a sort of "technification" of the security response. Whether assisting with public order, migration management, or complex peacekeeping operations, the good drone comes with the promise of both overview and precision – affording both greater knowledge and enhanced decision-making. Such promises are part of the aforementioned trend toward technological optimism (Sandvik et al. 2014) – that is, the belief that new technologies, particularly digital information and communications technologies, can solve virtually any problem.

The discourse of "techno optimism" is especially prone to offering technological solutions to security problems. According to Monahan and Mokos (2013), the creation of compelling narratives is an important element in justifying surveillance (or other security) systems. Crang and Graham (2007) refer to such narratives as "technological fantasies" that position emergent technological systems as necessary (and effective) responses to dire threats. These fantasies are not simply narrative devices used to achieve desired ends; they also actively shape larger security cultures and afford them influence (Monahan and Mokos 2013). Thus, it is important to understand the development of the "insecurity scenarios" that call on drones as a solution, and how those scenarios affect our perception of good drones.

In the cybersecurity field, *cyber-utopianism* refers to "a naïve belief in the emancipatory nature of online communication," along with a refusal to acknowledge any negative impact of the Internet on society (Mueller 2011). Borrowing from cybersecurity scholarship, we have created the term *drone utopianism*, which can be used as an analytical prism for understanding the promise of the good drone. In drone utopianism, technology replaces politics as the solution for a raft of problems – from insecurity to resource inequality and injustice.[4] At the same time, however, drone utopianism fails to recognize that the mere introduction of drones (like that of technologies that have preceded them) alters political context, social behavior, and even the trajectory of crises. Thus, one of the goals of this volume is to assess and critically address the drone as a technological fantasy, and drone utopianism as a key feature of contemporary technological optimism.

Conceptualizing the good drone

The characteristic of drones that has so far attracted the most attention is the "drone stare" – the presumed ability to see and strike with surgical precision, and thereby lessen human suffering.

The dominant politico–military rationale for the drone wars is the notion that the drone stare, with its near-real-time video feeds, allows unparalleled accuracy, not only minimizing civilian casualties but virtually eliminating the risk to one's own soldiers (Gregory 2011a; Chamayou 2013; and Krasmann,

Chapter 1). Although the drone-war literature critiques this rationale, little effort has so far been made to develop a more fine-grained understanding of the particularities of the "good drone" stare. What does it mean, for example, to "see" like a good drone, and how does the good drone interpret and act on what it observes? What does it mean to "be seen" by good drones? And what are the politics of the good drone stare?

We suggest that the good drone is accompanied by the same rhetoric of overview and precision as the military drone, but is also wrapped in notions of saving, protecting, or rescuing humans, animals, crops, and property. Whereas the attention given to the killer drone stare is focused almost exclusively on the drone pilots, making sense of the good drone stare requires a more expansive view, which takes account of the interface between technological performance, one the one hand,[5] and the interpretations of those who "see," on the other (those who see include not only pilots but the larger crews that are necessary to operate the bigger UAVs; manufacturers and their lobbyists; drone hobbyists; and commercial and government actors). It is also important to note that the drone stare is mediated by operational mandates, training requirements, and funding schemes.

By studying how hardware, software, professional cultures, and rhetoric travel with drone technology, we can begin to detect the ways in which the emergence of the good drone may be blurring the boundaries between civilian and military practices. In settings where the lines between war and peace are ever more uncertain, the consequences of such blurring – and of the dual uses of technology – become harder to distinguish, and more important to assess and understand.

With respect to the use of drones in civil airspace, a different type of blurring is at play: by moving the line of sight from the street to the air, drones relocate the boundary between the public and the private. Choi-Fiztpatrick notes that "this simple shift effectively pushes public space from the sidewalk to the stairwell, courtyard, rooftop, and so forth. Once private, these spaces are now subject to surveillance. Or have they now become public spaces?" (Choi-Fiztpatrick 2014: 21).

In other words, have drones simply increased the number and type of locations considered public? Or is a more profound conversation called for, through which we can examine how drones are disrupting our understanding of which spaces are private (Choi-Fitzpatrick 2014)?

To begin such a conversation, this volume explores the good drone as both a material and symbolic entity, considering both its direct practical effects (e.g. distributive effects, unintended effects, and the consequences of drones being put to uses other than those originally envisioned) as well as its indirect legitimating effects. We are interested in the good drone as an object of discourse; as a technosocial practice; and as an ethical, legal, and political concept. To explore these multiple dimensions, we must unpack the different meanings of "good" in the discourse surrounding the development and use of drones, whether that discourse comes from the realm of technological innovation, commercial imagination, or political rhetoric. We will also carefully attend to the paths along which the good drone discourse moves and shifts; in particular, we will explore the ways in which the good drone, as construed through discourses associated with high degrees of legitimacy (humanitarianism, peacekeeping, and crisis management), is reappropriated to strengthen the legitimacy of other operations or objectives.

Arguments about economy and efficiency are central to the discourse used to legitimate the good drone, as well as to support deregulation and the acquisition of drones by governmental, nonprofit, and private sector entities. In the economic realm, the drone industry argues that drones will allow savings on labor costs while generating new jobs. The industry also claims that existing restrictions are leading to large financial losses, and that deregulating civil airspace will yield enormous profit.[6]

So far, however, the drone industry has made no attempt to undertake comprehensive cost–benefit analyses that would, for example, account for losses that could occur in the traditional aviation industry, if some employees were replaced by drones.[7] In the case of border surveillance, for example, the argument that drones would be more cost-efficient than human patrols appears to be based on the notion that in order to achieve the coverage provided by drones, many more manned patrols than are currently employed would be needed. In fact, as is argued in this volume, the functionalities of drones, and their ability to cover relatively wide areas better than manned aircrafts, ground vehicles, boats, or satellites may lower the threshold for deploying drones, and thereby increase the overall number of operations – and thus the overall costs (see also Hayes, Jones, and Töpfer 2014: 9). In sum, the rationales (and calculations) underlying the industry's cost–benefit claims need further scrutiny, not least to engender broader discussions about various alternatives for future drone regulation. Unpacking the role and politics of cost–benefit claims is a valuable way of examining the distribution of resources that makes good drones possible.

Making sense of the good drone: an analytical framework

The terrain of the good drone

To appreciate what it takes to be "good" requires an analytical understanding of the terrain of the good drone. As indicated in the introduction, this volume explores the good drone as it is imagined, legally constituted, and deployed in three overlapping spaces: the global battlespace, the humanitarian emergency zone, and the field of everyday politics.

As a conceptual and material project, war is now everywhere: it is embedded in the matrix of contemporary social life. In particular, the global war on terror served to erase geographical distinctions and limitations (Graham 2006). Over a decade ago, Duffield (2004) described how a global "borderland" of failed states, shadow networks, and rogue states had emerged during the 1990s. As a metaphor for an imagined global space, the notion of borderlands – a form of "cartography of risk" – encapsulates the terrorist threat (Duffield 2004: 8).

In a similar vein, Gregory (2011b: 239) understands these spaces as shadowlands: "spaces that enter European and American imaginaries in phantasmatic [sic] form, barely known but vividly imagined." These spaces are also acutely material: Gregory (2011b: 239) notes that one of the characteristics of late modern war is the emergent, "event-full" quality of military, paramilitary, and terrorist violence that can, in principle, occur anywhere and everywhere. Through its potent ability to produce new enemies (Hayes and Sullivan 2010) by forging spatial linkages between targets and those who are "part of" or "associated with" terrorist enterprises, late modern warfare has been transformed into what Harald Koh (2013) has labelled "the Forever War."

This "everywhere and forever war" plays out on a vast global battlespace that is intrinsically connected to and co-constituted by the "humanitarian emergency zone" (Ferguson 2006), a field where a global regulatory system of international organizations, donor and troop-contributing nations, and non-governmental organizations (NGOs) operate parallel to and across domestic state structures to respond to and administer a permanent condition of "crisis." This perpetual crisis management apparatus results not only from the rise of new political and rhetorical humanitarianisms (e.g. "humanitarian interventions," "humanitarian soldiers" [Kotilainen 2011], "humanitarian violence") but also from the humanitarian governance regimes that have been devised for the borderlands. These regimes, in turn, reflect the ways in which non-territorialized power is deployed, legitimized, and imposed, in accordance with a planetary logic applied to "crisis" situations by an "international humanitarian rule of law" (Pandolfi 2003: 370).

Over the past century, leading governments, United Nations agencies, NGOs, and private companies have gained unprecedented access to, and varying degrees of influence over, the internal affairs of many weak or contested states in the global borderlands (Duffield 2001). We suggest that the humanitarian emergency zone also overlaps with, and co-constitutes how, the everyday "risk society" (see Beck 1992: 1) deals with hazards, uncertainties, and perceived future insecurities. Our perspective takes as its starting point the contemporary concern with "preparedness" (Lakoff 2008) and the societal need for "resilience" (Cavelty, Kaufmann, and Kristensen 2015) against threats to national security and human security. The view taken here is broad, ranging from how poor and disaster-prone societies grapple with actual risk, to how politically stable and relatively wealthy societies organize around imagined future risks.

Attributes, capabilities, and functions

Although the narrative of the good drone often focuses on particular iconic attributes, there is in fact a great deal of heterogeneity in the characteristics, capabilities, and functions of drones; it is from the shifting combinations of these qualities that the good drone emerges. Some drones are large, fly at medium or high altitudes, and have long endurance and a wide range; others are micro- or nano-sized, fly at relatively low altitudes, and can fly only for brief periods and within a short range. Drones can fly fast or slow, solo or in swarms. Some have fixed wing sets, reminiscent of those on airplanes, while others have rotary blades like helicopters. Drones have different levels of autonomy during take-off, flight, and landing. Some drones need a special runway, while others are handheld devices that fit in a backpack.

While some drones are mounted with simple cameras that provide grainy, soda-straw views, others (like the Gorgon Stare) are equipped with sophisticated, wide-area surveillance platforms. Most drones run on fuel or batteries, although models are being built that run on solar power or wind; if such designs are successful, they would allow drones to remain airborne for much longer.[8] Drones are made of metal or plastic, and are equipped with an endless array of software with varying levels of security and allowing for different modes of data collection and interpretation. Drones are made by military manufacturers or tech firms, by hobbyists modifying commercial off-the-shelf technology, or by individual innovators who build them from scratch. Given their different functions and capabilities, drones require various kinds of crews for maintenance and use: while the larger models deployed for combat air patrols require hundreds of people, hobbyist drones have a crew of one.

Drones have a range of different functions: they can perform overhead surveillance, offering enhanced situational awareness but also the possibility of mapping topographies, populations, or changes in the landscape. Drones come with various ranges and combinations of sensing platforms, including cameras, thermal cameras, and radar. Equipped with the right software, drones can intrude upon, disrupt, or destroy wireless networks. Drones that are equipped with lasers, missiles, bombs, or less lethal weapons such as Tasers, gas, or rubber bullets can be used for targeting. The ongoing miniaturization of drones dovetails with the weaponization of ever-smaller, faster, and more sophisticated drones, the so-called LMAMS (lethal miniature aerial munitions system, also known as "loitering munitions"). Using sling loads, drones can carry heavy cargo over long distances; they can also be used to transport small containers of medicine, blood, or other materials over short distances.

Significant efforts are being made to improve the seeing and sensing abilities of drones – allowing them, for example, to see at night, or through the tree canopy. Importantly, the exponential increase in the technical ability to see changes the act of seeing: even single-sensor platforms (which sport names like Gorgon Stare and Constant Hawk) can now replace armadas of drones.[9] The imaging system on the newly developed ARGUS (autonomous real-time ground ubiquitous surveillance), for example, allows the collection of six petabytes of video in a single day – roughly equivalent to eighty years of high-definition video. Leaving the Predator's soda-straw view of the world far behind, the ARGUS can track objects, people, and vehicles across an area of ten square kilometers (or more). And with the integration of long-endurance platforms, wide-area aerial surveillance is being transformed into wide-area *persistent* surveillance. This ever-increasing generation of data presents an unprecedented challenge to users, who must be able to detect highly specific bits of information (e.g. indicators of hostile action) among activities occurring across a large area. Such changes in the requirements for the act of "seeing" are rendering PED (processing, exploitation, and dissemination) cells increasingly central to contemporary warfare (Sandvik 2013).[10]

Finally, no discussion of drone attributes is complete without reference to how the drone is "seen," and the dynamics engendered by this visibility. The drone itself is a species of visual image (think of the iconic pictures of the Predator against a dark-blue sky). According to human rights reports, for those living under the drone stare, the continuous sight and sound of drones shapes the rhythm of everyday life. For example, residents who live near Goma, in the Democratic Republic of the Congo, describe the UN peacekeeping drones as "loud mosquitos" (*IRIN* 2014, see also Karlsrud and Rosén, Chapter 2).

What is "good"?

In addition to existing as a physical entity, the good drone is made up of narratives that incorporate abstract values and objectives; taken together, such narratives engender a vision of the good drone as utopian, yet technically possible – and as capable of yielding broad societal benefits. To understand how articulations of the "good" attach to the drone, we must first examine a set of background discourses that shape both (1) the ways in which drones are used and (2) the perception of drone activities. (As will be explored in several chapters, drones also shape the background discourses themselves, by adding elements of efficiency, protection, connectivity, etc.)

As part and parcel of "the forever war" and "the everywhere war," drones are intrinsically connected to contemporary debates about global governance. Much of the ethical debate on the use of armed drones, and the war on terror more generally, has been framed as a choice between two legal paradigms: international human rights law and international humanitarian law. Through having been integrated into peacekeeping missions, drones have also become firmly wedded to the protection-of-civilians agenda. In the aftermath of 9/11, control over civil airspace became an important component of domestic national security; by the same logic, control over hard-to-reach areas *beyond* national borders has become a priority.

Humanitarianism is a key moral discourse in the twenty-first century; it has also become more and more intertwined with notions of risk: in a world that is perceived as increasingly dangerous, drones help humanitarians do their jobs from a distance. For governments, preparedness for future eventualities is becoming tied to the politics of the present, and drones fulfill the promise of preparedness in both material and symbolic ways. Finally, as viewed through the lens of neoliberalism, drones are held to be efficient, effective, and cheap; supporters argue, for example, that as "smart" weapons, drones enhance military effectiveness, and that they are less expensive than fighter jets, boots on the ground, police helicopters, or safety-inspection teams. Finally, drones offer a dual promise: they represent both technological innovation (regarded as an inherent good) and the emergence of new business models and opportunities.

As noted earlier, "good" refers to assumptions about the economic advantages of drones: not only are they held to be less costly than the alternatives, but they are also reputed to yield better results from a cost–benefit perspective, which measures the raw cost of the drone against the value created. Drones are also held to increase the efficiency and effectiveness of the operations in which they participate, both because they can reach difficult locations more easily and because they are more precise than unassisted humans. Thus, drones are "good" because of their precise sensing capacities, whether those are applied to targeting, farming ("precision farming"), or search and rescue. Such formulations, however, assume that the technology functions as it has been programmed to do, and that the potential for errors can thereby be reduced to nearly zero.

Drones are imagined to be "virtuous" weapons for protecting the peace (Kennedy and Rogers 2015); they are also construed as "smart" in two senses: (1) they have built-in protections against misuse (whether deliberate or accidental), and (2) they reflect the ongoing push for a "smarter" defense – that is, one that combines effectiveness, cost-efficiency, and high technical standards (in this case, high-quality targeting).

"Good" is also often based on a multilayered invocation of a humanitarian ethos of assisting people in need: if the drones' greater efficiency (compared to that of human rescuers) enables more lives to be saved, the drone is endowed with something akin to a humanitarian sensibility – an acquired quality that then travels with the drone, and is transposed to similar tasks within different operations, which can then be relabeled as "humanitarian."

The "saving lives" rhetoric is also merging with traditional, business-sector cost–benefit calculations: an economic analysis conducted by the US Federal Aviation Administration, for example, suggested that drones might effectively cut the high costs of fatalities (of which there were ninety-five, between 2004 and 2012) among workers who climb cell towers and other similar structures. If standard practice called for a small drone instead of a tower climber, the prevention of just one fatality would save $9.2 million (the amount the government deems to be the economic value of a single life), which would exceed the entire societal cost of the regulations (Lowy 2015; McNeal 2015).

Drones also constitute a politics of the possible: first, they are in keeping with the vision of "unmanned technoscapes" conjured up by the industry; second, they are in accord with utopian images of what could be achieved if they were widely deployed. The former is reflected in the promulgation of drones as essential tools for a "twenty-first-century approach" to first response in various domains, including policing, firefighting, search and rescue, and flood management. For first responders, drones offer endless possibilities, promising not only better performance but also improved forms of public order and public safety – which is to say, *more* of a given public good for the cost incurred by the public purse, and *better* versions of that good.

So far, we have considered specific articulations of the "good" that have been attached to the work descriptions of the drone. It is also important to consider how the drone industry, policy, and academic discourse shape and define what it takes to be good across military, emergency, and civil sector uses. Generally speaking, these discourses hold that drones should be legal (that is, legally flown for legal purposes); however, the relationship between legality and legitimacy is somewhat murky: when drones are legal, as in the case of targeted killing, they will not necessarily be seen as legitimate by the public, civil society, or the international community. Similarly, a journalist drone that records violent methods of crowd control being used against unarmed protesters may be illegal but may be widely seen as legitimate. Although drones flying in civil airspace are generally seen as legitimate if they are flown "responsibly," with safe and technically sound hardware (and under the control of competent and responsible pilots), there is little agreement about what it means to fly responsibly – whether, for example, drones must remain within the line of sight, fly only during daylight hours, or not trespass over private property. Finally, there is increasing concern about the need for insurance for all types of drone use (Levin 2015), and flying without insurance (although perhaps common in practice) is widely regarded as illegitimate.

The "bad" drone

In addition to being defined positively, the good drone must be distinguished – technically, politically, and morally – from what is "bad." As noted earlier in the chapter, because drones make it possible to kill enemies or political opponents from a distance, they are regarded by some as an efficient and cost-effective means of avoiding putting boots on the ground. Yet to many observers, such organized killing – undertaken in accordance with so-called kill lists, and including signature strikes – appears unjust and mechanical. And double-tap strikes, which target survivors or rescue parties, seem particularly unreasonable and cruel. Some have alleged, moreover, that drones encourage killing by lowering the threshold for the use of force: having a weaponized Reaper at your disposal is in itself an incentive for using it. As Missy Ryan has commented in *The Washington Post*, "[t]he important thing to know with armed drones is that based on America's record, they lower the threshold for when countries use armed force ... And when you have that lower threshold, it can change the calculus of countries" (Ryan 2015).

Beyond the fact that drones allow killing at a distance, a number of characteristics of drone warfare – including the fallibility of technology, and the need for collaboration on the part of large, far-flung teams of potentially exhausted, frustrated, demotivated, and inadequately trained pilots – can engender lethal drone strikes that do not conform with the Rules of Engagement or international legal standards. For example, civilians may be targeted by mistake, or suffer as collateral damage. And for the generations growing up under the skies of killer drones, the human costs are high, affecting physical and mental health, education, family life, and participation in society (Stanford Law School Human Rights and Conflict Resolution Clinic and NYU School of Law Global Justice Clinic 2012). And while drones can be used for purposes such as detecting land grabs and raising awareness of conditions in slums, they also have the potential to *facilitate* land grabs or to support the eviction of squatters. Finally, drones can be used for stalking, spying, and trafficking drugs and weapons (including into prisons). In sum, drones are not predestined to be either "good" or "bad": they are tools that can be used in both good and bad ways.

Recently, some new conceptions of "bad" have emerged (Sandvik, Chapter 5). The first can be called "drone antisociality" – that is, the unsafe use of drones by untrained and irresponsible hobbyist pilots who endanger public safety or national security, or spy on or intimidate fellow citizens or the public. For example, amateurs flying near airports or emergency sites can endanger aircraft or obstruct the work of first responders, and reports of drones crashing onto lawns, into buildings, onto highways, or in crowded public spaces are on the rise. In January 2015, a drone crashed on the White House lawn; later that year – and less than a month after the *Charlie Hebdo* attacks – "rogue" drones were detected flying over Paris, as well as over French nuclear plants. Such events highlight the problem of drone pilots' ethics: in an environment where anyone can become a small drone operator, who is to say what a pilot's intentions might be? In a sense, these events also illustrate an expansion of the territory subject to the drone stare, with all that such an expansion entails.

A second type of "bad" arises from cybersecurity issues: drones can be hacked to dive or change course, and the data they collect can be stolen, manipulated, or destroyed. In the conflict in Ukraine, for example, Russian forces traced Ukrainian do-it-yourself drones back to ground-control units that were subsequently wiped out (Tucker 2015).

Both antisociality and cybersecurity raise new questions about technological management, data management, and the drone as a security multiplier. In the case of antisociality, drones become threats through a combination of inherent features and the popular proliferation that is an inevitable result of the push to open civil airspace. In the case of cybersecurity, the drone becomes an *insecurity* multiplier, as the actors with the least sophisticated technology eventually lose; the same technology that allows for unmanned targeting can be manipulated to link the man to the drone – reversing the boots-on-the-ground equation by selecting the drone pilot as the target.

Shifting discourses: the definition dogfight and public airspace as a common good

The notion of the "good drone" is entangled in a number of different discourses, two of which will be highlighted here: the first concerns the definition of the term *drone*, and the second concerns the growing sense of civil airspace as both a public good, and as a space that can be "personalized."

For a number of years, both the military and the drone industry have vehemently resisted the use of the term *drone*, arguing that it had become value laden through its association with targeted killings, and that it was central to efforts to denounce such killings. In place of *drone*, military and industry actors have insisted on a host of acronyms, including UAV (unmanned aerial vehicle), RPA (remotely piloted aircraft), and RPV (remotely piloted vehicle). For their part, civil society and the mainstream media resisted military and industry demands that they use the "correct" terms.

Until recently, both sides continued to insist on the neutrality of their own terminology, arguing that only their definition avoided stigmatization and obfuscation. Over the past several years, however, leaders of the main lobbying groups, including the Association for Unmanned Vehicle Systems International, have begun to use the term *drone*. It is as if the industry, having realized that acceptance of the term may be a potentially profit-generating move, is attempting to demonstrate that it is attuned to the public preference for the term. As one senior drone lobbyist observed, "I'm going to roll over on this one, and call them drones from now on. There are just some fights you are not going to win" (*ABC News* 2013). Another industry representative explained his new position by pointing to "the changed meaning of the drone":

> Back almost two years ago, when someone said the word "drone," they thought military, hostile, weaponized, large, and autonomous ... Today ... most people think of Amazon ... They think of the small ones ... You're going to have hundreds of thousands of individuals that are going to receive a drone, and that's what they're going to call it – a drone ... I have no problem if they call it that, because now they know what it is, whereas before, when you said the word "drone," people didn't have one, and what they thought it was, was the Predator with a Hellfire missile ... I never had a problem with the word "drone."
>
> (Whittle 2014)

In our view, even with the concession that a Predator armed with a Hellfire missile *is* potentially bad, this detoxification narrative is too simple: as "everybody" gets their own drone, new "bads," examples of runaway or malfunctioning drones, are being loaded onto old ones. Hence, one well-established hobbyist drone group is reported to be

> nostalgic for the days when the word "drone" didn't conjure military strikes in Pakistan with civilian casualties, a toy veering out of a hobbyist's

control and crashing on the White House lawn, or Parisians unnerved by unidentified flying objects buzzing the Eiffel Tower.

(Dufresne 2015)

The drone industry's acceptance of the term strands those who have supported the use of *drone* as a form of resistance. Thus, we feel that more reflection is needed on the ways in which the word is losing its critical potential. This loss is occurring not only because the term is being embraced by the industry, but because the term is beginning to obscure rather than clarify: while it is true that all drones in the past were not spy or killer drones, all drones in the present are not out looking for criminals, lost children, or endangered species. As discussed earlier in the chapter, unmanned platforms come in an enormous variety of sizes, shapes, and capabilities.

The conception of civil airspace as a public good, in which individuals and communities have a stake, is gaining increasing strength in the eyes of both governments and the public. Making sense of a common good that can also be personalized, however, requires better conceptual tools.

Airspace is that portion of the atmosphere that is above a country's territory (including its territorial waters) and is controlled by that country. More generally, airspace is any specific, three-dimensional portion of the atmosphere. In the words of the International Civil Aviation Organization, "aviation relies on the scarce resource that is airspace to ensure that passengers, businesses, the military and leisure flyers enjoy the many benefits aviation brings" (Civil Aviation Authority 2012: 1).

In the past, discussions about air traffic have focused on the noise produced by low-flying commercial craft, on concerns about trespassing by military aircraft, on the risks associated with helicopters in urban areas, and on the need to effectively control civil airspace after 9/11; there has been little emphasis on the notion of civil airspace as a global commons. The proliferation of drones, however, is reshaping the regulation of civil airspace, transforming it into a matter of distributing access to a scare commodity that everyone could technically access.

In response to concerns about general safety, hobbyist misuse, and industry fears that "just one disastrous accident" (Perraudin 2015) could severely undermine demand, both governments and the drone industry are engaging in rhetoric that emphasizes "the controllable drone." An emerging commercial sector is marketing a range of products for the defense of both public and personal airspace. Compulsory registration of drones has been proposed (Gibbs 2015), and technical proposals have been made for "geofencing" drones, to stop them from flying near airports.[11] Innovative solutions for protection against drones have also been offered: these include a database that promises to geofence registered customers and provide "personalized airspace" (Newman 2015); drone shields, which detect drones by means of radar or recognize their distinctive noise; personal jammers, which can disrupt wireless networks, including drone connections

(Pilkington 2015); and devices that can find and crash nearby drones (see, for example, Ackerman 2015; Mathews 2014).

Taken together, the contributions to this volume investigate how drones are used in a range of contexts. By providing a sense of what is similar and distinctive across these spheres, and how the narrative of the good drone travels from one sphere to another, the contributions demonstrate how the political currency of good drones is being appropriated, so as to open doors to new fields of use.

Chapter previews

In the first contribution, "Targeted 'Killer Drones' and the Humanitarian Discourse: On a Liaison," Susanne Krasmann discusses the "killer drone" as the term that perhaps most explicitly repudiates targeted killing by attributing responsibility for the practice to the technology itself. Krasmann focuses on the incongruity of weaponized drones being presented as humanitarian – a strategy that seems designed to bolster their legitimacy, along with that of the practice of targeted killing. The promise of precision plays a key role in the process of legitimization: first through an association with the Western idea of the reasonable use of force; second by linking the technology to contemporary ethical and legal requirements (notably those of international humanitarian law); and third by supporting the ambition of effective warfare. As Krasmann demonstrates, the promise of precision is what enables drones to be regarded as the most suitable tool for combating terrorism and counterinsurgency at a global scale. If the good drone is one that is able to meet ethical and legal standards, it does so, Krasmann argues, precisely because it reflects particular political conceptions, both of the social body that is to be protected and the social body that is to be defeated.

Moving from targeted killing to peacekeeping and from the promise of precision to the promise of protection, "Lifting the Fog of War? Opportunities and Challenges of Drones in UN Peace Operations," by John Karlsrud and Frederik Rosén, discusses the increasing use of surveillance drones within UN peacekeeping operations, as viewed at the dawn of 2016. The first mission to acquire such capability was the UN mission in the Democratic Republic of the Congo (MONUSCO). At the same time that it received surveillance drones, MONUSCO received a new and more robust mandate from the UN Security Council, which allows for greater use of force and is to be implemented through the Force Intervention Brigade (consisting of troops from Malawi, Tanzania, and South Africa). Meanwhile, to enable it to respond to a challenging environment, the UN mission in Mali (MINUSMA), was also given a strengthened mandate, and the UN is in the process of adding drones to MINUSMA's mission capabilities. While contributing to the broader critical debate about "good drones," Karlsrud and Rosén also argue for the desirability of drone use – in particular, the use of surveillance drones as a tool of UN peacekeeping. Building on the authors' research on international peacekeeping (including interviews with key staff at the UN Department for Peacekeeping Operations), media reports, and academic literature, Karlsrud and Rosén discuss the benefits drones can bring, and the challenges they stir up, particularly when viewed against the backdrop of increasingly robust peacekeeping mandates.

The next chapter, by Kristoffer Lidén and Kristin Bergtora Sandvik, "Poison Pill or Cure-All: Drones and the Protection of Civilians" explores the relationship between the protection of civilians (PoC) and the use of drones in combat, peacekeeping, and humanitarian aid. Lidén and Sandvik observe that although drones afford some support to PoC efforts, they also offer solutions that lead warfare, peacekeeping, and humanitarianism in new directions. Regarding the protection of civilians by combatants, drones have created a new, worldwide battlefield by lowering both the risks and costs of engagement. Because of their capacity to improve intelligence, surveillance, reconnaissance, target selection, and precision in targeting, drones can be viewed as supporting PoC. Such improvements can also be used to target civilians, however, and offensive uses in general can spark or exacerbate conventional war. Karlsrud and Rosén note in their chapter that drones offer a number of advantages in the realm of peacekeeping; Lidén and Sandvik argue, however, that drones can compromise neutral, third-party attempts to keep the peace, and thereby indirectly undermine PoC. For humanitarians, drones offer improved crisis mapping and transportation for PoC; at the same time, they are likely to exacerbate the shift toward the remote management of crises and the removal of staff from the field.

"Creating the EU Drone: Control, Sorting, and Search and Rescue at Sea," by Maria Gabrielsen Jumbert, analyzes the "good" drone as imagined and expected to be deployed for the purpose of border control in the European Union (EU). Each year, hundreds of migrants attempting to reach Europe die in the Mediterranean Sea, and the numbers have risen tremendously since 2013. Meanwhile, surveillance of the EU's external maritime borders has intensified, and includes the deployment of increasingly sophisticated surveillance technologies. In 2013, Frontex (the EU border management agency) sought to acquire drones to improve its border surveillance capacities. Although the prevention of unwanted migration is the general rationale for EU border surveillance, aims such as strengthening EU borders against terrorist threats and cross-border crime have also been added to the list, in order to increase the "security stakes." Nevertheless, in their effort to justify the need for drones for border surveillance, both Frontex and security-industry representatives have put forth, as their central argument, the fact that drones will improve the detection of migrants in distress at sea. Jumbert discusses two specific ideas of "good" that are driving the EU's broader deployment of drones: first to increase control, and second to support migrant rescues. Jumbert argues that drones are more likely to provide a *sense* of control than to fill any actual social-sorting role at the border. Despite this limitation (or perhaps to cover up this limitation), and as a means of legitimating the acquisition of drones,

Frontex officials continue to emphasize the potential for drones in providing life-saving information and assisting with search and rescue.

In "The Public Order Drone: Proliferation and Disorder in Civil Airspace," Kristin Bergtora Sandvik offers a critical narrative of the relationship between drone proliferation and public order, giving particular attention to the types of "drone disorder" that are emerging from the current explosion in the recreational use of drones. As Sandvik observes, the drone industry's central project is to gain access to civil airspace in the United States and the European Union. Despite considerable success in shaping the political and legislative debates about access, industry groups remain frustrated by public and government resistance to the notion of integrating drones into civilian airspace. Given public skepticism about the drone wars and the perceived threats to privacy associated with domestic drone surveillance, promoting "good uses" for drones is central to industry efforts to strengthen the legitimacy of drones and drone usage. Sandvik examines how the "public order drone" has emerged as an important part of this project.

In "A Revolution in Agricultural Affairs: Dronoculture, Precision, Capital," Brad Bolman explores the fastest-growing segment of the drone industry: the agricultural drone. Pioneered in Japan and later adopted in South Korea in response to labor shortages, agricultural drones have predominantly been used for crop spraying and fertilizing. In the contemporary Western context, interest in the promise of "precision agriculture" has been coupled with a desire to deploy drones more broadly for land mapping, meteorological sensing, and geological analysis. Massive investments are being made in innovative solutions to classic agricultural challenges, and advertising campaigns and media reports are trying to sell "drone farming" to Western agribusiness. As mapping technology and unmanned technology transition from the mountains of Afghanistan to the fields of North Dakota, what was once characterized as a "revolution in military affairs" is becoming a "revolution in agricultural affairs." Bolman argues that, along with technological innovations, the manufacture of agricultural drones will provide economies of scale for the manufacture of military drones. Equally important, Western enthusiasm for drone farming risks whitewashing the capacity of agricultural drones to intensify the land grabbing that, outside the West, has become part and parcel of modern agribusiness.

In "Wings for Wildlife: the Use of Conservation Drones, Challenges and Opportunities," Serge Wich, Lorna Scott, and Lian Pin Koh observe that monitoring wildlife and their habitats is essential to protecting global biodiversity; but because traditional means of doing so face cost, efficiency, and practical constraints, drones are being used to monitor habitats and both terrestrial and marine wildlife; to detect changes in land use; and, more recently, to protect against illegal poaching. The authors note, however, that conservation drones do not represent an uncomplicated good; as they gain popularity in the scientific community, drones are beginning to raise ethical issues concerning data protection and the privacy of local communities. Even the use of drones in anti-poaching efforts raises problematic questions. Although drones can be useful for intercepting poachers, the consequences can be lethal when armed rangers use drone footage to track down the poachers.

In the volume's final chapter, "Drone/Body: the Drone's Power to Sense and Construct Emergencies," Mareile Kaufmann explores the unknown terrain being created by the increasing acceptance of drone deployment in humanitarian and civilian emergencies. Drones can, for example, find victims, photograph territory, indicate where aid is needed, guide survivors out of disaster zones, and provide data for early-warning systems. Drones equipped with novel sensing technologies can do even more: they can hear sounds, feel radiation, and smell chemicals. Drones are also "smart" – capable not only of gathering data but of interpreting it. Given such capacities, drones may appear to be better suited to coordinating and providing assistance in disasters than humans – in fact, drones are being promoted as tools for reaching beyond human physical capacities. As valuable as the superhuman abilities of the "sensing drone" may be in the support of disaster management, however, Kaufmann observes that such drones contribute to the construction of what emergencies are, and how emergency responses are regulated and reasoned about. Thus, a drone is not only a powerful technological quasi-body, but, as an entity that is capable of sensing and processing information, it also exercises power over human bodies. So far, critical discussions of the power of drones over human bodies has focused primarily on the destruction of bodies in targeted killings. Kaufmann argues that, through their hyperphysical characteristics as well as through their increased deployment in humanitarian and civil disasters, drones are contributing to the construction of bodies, and that this is a form of power that needs further critical investigation.

Notes

1 See, for example, Singer (2009); Wall and Monahan (2011); Gregory (2011a, 2011b); Kreps and Kaag (2012); Krasmann (2012); Leander (2013); Brunstetter and Braun (2011); and Chamayou (2013).
2 There have been scattered discussions of the technical aspects of drone use in agriculture, conservation, and the environment (Marks 2014; Spillane 2013; Gómez-Candón et al. 2014); there is also an emerging body of work on the role of drones in peacekeeping (Karlsrud and Rosén 2013; Piiparinen 2015; Whetham 2015; Kennedy and Rogers 2015), humanitarian aid (Sandvik and Lohne 2014), and border control and crime management (Salter 2013; Bergenas et al. 2013).
3 Mainstream accounts of recent drone proliferation usually overlook these decades of previous drone use. Similarly, discussions of drone manufacturers tend to assume that the industry is a monolithic, geographically concentrated entity, which is not the case.
4 By its very nature, humanitarian aid seems to be particularly prone to drone utopianism: drones have been rhetorically tasked, for example, with "connecting Africa," ending hunger, and providing health care (Chow 2012; Lagesse 2015).
5 It is worth noting here that technological performance is likely to change radically in the years to come, as new sensing technology enables drones to smell, hear, read, and so forth (see Kaufmann, Chapter 8).

6 We have observed a general resistance, in the drone industry and among its political supporters, to engage in critical discussions about alternatives with respect to regulation. Those who attempt to begin such discussions are often accused of "being negative" or having Luddite tendencies; alternatively, the conversation gets sidetracked by the "definition dogfight" – the claim that disagreements over terminology (*drone* vs. the more neutral *UAV* or other terms) need to be settled before any substantive discussions can proceed.
7 The Association of Unmanned Vehicle Systems International, an industry trade association, did undertake an interesting cost–benefit analysis, which estimated that small commercial drones would create 70,000 jobs – with an economic impact of more than $13.6 billion – in the first three years after their integration into US skies. The analysis did not, however, address jobs that might be displaced by drones, like those of some types of pilots (*The New York Times* 2015).
8 Suspected (and controversial) proposals for nuclear-fueled drones are thought to have been shelved (Biddle 2012).
9 Whereas single-sensor platforms can monitor, for example, motion only, multi-sensor platforms can monitor motion, temperature, humidity, etc.
10 A PED cell is a special group of soldiers and analysts who work to produce intelligence products from a steady stream of imagery delivered by drones.
11 Geofencing relies on radio-frequency identification to create a geographic boundary that location-aware devices are able to avoid.

References

ABC News (2013) Drone Wars: The Definition Dogfight. *ABC*, March 1. Available at: www.abc.net.au/news/2013-03-01/drone-wars-the-definition-dogfight/4546598 (Accessed April 10, 2016).

Ackerman, E. (2015) Rapere: An Intercept Drone to Seek and Destroy Other Drones. *IEEE Spectrum*, January 14. Available at: http://spectrum.iccc.org/automaton/robotics/aerial-robots/rapere-intercept-drone (Accessed April 10, 2016).

Adey, P., Whitehead, M., and Williams, A.J. (2011) Introduction: Air-target distance, reach and the politics of verticality. *Theory, Culture & Society*, 28 (7–8): 173–187.

Amnesty International (2012) *Will I be Next? US Drone Strikes in Pakistan.* London: Amnesty International. Available at: www.amnestyusa.org/research/reports/will-i-be-next-us-drone-strikes-in-pakistan (Accessed April 10, 2016).

Beck, U. (1992) *Risk Society: Towards a New Modernity.* London; Thousand Oaks, CA: Sage Publications.

Bergenas, J., Stohl, R., and Georgieff, A. (2013) The other side of drones: Saving wildlife in Africa and managing global crime. *Conflict Trends*, 3: 3–9.

Biddle, S. (2012) Secret Nuclear Drone Plan Nixed by "Political Realities." *Wired*, March 22. Available at: www.wired.com/2012/03/secret-nuclear-drone/.(Accessed April 10, 2016).

Bijker, W.E. and Law, J. (1992) *Shaping Technology/Building Society: Studies in Sociotechnical Change.* Cambridge, MA: MIT press.

Brunstetter, D. and Braun, M. (2011) The implications of drones on the Just War tradition. *Ethics and International Affairs*, 25 (3): 337–358.

Buzan, B., Wæver, O., and de Wilde, J. (1998) *Security: A New Framework of Analysis.* Boulder, London: Lynne Rienner Publishers.

Cavelty, M.D., Kaufmann, M., and Kristensen, K.S. (2015) Resilience and (in)security: Practices, subjects, temporalities. *Security Dialogue*, 46 (1): 3–14.

Center for Civilians in Conflict and Columbia Law School Human Rights Clinic (2012) *The Civilian Impact of Drones: Unexamined Costs, Unanswered Questions.* New York: Columbia Law School. Available at: http://civiliansinconflict.org/uploads/files/publications/The_Civilian_Impact_of_Drones_w_cover.pdf (Accessed April 10, 2016).

Chamayou, G. (2013) *La théorie du drone.* Paris: Edition La Fabrique.

Choi-Fitzpatrick, A. (2014) Drones for good: Technological innovations, social movements, and the state. *Journal of International Affairs*, 68 (1): 19–36.

Chow, J. (2012) Predators for Peace. *Foreign Policy.* Available at: www.foreignpolicy.com/articles/2012/04/27/predators_for_peace (Accessed April 10, 2016).

Civil Aviation Authority (2012) Updating the UK's Airspace – The Future Airspace Strategy (FAS). *In Focus.* Available at: www.caa.co.uk/docs/2408/FAS%20brief.pdf (Accessed April 10, 2016).

Crang, M. and Graham, S. (2007) Sentient cities: Ambient intelligence and the politics of urban space. *Information, Communication, Society*, 10 (6): 789–817.

Dolan, A.M. and Thompson, R.M. (2013) Integration of Drones into Domestic Airspace: Selected Legal Issues. *Congressional Research Service.* Available at: www.fas.org/sgp/crs/natsec/R42940.pdf (Accessed April 10, 2016).

Duffield, M. (2001) Governing the borderlands: Decoding the power of aid. *Disasters*, 25 (4): 308–320.

Duffield, M. (2004) *Carry on Killing: Global Governance, Humanitarianism and Terror.* DIIS Working Paper 23. Copenhagen: DIIS.

Dufresne, B. (2015) CT Drone Enthusiasts Worry About Future of Their Hobby. *Hartford Courant*, March 9. Available at: www.courant.com/features/hc-connecticut-hobbyists-with-drones-20150309-story.html#page=1 (Accessed April 10, 2016).

FAA (2013) Federal Aviation Administration, U.S. Department of Transportation. Integration of Civil Unmanned Aircraft Systems (UAS) in the National Airspace System (NAS) Roadmap. Available at: www.faa.gov/uas/publications/ (Accessed April 10, 2016).

Ferguson, J. (2006) *Global Shadows: Africa in the Neoliberal World Order*, Durham, NC: Duke University Press.

Fritsch, S. (2011) Technology and global affairs. *International Studies Perspectives*, 12 (1): 27–45.

Gibbs, S. (2015) Lords Urge Compulsory Registration of all Civilian Drones. *The Guardian*, March 5. Available at: www.theguardian.com/news/2015/mar/05/lords-urge-compulsory-registration-of-all-civilian-drones (Accessed April 10, 2016).

Gómez-Candón, D., De Castro, A.I., and López-Granados, F. (2014) Assessing the accuracy of mosaics from unmanned aerial vehicle (UAV) imagery for precision agriculture purposes in wheat. *Precision Agriculture*, 15 (1): 44–56.

Graham, S. (2006) Cities and the "War on Terror." *International Journal of Urban and Regional Research*, 30 (2): 255–276.

Gregory, D. (2011a) From a view to a kill: Drones and late modern war. *Theory, Culture & Society*, 28 (7–8): 188–215.

(2011b) The Everywhere War. *The Geographical Journal*, 177 (3): 238–250.

Hayes, B. and Sullivan, G. (2010) *Blacklisted: Targeted Sanctions, Preemptive Security and Fundamental Rights.* London: Transnational Institute. Available at: www.tni.org/paper/blacklisted (Accessed April 10, 2016).

Hayes, B., Jones, C., and Töpfer, E., (2014) *Eurodrones Inc*. London: Transnational Institute and Statewatch. Available at: www.tni.org/en/eurodrones (Accessed April 10, 2016).

Herrera, G.L. (2003) Technology and international systems. *Millennium: Journal of International Studies*, 32 (3): 559–593.

Holmqvist, C. (2013) Undoing war: War ontologies and the materiality of drone warfare. *Millennium: Journal of International Studies*, 41 (3): 535–552.

IRIN (2014) NGOs against MONUSCO drones for humanitarian work. *IRIN*, July 23. Available at: www.irinnews.org/report/100391/ngos-against-monusco-drones-for-humanitarian-work.(Accessed April 10, 2016).

Karlsrud, J. and Rosén, F. (2013) In the eye of the beholder? UN and the use of drones to protect civilians. *Stability: International Journal of Security and Development*, 2 (2).

Kennedy, C. and Rogers, J.I. (2015) Virtuous drones? *International Journal of Human Rights*, 19 (2): 211–227.

Koh, H. (2013) How to End the Forever War? – A Speech by Professor Harold Hongju Koh. Oxford University, May 7. Available at: http://yaleglobal.yale.edu/content/how-end-forever-war (Accessed 10 April 2016).

Kotilainen, N. (2011) Humanitarian Soldiers, Colonialised Others and Invisible Enemies: Visual Strategic Communication Narratives of the Afghan War. *The Finnish Institute of International Affairs*, Working Paper 72.

Krasmann, S. (2012) Targeted killing and its law: On a mutually constitutive relationship. *Leiden Journal of International Law*, 25 (3): 665–682.

Kreps, S. and Kaag, J. (2012) The use of unmanned aerial vehicles in contemporary conflict: A legal and ethical analysis. *Polity*, 44 (2): 260–285.

Kroener, I. and Neyland, D. (2012) New Technologies, Security and Surveillance, in Lyon, D., Ball, K., and Haggerty, K.D. (eds.), *Routledge Handbook of Surveillance Studies*. Abingdon: Routledge.

Lagesse, D. (2015) If Drones Make You Nervous, Think of them as Flying Donkeys. *National Public Radio*, March 31. Available at: www.npr.org/sections/goatsandsoda/2015/03/31/395316686/if-drones-make-you-nervous-think-of-them-as-flying-donkeys (Accessed April 10, 2016).

Lakoff, A. (2008) The generic biothreat, or, how we became unprepared. *Cultural Anthropology*, 23 (3): 399–428.

Leander, A. (2013) Technological agency in the co-constitution of legal expertise and the US drone program. *Leiden Journal of International Law*, 26 (4): 811–831.

Levin, A. (2015) Insurers Step Up for Drone Pilots Unwilling to Wait on FAA Rules, *Bloomberg*, March 6. Available at: www.bloomberg.com/news/articles/2015-03-06/insurers-step-up-for-drone-pilots-unwilling-to-wait-on-faa-rules (Accessed April 10, 2016).

Lowy, Joan (2015) FAA seeking drone rules favorable to commercial operators, February 14. Available at: www.salon.com/2015/02/14/faa_seeking_drone_rules_favorable_to_commercial_operators/ (Accessed April 10, 2016).

Marks, C. (2014) Elephants and Rhinos Benefit from Drone Surveillance. *New Scientist*, February 14. Available at: www.newscientist.com/article/dn25056-elephants-and-rhinos-benefit-from-drone-surveillance.html#.VRmyl2akEy4 (Accessed April 10, 2016).

Mathews, L. (2014) This $50 Device Let's You Kick People off Wireless Networks. *Geek*, November 12. Available at: www.geek.com/chips/this-50-device-lets-you-kick-people-off-wireless-networks-1609283/ (Accessed April 10, 2016).

McCarthy, D.R. (2013) Technology and "the International" or: How I learned to stop worrying and love determinism. *Millennium: Journal of International Studies*, 41 (3): 470–490.

McNeal, G. (2015) Leaked FAA Document Provides Glimpse into Drone Regulations. *Forbes*, February 14. Available at: www.forbes.com/sites/gregorymcneal/2015/02/14/the-faa-may-get-drones-right-after-all-9-insights-into-forthcoming-regulations/.

Monahan, T. and Mokos, J.T. (2013) Crowdsourcing urban surveillance: The development of homeland security markets for environmental sensor networks. *Geoforum*, 49: 279–288.

Mueller, M. (2011) What is Evgeny Morozov Trying to Prove? A Review of the Net Delusion. *Internet Governance Project*. Available at: www.internetgovernance.org/2011/01/13/what-is-evgeny-morozov-trying-to-prove-a-review-of-the-net-delusion/ (Accessed April 10, 2016).

Newman, L.H. (2015) Here's How to Set Up a No-Fly Zone Over Your House. *Slate*: *Future Tense*, February 10. Available at: www.slate.com/blogs/future_tense/2015/02/10/noflyzone_org_lets_you_geofence_the_area_over_your_house_for_drones_to_avoid.html (Accessed April 10, 2016).

Pandolfi, M. (2003) Contract of mutual (in)difference: Government and the humanitarian apparatus in contemporary Albania and Kosovo. *Indiana Journal of Global Legal Studies*, 10 (1): 369–381.

Perraudin, F. (2015) Just One "Disastrous Accident" Could Set Drone Industry Back, Warn Lords. *The Guardian*, March 5. Available at: www.theguardian.com/technology/2015/mar/05/just-one-disastrous-accident-could-set-drone-industry-back-warn-lords (Accessed April 10, 2016).

Piiparinen, T. (2015) Beyond the technological turn: Reconsidering the significance of the intervention brigade and peacekeeping drones for UN conflict management. *Global Governance: A Review of Multilateralism and International Organizations*, 21 (1): 141–160.

Pilkington, E. (2015) US Experts Join Companies Protesting FAA Commercial Drones Proposals. *The Guardian*, February 22. Available at: www.theguardian.com/world/2015/feb/22/experts-companies-protest-faa-commercial-drones-proposals.

Ryan, M. (2015) Obama Administration to Allow Sales of Armed Drones to Allies. *The Washington Post*, February 17. Available at: www.washingtonpost.com/world/national-security/us-cracks-open-door-to-the-export-of-armed-drones-to-allied-nations/2015/02/17/c5595988-b6b2-11e4-9423-f3d0a1ec335c_story.html (Accessed April 10, 2016).

Salter, M. (2013) Toys for the boys? Drones, pleasure and popular culture in the militarisation of policing. *Critical Criminology*, 22 (2): 163–177.

Sandvik, K.B. (2013) Drone Pilots, Humanitarians and the Videogame Analogy: Unpacking the Conversation, in *UAV – bare ny teknologi eller en ny strategisk virkelighet? Luftkrigsskolens skriftserie* 29. Trondheim: Luftkrigsskolen.

Sandvik, K.B. and Lohne, K. (2014) The rise of the humanitarian drone: Giving content to an emerging concept. *Millennium: Journal of International Studies*, 43 (1): 145–164.

Sandvik, K.B., Jumbert, M.G., Karlsrud, J., and Kaufmann, M. (2014) Humanitarian technology: A critical research agenda. *International Review of the Red Cross*, 96 (893): 219–242.

Singer, P.W. (2009) *Wired for War: The Robotics Revolution and Conflict in the Twenty-first Century*. New York: Penguin.

Spillane, C. (2013) How Google Earth and Drones are Saving Elephants in Africa. *The Sydney Morning Herald*, October 14. Available at: www.smh.com.au/technology/technology-news/how-google-earth-and-drones-are-saving-elephants-in-africa-20131010-2v9na.html (Accessed April 10, 2016).

Stanford Law School Human Rights and Conflict Resolution Clinic and NYU School of Law Global Justice Clinic (2012) Living under Drones: Death, Injury, and Trauma to Civilians from US Drone Practices in Pakistan. Available at: http://chrgj.org/wp-content/uploads/2012/10/Living-Under-Drones.pdf (Accessed April 10, 2016).

Tucker, P. (2015) In Ukraine, Tomorrow's Drone War is Alive Today. *Defense One*, March 9. Available at: www.defenseone.com/technology/2015/03/ukraine-tomorrows-drone-war-alive-today/107085/ (Accessed April 10, 2016).

Wæver, O. (1993) *Securitization and Desecuritization*, Centre for Peace and Conflict Research.

Wall, T. and Monahan, T. (2011) Surveillance and violence from afar: The politics of drones and liminal security-scapes. *Theoretical Criminology*, 15 (3): 239–254.

Whetham, D. (2015) Drones to protect. *The International Journal of Human Rights*, 19 (2): 199–210.

Whittle, R. (2014) Drone Defender Drops D-word Denial. *Breaking Defense*, December 23. Available at: http://breakingdefense.com/2014/12/drone-defender-drops-d-word-denial/ (Accessed April 10, 2016).

1 Targeted "killer drones" and the humanitarian discourse

On a liaison

Susanne Krasmann

Introduction: the promise of precision and the problem of reasonable use of force

There is no such thing as a "good drone" as opposed to a "bad drone," despite suggestions to the contrary in public discourse. This discourse seeks to distinguish between weaponized drones employed in the fight against terrorism and more praiseworthy "humanitarian drones." As Andrew Stobo Sniderman and Mark Hanis (2013), co-founders of the Genocide Intervention Network, point out: "[...] humanitarian drones [...] should assume their place in the arsenal of human rights advocates [...] Drones can reach places and see things cell phones cannot." Hence, Remotely Piloted Aircraft Systems (RPAS) may spot human rights violations that are otherwise hidden from the public eye, and thus substantially contribute to saving the lives of innocent and endangered people.[1] "Why not get drones to assist the good work?" the authors contend, effectively brushing aside the general scepticism about the technology due to its association with the practice of targeted killing in the fight against terrorism.[2] Yet, this explicit and more often implicit distinction between "killer drones" (Sauer and Schörnig 2012), as the "reprehensible" ones, and "humanitarian drones," as the "good" ones, is not tenable. This is not only because, in principle, all types of drones, even the smallest flying robots,[3] may be armed,[4] or because various drone types, serving different purposes like reconnaissance or surveillance, work hand in hand within a single joint killing operation (Niva 2013; Rosén 2014; Sandvik and Lohne 2014). Rather, the weaponized drone locates itself within the humanitarian discourse. The promise of precision plays a key role here. It addresses the legal principles of international humanitarian law, notably regarding proportionality, discrimination and humanity, as contained in the Geneva Conventions of 1949 and the Additional Protocols of 1979 related to the protection of victims of armed conflict. These principles are geared towards a limited use of force, in relation to the military objective, and in particular the avoidance of civilian casualties and unnecessary suffering. As a weapon of warfare, drones therefore are even welcomed by human rights organizations, as the statement by Peter Maurer (2013), President of the International Committee of the Red Cross, reveals:

from the perspective of international humanitarian law, any weapon that makes it possible to carry out more precise attacks, and helps avoid or minimize incidental loss of civilian life, injury to civilians, or damage to civilian objects, should be given preference over weapons that do not.[5]

Similarly, the Special Rapporteur for the UN, Ben Emmerson (2013: 7), also embraces the promise of precision in a recent report: "The ability of drones to loiter and gather intelligence for long periods before a strike, coupled with the use of precision-guided munitions, is therefore a positive advantage from a humanitarian law perspective."

It is, moreover, against this backdrop that the US administration is able to plausibly praise the advantages of the technology. As the former Assistant for Homeland Security and Counterterrorism, John Brennan (2012), maintains: "Never before has there been a weapon that allows us to distinguish more effectively between an al-Qa'ida terrorist and innocent civilians, it is hard to imagine a tool that can better minimize the risk to civilians than remotely piloted aircraft."

This statement also reveals that the promise of precision echoes the fundamental ambivalence of the Western, liberal understanding of the use of force.[6] "Killer drones" have been recognized as "the silver bullet of democratic warfare" (Sauer and Schörnig 2012). The good drone is "uninhabited" and spares the lives of our warriors, and it is praised as an intelligent, "smart weapon." It is capable of targeted interventions, that is, of a limited and reasonable use of force. It thus addresses our moral and legal concerns about state-sponsored killing as well as the aspiration of effective warfare.[7]

Drawing on the recent debate in social theory that takes the interplay of the material and the social, of matter and meaning into account, allows us to capture the active role the drone technology plays in producing the legitimacy of the practice of targeted killing – and this will be the topic of the following sections: how the drone technology activates and shapes our moral and legal concerns by actually tying in with currently predominant conceptions of the nature of the threat of terrorist networks. The crucial notion of networks is cherished both in military strategic thinking and with regard to matters of inner security or, to be more precise, the securitization of vulnerable vital systems and their resilience. It is the thinking in terms of connectivity that is characteristic here and, accordingly, the suggestion of targeted forms of intervention. Rather than merely being a rhetorical figure, the drone's promise of precision appears as a strategy that, in response to emerging terror networks, generates its own dynamic. 'Reasonable' then may signify a limited use of force, but also includes the option of sounding out ever more targets. According to critical security studies, legal concerns fade away with rather informal forms of protecting complex "living milieus." The final section, in contrast, observes that targeted interventions and their propensity for expansion in the name of security actually go well together with today's requirements of legality. The drone seems to be made to satisfy these. "Signature strikes," operating on the basis that biological life forms can be numerically codified, come to appear as the point of culmination of this development. They are deemed to be legitimate once behaviour and movements of anonymous entities on the ground are identified as suspicious patterns that match certain risk profiles.

The drone as an active player in the political game of securitization

What is deemed to be appropriate or suitable, Michel Foucault's notion of the rationalities of government teaches us, always depends on the nature of the problem at hand, and on our conception of it. It is a question of the "right disposition of things" (Foucault 2007: 99),[8] that is, of how our aims, taking the nature of the problem into account, are to be best achieved (see ibid.: 95; 2008: 2). The articulation of aims thereby itself depends on and changes with the problem, which also implies with the technologies at hand and the forms of knowledge that render the problem accessible to us in a particular manner. Hence, the question of the "right" use of drones and their suitability in the fight against terrorism unfolds within a matrix of the presumed nature of the threat, the object of protection, the technology's capabilities and related ethical, tactical and strategic considerations. Accordingly, the bio-political body to be defended against or defeated is indissolubly linked to the knowledge techniques, for example, statistics, algorithms or network theory, and the related technologies, for example, video cameras, computer systems or GPS, that render it accessible in the first place (Foucault 2003; 2008). Securitization is thus always also a response to vulnerability that becomes visible in this way.

If the drone appears to be a suitable weapon for facing today's security challenges, we may conclude that this is also because the technology somehow fits into the current cartography of our politico–legal thinking. In fact, the "rise of the drone"[9] goes hand in hand with the development of a new conception of the social body to be protected, which can be noticed both in social theory and the governance of security. Concepts like network centric warfare, which have been prevalent in recent military doctrines, are consistent with this. It is also no coincidence that they find their complement in new conceptions of securitization, like critical infrastructure and resilience in the civilian sector. These concepts have in common that they transcend the traditional distinction in politico–legal thinking between military affairs and policing, national and internal security as well as the established boundary between different spheres of the economic and the social, the human and the non-human. They are understood as a response to a new quality of security challenge, namely, a world of complex systems that deploy their own protocols and logics of expansion. Moreover, the recent debate on "matter" (Barad 2003) and the relevance of "materiality" in social theory can be seen as a reflection of these developments in the governance of security.[10] Rather than in terms of the classical coordinates of politico–legal representation, nation-state, or the rule of law, "post-hegemonic" accounts (Lash 2007; Urry 2005) conceive of the interplay of human and non-human action, or forces, and, notably, the material fabrication of the social (Law and Urry 2004).[11]

Focusing analytically on "matter," furthermore, allows us to capture the drone technology's active role in its own localization within the socio-material inscription of our world. However, rather than speaking of "actants" as "things" with "agency" (Leander 2013: 813), and thus losing sight of the intrinsic entanglement of human agency with technology as well as of the involvement of technology in strategic configurations,[12] we should conceive of the drone more dynamically as a technology, and in this sense as an artefact.[13] It is a *téchnē* (*gr.*, entailing the notions of art, craft, science), which involves certain techniques, practices and procedures as well as certain forms of knowledge. Drone operations require not only a certain know-how for their use, but also produce certain forms of knowledge and visibility. They enable a "view from above" (Adey, Whitehead and Williams 2013) and a particular practice of state sponsored killing in the first place. They also produce certain imageries of the target or enemy and of the nature of the problem in question, which in turn may be tied to certain imageries of warfare or the fight against terrorism (Van Veeren 2013). This, of course, is neither to say that respective images would overwhelmingly endorse the practice of targeted killing (Leander 2013), nor that this is merely a question of rhetoric and symbolic meaning. On the contrary, drones *matter* in that they determine not only what can be said and be seen, but also what can be done in a material or ontological sense (Barad 2003; Walters 2014). They are material "devices" that "*do* things" (Law and Ruppert 2013: 230; emphasis in original) and render the world, in a particular manner, accessible.[14] Drones therefore are always "'already' political agents" (Holmqvist 2013: 545). As a military weapon, they are tied to the politico–legal discourse and in a way do not exist prior to it. The very notion of targeted killing, echoing the promise of precision, may be read as the product of a legal discourse that addresses the pertinent legal principles of international humanitarian law (Gunneflo 2014). Drones epitomizing this capacity to enact targeted interventions, in this sense, are literally made for contemporary warfare. If there is a "prescriptive force of legality" (Rajkovic 2012: 31), however, legality is never already there. It does not pre-exist the practices in question but is something to be fabricated. It is the practices themselves that invoke and effectuate certain norms. Drone operations, in this sense, also shape the imagery of contemporary warfare and, correspondingly, the understanding of legitimate and legal state-sponsored killing. Let us then take a closer look at how drone technology and the logic of targeted intervention appear to correspond to currently predominant conceptions of threats and the social body to be protected both in the field of everyday life securitization and in the context of counterterrorism and counter-insurgency. As we will see, the notions of "resilience" and "preparedness," as well as that of terror networks, are based on an idea of connectivity that renders the respective matter calculable and incalculable at the same time, and precisely therefore requires specific countermeasures.

Complex systems as actors and objects of threats

In the governance of security, the notions of "resilience" and "preparedness" (Lentzos and Rose 2009) emerged in the face of a new dimension of catastrophic threats that were perceived as resisting calculability and controllability while, at the same time, demanding attention because of the intolerable harm they caused (Amoore and de Goede 2008). Resilience is widely applicable (see exemplarily: United Nations 2005).[15] Framed in terms of empowerment, the concept aims at strengthening the sustainability of systems and their mechanisms of self-defence. Citizens are supposed to improve their capabilities as "resistant" subjects within their environments and to be prepared for the possible next catastrophic event. Resilience, to be sure, is not to be confused with resistance as a force of civil society (Reid 2013: 362–3). On the contrary, it is a governmental technology where security is deemed to be a permanent endeavour of everyday life and which allows for governmental authorities to resign from the exclusive responsibility of their traditional role of the providing of security.[16] The subject is being "responsibilized" for its own and the community's safety. As David Chandler (2013: 211) observes, "security has become societalized." Hence, "civil security" is a typical signification of this paradigm shift (Zoche, Kaufmann and Haverkamp 2011), indicating the establishment of a new relationship between state and citizen.

While this process of a "societalization of security" and responsibilization through participation has received much attention in security studies so far (e.g. Joseph 2013), a different aspect is of interest for our purposes that comes with the rise of resilience. What is at issue is the re-configuration of the biopolitical body as the object of protection. Rather than alluding to entities like the state, nation or citizen, as political thinking in terms of a genuinely symbolically constituted order would have it, today the concern is about the vulnerability of "vital systems" (Collier and Lakoff 2015). Systems like 'critical infrastructures' and the corresponding threats are assumed to be 'complex' in several respects. Being organized in the form of a network, they emerge and reproduce themselves in a non-linear and contingent manner (Dillon 2007). Independent of human action, they deploy their own forms of connectivity and expansion, and intervention in the name of security, accordingly, addresses the very rules and modes of connectivity that constitute these systems.

Social theory reflects this shift in thinking when it literally centres on the nature of the problem. Critical infrastructure, it has been suggested, is to be taken into account 'as an object whose *materiality* has both enabling and constraining effects on what can be said and done to secure it' (Aradau 2010: 492; emphasis added). Moreover, the notion of critical infrastructures, which includes key locations of trade like the harbour, and key technologies like computers and the Internet, exceeds the established distinction between the economic, the social and the political sphere of government. What needs to be secured are the modes of operation and the functioning of the systems: the services and exchanges, the chains of communication or goods. The "breakdown or impairment" of critical infrastructures as vital systems, a strategic paper of the German Federal Ministry of Interior holds, may cause "long term supply bottlenecks" and eventually "a substantial disruption of the public order or other dramatic consequences" (BMI 2009: 3).

When citizens are addressed in the interest of fostering a "culture of resilience," they are themselves conceived as resources. They are to be mobilized via the so-called new media, the Internet, Web platforms, or Twitter. Connectivity, once again, is considered essential. Rather than merely a biological or social entity, the social body is deemed to be an "assemblage" (de Landa 2006) of human and non-human entities and interconnected processes. The nature of politics, or government, is consequently performative and inscriptive. Instead of representation and hegemony, it emphasizes communication, connectivity and materialization (Lash 2007). Within these governmental programmes and practices, the sociological notion of society, and along with it the object of security, divides up into "multiplicities" (Foucault 2007: 11).

For good reason, these observations may remind us of Foucault's differentiation between exercising power *upon* things and modes of governing "circulations" (Foucault 2007: 18) *through* the elements of an empirical reality (see ibid.: 46–7) that comes to be codified and represented, for example, in data doubles and numbers for calculation. In modern terms, security is the response to what Foucault designates as "the sudden emergence of the problem of the 'naturalness' of the human species within an artificial milieu" (ibid.: 21–2). This is in line with the discovery of the population as a biopolitical body which assumes a life of its own: "Security will rely on a number of material givens" (ibid.: 19), ranging from the climate and economic resources to cultural codes of behaviour that shape the everyday existence of the population. These "material givens," however, are rendered accessible to governmental intervention only by way of translating them into artificial data. As a subject of knowledge and object of government, the biopolitical body is necessarily subjected to "informatic methods," and as such, of a "fundamentally unhuman quality" (Thacker 2013). As Nathaniel O'Grady has also pointed out recently, this artificial configuration of a living "milieu" – that is, of a space of "possible elements" (Foucault 2007: 20) that are to be assessed and organized in their circulations, interactions and varying constellations – is what gives way to a "speculative thinking" (O'Grady 2013). Demarcating the birth of the liberal security dispositif, this thinking, according to Foucault (2007: 20), "takes into account precisely what might happen" without ever being able to control the unknown, unforeseeable future. Complexity theory, we may therefore argue with Foucault, is only the logical outcome of this entering of the biopolitical body onto the historical scene. If this observation is true, then today's talk about networks that are incalculable in their moves and proceedings would only be the continuation of the modern experience of contingency. It suggests a shift of awareness in the face of only putatively new dimensions of threats. The continuity, on the one hand, lies in the awareness of a "naturalness" and internal dynamic that goes beyond one's control. The difference to the classical liberal order, on the other hand, consists in the focus on a non-linear contingency that constantly indicates a possible rupture with the (just) established order.

Yet, a further aspect needs to be taken into account. As David Chandler (2013: 211–12) points out, those rather indirect and "informal" ways of intervening in the "societal milieus" that the concept of resilience – exemplarily – stands for, denote a rupture with the traditional liberal understanding of legally shaped state–society relations operating "through the formal framework of public law" as well as with the idea of individuals being addressed in a normative fashion. With distinctive and targeted forms of intervention, governance in the name of security and protecting life, decentralizes, spreads and disperses while at the same time remaining open to permanent modification and adaptation.

In the context of counterterrorism and counter-insurgency, this state of affairs finds its counterpart in the figure of terror networks. The advocates of the information revolution in military affairs, John Arquilla and David Ronfeldt (2001a; see also Cebrowski and Garstka 1998), hold that network-like organized and dispersed forms of resistance must be countered by "network centric" forms of warfare. Consequently, the doctrine of counter-insurgency of 2006, authored by David Petraeus and James Mattis (2006, Chapter 1, para. 103), promotes the idea of intelligent and literally clean warfare. Targeted interventions are designated as "surgical" interventions: "With good intelligence, a counter-insurgent is like a surgeon, cutting out cancerous tissue while keeping other vital organs intact." John Brennan (2012), remarkably, borrows from this wording in his statement on the use of drones: "It's this surgical precision, the ability, with laser-like focus, to eliminate the cancerous tumor called an al-Qaida terrorist while limiting damage to the tissue around it, that makes this counterterrorism tool so essential." As Markus Gunneflo (2014: 29) observes, the pervasive use of medical metaphors here indicates how "targeted killing emerges as a means for the protection of the political body." The language carries with it the idea of a co-existence within a political community that takes the elimination of life as 'a precondition for sustaining life' (ibid.: 222). As "drone stake-holders" argue: "drones don't just end human life, they also save it" (Harwood 2011, quoted in Sandvik and Lohne 2014: 7). Yet, it is also the very notion of terrorist networks that gives rise to respective modes of thinking and intervention.

Terrorist networks no longer conform to the classical idea of war as a confrontation between states. In terms of modern politico–legal thinking, whereas sovereign states constitute themselves through a legal order within discrete territorial spaces, terrorist networks constitute themselves through "connectivity" (Galloway and Thacker 2007: 16). Further, whereas the former are rather conceived in terms of a symbolic order and representation, the logic of networks is determined by the logic of protocols and the interaction of technical devices and human beings. Moreover, due to their modular forms of organization, terrorist networks literally and figuratively transgress territorial boundaries and the established coordinates of the order of sovereign states. Compared to the traditional logic of a confrontation between states, the actions of terrorist networks are deemed rather to be unknowable. They employ a different, if not deviant, morality of asymmetrical warfare. "Transnational terrorists organized in widely dispersed, networked nodes have shown how it is possible to swarm together swiftly, on cue, then pulse to the attack simultaneously" (Arquilla and Ronfeldt 2001b). The combatants are also able to "blend perfectly into the background of society until needed and then [become] visible momentarily" (Mendel 2010: 735). Here, enemy combatant and civilian become indistinguishable.

Although denied equal legal status and sovereign rights, in view of their ability to utilize, or morph into, weapons of mass destruction, terrorist networks are at the same time viewed as being on a par with states (Kahn 2008). Pre-emptive action is therefore required against the emerging threat. The relationship between the terror network and the sovereign state that sees itself acting in self-defence is an at once asymmetric and symmetric relationship between "unequal sovereigns" (Gunneflo 2014: 239). It is at this point at the latest that we may become aware that the talk about networks is not merely metaphorical, but also a form of employing "devices" (de Goede 2012: 216) – of deciphering and enacting a vision of the world and corresponding threats, so as to render them accessible to strategic intervention. Networks are 'metaphorical totalities' and, at the same time, "material social infrastructures" (Jagoda 2010: 67). It is the particular mode of connectivity that makes for their constitution and their expansion. Their "power is additive, not exclusive," they follow a logic of "and" rather than "or" (Galloway and Thacker 2007: 18). Networks are "never integral whole objects in the first place." Identifying them therefore also means recognizing them in their very existence. "To name a network is to acknowledge a process of individuation ('the Internet,' 'al-Quaeda')" (ibid.: 12). It is to take part in their constitution and to *render* them identifiable in the first instance. And as the next section will show, it is this logic of self-assertion that makes for targeted interventions producing their own legitimacy.

Targeting: the logic of precision and expansion

Networks, then, are epistemic as well as ontic configurations, they are objects of knowledge as well as material entities that deploy their own logic. Combat drones and their targeted interventions correspond to these configurations in both a literal and a material sense. They address the "hot spots" of terrorist organizations. They aim at destroying the hubs of the networks, represented by their leading figures, so as to intercept their communication and any preparatory action, and to eventually destroy the entire network. Indeed, it is in this sense that drones are anything but "just another weapon system" (Henriksen 2014: 217). As the German political scientist Herfried Muenkler

(2013) claims drones "re-symmetrize" warfare. Yet, they reproduce the logic of the networks they encounter. As Samuel Weber (2005: 101; emphasis in original) observes: "Is *targeting* something that occurs independently of the network or is it part and parcel of how the 'net' works?" If we assume that networks are self-reproducing systems and hence the threat continues to persist, this establishes the *option* of targeted interventions as a reasonable use of force.[17]

The promise of precision thereby develops its own script. As a promise, it demands sticking to it as well as fulfilling it. We *keep* our promise, we say. And, with the promise, the idea is cherished that precision is possible and made possible thanks to the implementation of techniques like algorithmic calculation and the prediction of threats, or thanks to precautions like targeting and observing a suspected subject and, not least, thanks to the use of technologies like the drone that are able to zoom in on the object and strike precisely. Political rhetoric thereby upholds the suggestion that precision by itself is morally good (Kreps and Kaag 2012).[18]

Indeed, the idea of precision deploys its own logic as well. Rather than concerning limitation, it is one of expansion. Five moments can be distinguished here: the very definition of precision, which includes imprecision; its rhetoric, which is also one of distinction between the legitimate and illegitimate target; the problem of discrimination; the rationality of proportionality, which invokes the idea of excess; and the proposition of the right disposition of things which renders targeted intervention appropriate compared to the expected catastrophic threat. First of all, imprecision is inscribed into the very definition of precision itself. "'Precision' weapons," as Maja Zehfuss (2011: 548) has pointed out in the context of high-tech weaponry, are "inherently imprecise." Like accuracy, precision is always relational and as such determined by a radial space around an aim point, that is, by a scope that can be hit with a certain probability. Collateral effects are, in this sense, always already anticipated. Second, rhetorically, talk about precision and the possibility of discrimination suggests that a distinction exists between the illegitimate target that may not be hit and the legitimate target that may in fact be eliminated. The goal of limiting collateral damage thereby also involves accepting a certain degree of collateral damage. The promise of precision – of "smart," "surgical" interventions – thus sets forth the conditions for the legitimate use of force. As the etymology of the term already indicates, "'smart bombs' are really not 'smart'" (Kreps and Kaag 2012: 276) in the sense of "clever" or "neat." The term (from the Anglo-Saxon *smeart*) actually implies "painful," "stinging" and "sharp." Third, if the use of drones is a response to an asymmetric constellation where combatants are no longer members of a regular army, but have blended into the civilian population (so that none of them wear distinctive insignia or, conversely, everybody can potentially become involved in an effective conflict, etc.), the difficulty in discriminating between legitimate and illegitimate targets, participants and non-participants, is inherent. Obviously, indeterminacy raises the rate of suspects: According to several administration officials, the problem is or was that the Obama administration "in effect counts all military-age males in a strike zone as combatants [...], unless there is explicit intelligence posthumously proving them innocent" (Becker and Shane 2012).[19] Fourth, as with the legal principle of proportionality, thinking of precision always already includes and invokes its opposite. The rationality of the proportionality principle stipulates that the expected loss of the civilian population should not be disproportionate, that is, not excessive in relation to the anticipated military advantage (see Gregory 2011: 199). Similarly, rather than entirely excluding damage and suffering, the promise of precision concerns minimizing harm and collateral damage. Finally, through the lens of the "right" arrangement and distribution of things, anticipating the worst possible predictable outcome of catastrophic threats always renders targeted interventions proportionate. They are the least of all possible evil choices (see Weizman 2011: 2). Collateral damage is to be taken into account in the expectation of a better future. Yet, as long as one is supposed to assume that the threat – the unwanted possible catastrophe – will continue to loom, this putative better future will never be reached.

In light of the above we may presume that the practice of targeted killing develops a tendency of self-assertion including the option of expansion. This is due to the promise of precision that the drone technology carries with it. It associates ethical concerns with the aspiration of effectiveness by addressing an object that seems to require targeted interventions. Concerns on the part of the critics, nonetheless, may persist. They appear as the reverse image of the prevailing perspective: "For many, the drone promises to be the technological 'game changer' that can produce insurmountable, asymmetrical advantage: the capacity to kill literally anywhere and at any time without exposure to risk" (Kahn 2013: 200). In the eye of the critics, by contrast, this strategic and tactical advantage is exactly what constitutes the problem (Zenko and Kreps 2014): "drones may spare more innocents but they may also create more war" (Coll 2014). The versatile, smart and uninhabited drone allows for figuring out ever more targets literally anywhere and at any time without exposure to risk, above all leaving the targeted subject in an unequal and unfair constellation without any chance of legally objecting their situation (Coeckelbergh 2013; Kahn 2013).[20] Even if there is a "leap in precision" to be recorded over the course of the years, there is a predominant 'mentality [that] drives it all: if only we can get enough of these bastards we will win the war' (Coll 2014, quoting NYU law professor Philipp Alston). Yet, as is to be shown in the final section, the law is prepared to also accommodate the expanding logic of the practice of targeted killing.

Targeted killing and its law

Although targeted killing is a particular form of intervening into "living milieus," where the juridical tends to be substituted by informal modes of governing security (Chandler 2013), this in no way indicates that the US administration would not be eager to comply with the law and cherish the "rule of law." On the contrary, as mentioned above, the very notion of targeted killing itself embraces and promotes the legality and legitimacy of state-sponsored killing in the context of counterterrorism (see Gunneflo 2014, 11). Furthermore, the discursive figure of the terrorist network provides further corroboration here. It facilitates a reinterpretation of the limited right of states to use force in relation to another state, which according to Art. 51 of the UN Charter is ensured by the principle of self-defence. Since 9/11, there has been a gradual shift in the interpretation of this legal precondition, namely, from a temporal understanding to a qualitative one. The traditional criterion concerning a singular massive attack that has already occurred or is about to occur continues to be substituted by a focus on cumulative patterns of distributed and incalculable terrorist attacks,[21] which results in invoking the impression of a terror network. A confidential White Paper of the Department of Justice extrapolates that targeted interventions, as acts of "anticipatory" self-defence (Tams 2009), are now deemed to be reasonable, if not imperative, even without "specific evidence" about an *imminent attack*, if there is intelligence about a *continuing threat* of systematically planned terror attacks (Department of Justice n.d.: 7).[22] Furthermore, the figure of the network relocates the conception of sovereignty and, along with it, not only the question of territorial integrity but also of the binary distinction between warfare and law enforcement, symmetric and asymmetric warfare. To combat an enemy that is deterritorialized (see Gunneflo 2014: 235–44) implies no longer addressing the state where the combat takes place. Talk about a "war" against the terror organization and its affiliates, consequently, indicates that "the war goes where the combatant goes" (Anderson 2010: 4) and, notably, that this "war" is still warfare, or at least self-defence, but not police action.[23] An armed attack can be detected anywhere where joint terrorist networks' activities emerge (see Shaw 2013: 542) and, accordingly, must be countered by military means.

What is more, the introduction of the practice of "signature strikes," in contrast to "personality strikes" against "high-value" targets focusing on anonymous suspects, is to some extent consistent with a security regime that is focused on connectivity. It may therefore be read as an indicator of what we have to expect in the future. "Signature strikes target 'large groups of people whose identities are not known' but who are seen to display patterns of behaviour that render them suspicious" (Pugliese 2013: 195). In essence, this procedure relies on algorithmically generated patterns of anonymous behaviour and movements inspired by intelligence and measured against indicators of suspicion. Numerically codified biological life (Thacker 2013), abstracted from the individual human beings, is rendered meaningful on the basis of risk profiles and through the lens of the "objectifying" screen technology, which ultimately justifies the lethal strike. The targets are objects, and in effect victims, of an automatized "calculus of probabilities" (Pugliese 2013: 208).[24] Compared to the procedure of personality strikes, the effort to meticulously gather intelligence as well as to conduct a judicial review and provide a legal justification is reduced to a minimum.

Conclusion

Despite, but also because of, Obama's famous proclamation concerning a more restricted and controlled practice of air strikes in May 2013 (and reinforced in January 2014: The White House 2013; 2014), the practice of drone strikes may very well persist and normalize. It is not finally even necessary that the use of drones serves the purpose of killing, for the technology is also a tool of governing at a distance. Not only does it impinge upon the everyday life and behaviour of civilians who are frightened in the face of the actual or potential presence of drones, but it also mobilizes the enemy to look for a place to hide and thus leave aside for the moment any preparatory terrorist action (see Benjamin 2013: 101–18; Niva 2013). In this sense, drone operations somehow pervert the principle of resilience and instil in its victims that of preparedness.

The good drone, we may conclude, is the one that provides us with an appropriate response to the identified, non-ignorable threats. With its capacity of targeted interventions, the technology not only presents itself as the exact correspondence to the figure of terrorist networks. It also ties in with Western values and attendant legal norms that seem to require limited and effective use of force. And it is on this basis that the promise of precision makes for its own perpetuation. There is, to be sure, always enough space to read things otherwise and to object, even if we are already entangled in these conceptions of resilience.

Notes

1 Although Remotely Piloted Aircraft Systems (RPAS) or Unmanned Aerial Vehicles (UAV) figure among the official terms. The more concise notion of "drones" was gradually adopted by the public as well as the professional discourse, see Goldberg, Corcoran and Picard (2013: 4).

2 See, for example, the German anti-combat drone initiative 'Campaign on Drones': https://drohnen-kampagne.de/appell-keine-kampfdrohnen/international/; and the 'Campaign to stop Killer Robots', initiated by Human Rights Watch, focusing especially on autonomous weapons systems: www.stopkillerrobots.org/.

3 For a miniature prototype, see the "Skunk riot control drone" presented recently by the South African company, Desert Wolf: www.defenceweb.co.za/index.php?option =com_content&view=article&id=34659.

4 Even one of the most well-known combat drones of the first generation, the Predator, was originally constructed as a reconnaissance drone and is still available today in both versions (Shaw 2012).

5 Whereas some legal scholars tend to consider the practice of targeted killing through drones, by its very nature, to be a "calculated, precise use of lethal force" (e.g. Ulrich 2005), others are more cautious and demand a careful revision of the particular practice, as Maurer (2013) explains: "Whether the use of armed drones does indeed offer these advantages will depend on the specific circumstances. This issue is the subject of on-going debate due, among other things, to lack of

information on the effects of most of the drone strikes." For a critique of the lack of transparency regarding the disclosure of the full legal basis and procedural safeguards for targeted killing operations, the criteria of 'targetability' and the details of the decision-making procedure as a precondition of democratic control and accountability, see, among others, the websites of the American Civil Liberty Union (ACLU), for example, www.aclu.org/blog/national-security-human-rights/year-targeted-killing-small-steps-forward-transparency-still-no, the UN-Report by Alston (2010) and the expertise of the Stanford Law School and NYU School of Law (2012).

6 On this matter with regard to the idea of targeted governance, see also Valverde and Mopas (2004).

7 This is not to say that the questions about the ethics or morality of state sponsored killing and its legality were the same, but that they both relate to considerations of effectiveness. The question of legality, which goes beyond the scope of this article, of course requires a complex examination of different bodies of law. Among others, the crucial question is whether the law of armed conflict applies at all. Within the paradigm of law enforcement, international human rights law would otherwise, for example, place special emphasis on the individual right to life. For a related critique, see Klaidman (2012), and for a more detailed analysis of these questions taking shape with the drone technology in action, see Krasmann (2014).

8 Foucault quoting La Perrière.

9 This is the title of a film from 2012 about the advancement and multiple uses of the technology: www.pbs.org/wgbh/nova/military/rise-of-the-drones.html; see also Anderson (2010); Shaw (2012) using the same phrase. The market is expecting high growth rates in the upcoming decade; for the military sector and border control in the EU, see Hayes, Jones and Töpfer (2014); for the civilian sector, European Commission (2012).

10 On this observation with a focus on the notion of resilience, see also Schmidt (2013).

11 Whereas John Law and John Urry (2004, 397) address a shift in focus in social theory "from epistemology (where what is known depends on perspective) to ontology ([where] what is known is also being *made* differently)," I would rather speak of a shift from hegemonic thinking and social constructivism towards onto-epistemological approaches that insist on the 'mutual entailment' of discursive practices and material phenomena (Barad 2003: 822). Objects never exist prior to their fabrication.

12 For a respective and general critique of the reception of the actor-network theory, which Latour himself made a contribution towards in speaking of actants, things, and non-human beings, see Schüttpelz (2008). For a critique of the fetishization of drones that ignores the strategic-military apparatus employing the technology, see also Shaw and Akhter (2012).

13 Here, I draw on my own account, based on Foucault's notion of "dispositif" (Krasmann 2012), though this time with a more specified focus on the role of 'matter' for politico–legal analyses. The notion of technology thus features a conception of the ontological that cannot be dissolved from the epistemological or vice versa. See, accordingly, Lemke (2015) on correspondences between Foucault's and 'new materialism's' accounts. Similarly, Walters (2014: 103), in his reading of 'drone strikes' and 'dingpolitik', based on Latour and Foucault, insists on the 'fleeting, ambiguous, partial' and ungraspable nature of object and things.

14 For an early approach on technological that embodies its own rationality ("technological rationality") and at the same time can be transformed positively – and in this sense be "good" – in a way that it realizes the potentialities we experience in the 'nature' of things, see Marcuse (1982).

15 For an instructive overview over the genealogy of the concept of resilience, see for example, Rosenow (2012).

16 Aradau (2014: 75) even speaks of "the suspension of the promise of security."

17 It is part of this option that empirical facts and tactical considerations may lead to a temporary suspension of the practice or a shift in focus.

18 This is not to talk about the contingencies of actually hitting a target, that are due to practical reasons like the quality of the video feeds or the reliability of information and informants (Mayer 2009). The promise of precision, of course, is not the same as being precise.

19 There are no reliable figures to date on the military and civilian victims of drone strikes. Reliable estimates have been made, however, on the basis of journalistic research. Still, the range of these figures – for example, between 2004 and 2013, anywhere from 2,537 to 3,646 people died in 381 drone strikes in Pakistan, 416 to 951 of whom were civilians (The Bureau of Investigative Journalism: www.thebureauinvestigates.com/category/projects/drones/. Accessed 4 February 2014) – indicates not only the unsatisfactory level of information but also the varying, and controversial, criteria of distinction between civilian victims and combatants.

20 For a critique on the basis of "forensic architecture," including the interrogation of eye witnesses and family members of victims of drone strikes in Pakistan, see the research project at Goldsmith College: www.forensic-architecture.org/case/drone-strikes/ and the expertise of Stanford Law School and NYU School of Law (2012).

21 According to Christian Tams (2009), the rather defensive reading of self-defence that predominated during the period of the Cold War gradually shifted towards a more active or anticipatory form of pre-emptive or preventive self-defence. With the combat of terrorism in the aftermath of 9/11, the "accumulation-of-events" doctrine gained wider acceptance internationally (Henriksen 2014: 223; Erakat 2014).

22 This White Paper was distributed to members of the Senate Intelligence and Judiciary committees in June 2012 and obtained by the media in February 2013 (see Etzioni 2013: 5).

23 The European Parliament (2014) only recently expressed concerns about drone strikes on a foreign territory without the sovereign state's consent and urged the European Commission to adopt a common position. However, as Markus Gunneflo (2014: 161) has elaborated, the argument of "the 'right of a State to strike terrorists within the territory of another State where terrorists are using that territory as a location from which to launch terrorist attacks and where the State involved has failed to respond effectively to a demand that the attacks be stopped'" (Anderson 2010: 4, quoting a speech of the then-State Department Legal Advisor Abraham Sofaer held in 1989) goes as far back as the 1980s and had been since integrated into the legal discourse.

24 The practice of signature strikes has been known as a US counterterrorism tactic since 2008. It started under President Bush and expanded under President Obama, leading to a significant increase of drone strikes in Pakistan.

References

Adey, P., Whitehead, M. and Williams, A.J. (2013) *From Above. War, Violence and Verticality*. London: Hurst & Company.

Alston, P. (2010) 'Report of the Special Rapporteur on Extrajudicial, Summary or Arbitrary Executions: Study on Targeted Killings', UN Doc. A/HRC/14/24/Add.6, 28 May. Available at: www2.ohchr.org/english/bodies/hrcouncil/docs/14session/A.HRC.14.24.Add6.pdf (Accessed 10 April 2016).

Amoore, L. and de Goede, M. (2008) Introduction. Governing by risk in the war on terror, pp. 5–19 in Louise Amoore and Marieke de Goede (eds.), *Risk and the War on Terror*. London, New York: Routledge.

Anderson, K. (2010) Rise of the Drones: Unmanned Systems and the Future of War. Written Testimony Submitted to Subcommittee on National Security and Foreign Affairs, Committee on Oversight and Government Reform, US House of Representatives. Subcommittee Hearing. 23 March, 111th Cong., 2nd sess. 2010.

Aradau, C. (2010) Security that matters: Critical infrastructure and objects of protection. *Security Dialogue*, 41 (5): 491–514.

Aradau, C. (2014) The promise of security: Resilience, surprise and epistemic politics. *Resilience: International Policies, Practices and Discourses*, 2 (2): 73–87.

Arquilla, J. and Ronfeldt, D. (2001a) *Networks and Netwars: The Future of Terror, Crime, and Militancy*. Santa Monica, CA: RAND Corporation. Available at: www.rand.org/pubs/monograph_reports/MR1382 (Accessed 10 April 2016).

Arquilla, J. and Ronfeldt, D. (2001b) Osama bin Laden and the Advent of Netwar. *New Perspectives Quarterly*, 18 (4). Available at: www.digitalnpq.org/archive/2001_fall/osama.html (Accessed 10 April 2016).

Barad, K. (2003) Posthumanist performativity: Toward an understanding of how matter comes to matter. *Signs: Journal of Women in Culture and Society*, 28 (3): 801–31.

Becker, J. and Shane, S. (2012) "Secret 'Kill List' Proves a Test of Obama's Principles and Will." *The New York Times*, 29 May. Available at: www.nytimes.com/2012/05/29/world/obamas-leadership-in-war-on-al-qaeda.html?_r=0 (Accessed 10 April 2016).

Benjamin, M. (2013) *Drone Warfare. Killing by Remote Control*. Fully revised and updated version. London, New York: Verso.

BMI (Federal Ministry of Interior) (2009) *Nationale Strategie zum Schutz kritischer Infrastrukturen (kritis-Strategie)*. Available at: www.bmi.bund.de/SharedDocs/Downloads/DE/Broschueren/2009/kritis.pdf?__blob=publicationFile (Accessed 10 April 2016).

Brennan, J. (2012) "The Efficacy and Ethics of U.S. Counterterrorism Strategy": Transcript of Remarks, Woodrow Wilson International Center for Scholars, Washington, DC, 30 April. Available at: www.wilsoncenter.org/event/the-efficacy-and-ethics-us-counterterrorism-strategy (Accessed 10 April 2016).

Cebrowski, Vice Admiral A. and Garstka, J. (1998) *Network-Centric Warfare*. Proceedings of the United States Naval Institute 24 (1): 28–35.

Chandler, D. (2013) Resilience and the autotelic subject: Toward a critique of the societalization of security. *International Political Sociology*, 7: 210–26.

Coeckelbergh, M. (2013) Drones, information technology, and distance: Mapping the moral epistemology of remote fighting. *Ethics and Information Technology*, 15 (2): 87–98.

Coll, S. (2014) "The Unblinking Stare. The drone war in Pakistan," *The New Yorker*, 24 November. Available at: www.newyorker.com/magazine/2014/11/24/unblinking-stare (Accessed 10 April 2016).

Collier, S.J. and Lakoff, A. (2015) Vital systems security: Reflexive biopolitics and the government of emergency. *Theory, Culture & Society*, 32 (2): 19–51.

de Goede, M. (2012) Fighting the network: A critique of the network as a security technology. *Distinktion*, 13 (3): 215–32.

de Landa, M. (2006) *A New Philosophy of Society. Assemblage Theory and Social Complexity*. London, New York: Continuum.

Department of Justice (n.d.) "White Paper: Lawfulness of a Lethal Operation Directed Against a U.S. Citizen Who Is a Senior Operational Leader of Al-Qa'ida or An Associated Force." Available at: http://msnbcmedia.msn.com/i/msnbc/sections/news/020413_DOJ_White_Paper.pdf (Accessed 10 April 2016).

Dillon, M. (2007) Governing terror: The state of emergency of biopolitical emergence. *International Political Sociology*, 1: 7–28.

Emmerson, B. (2013) "Promotion and Protection of Human Rights and Fundamental Freedoms While Countering Terrorism. Note by the Secretary-General," UN Doc. A/68/389, 18 September.

Erakat, N.S. (2014: New imminence in the time of Obama: The impact of targeted killings on the law of self-defense. *Arizona Law Review*, 56: 195–248.

Etzioni, A. (2013) "The Great Drone Debate," *Military Review*, March–April. Available at: http://usacac.army.mil/CAC2/MilitaryReview/Archives/English/MilitaryReview_20130430_art004.pdf (Accessed 10 April 2016).

European Commission (2012) 'Commission Staff Working Document: Towards a European strategy for the development of civil applications of Remotely Piloted Aircraft Systems (RPAS)', 4 September (SWD(2012) 259 final).

European Parliament (2014) "Joint Motion for a Resolution on the use of armed drones," 25 February (2014/2567(RSP)) RC\1021121EN.doc.

Foucault, M. (2003) *Society Must Be Defended: Lectures at the Collège de France, 1975–76*, trans. D. Macey. New York: Picador.

Foucault, M. (2007) *Security, Territory, Population: Lectures at the Collège de France, 1977–78*, trans. G. Burchell. Hampshire/New York: Palgrave Macmillan.

Foucault, M. (2008) *The Birth of Biopolitics: Lectures at the Collège de France, 1978–79*, trans. G. Burchell. Hampshire/New York: Palgrave Macmillan.

Galloway, A.R. and Thacker, E. (2007) *The Exploit: A Theory of Networks*. Minneapolis: University of Minnesota Press.

Goldberg, D., Corcoran, M. and Picard, R.G. (2013) *Remotely Piloted Aircraft Systems & Journalism. Opportunities and Challenges of Drones in News Gathering* (Report of the Reuters Institute for the Study of Journalism, University of Oxford). Available at: http://reutersinstitute.politics.ox.ac.uk/publication/remotely-piloted-aircraft-systems-and-journalism (Accessed 10 April 2016).

Gregory, D. (2011) From a view to a kill: Drones and late modern war. *Theory, Culture & Society*, 28 (7–8): 188–215.

Gunneflo, M. (2014) *The Life and Times of Targeted Killing*. Lund: Lund University Press.

Harwood, M. (2011) "Drone Stakeholders Stress Robots' Humanitarian Upside," *Security Management*, 8 November.

Hayes, B., Jones, C. and Töpfer, E. (2014) *Eurodrones Inc*. Amsterdam: Transnational Institute and Statewatch. Available at: www.tni.org/eurodrones (Accessed 10 April 2016).

Henriksen, A. (2014) Jus ad bellum and American targeted use of force to fight terrorism around the world. *Journal of Conflict & Security Law*, 19 (2): 211–50.

Holmquvist, C. (2013) Undoing war: War ontologies and the materiality of drone warfare. *Millennium: Journal of International Studies*, 41 (3): 535–52.

Jagoda, P. (2010) Terror networks and the aesthetics of interconnection. *Social Text*, 105, 28 (4): 65–90.

Joseph, J. (2013) Resilience as embedded neoliberalism: A governmentality approach, Resilience. *International Policies, Practices and Discourses*, 1 (1): 38–52.

Kahn, P.W. (2008) *Sacred Violence. Torture, Terror, and Sovereignty*. Ann Arbor: University of Michigan Press.

Kahn, P.W. (2013) Imagining warfare. *The European Journal of International Law*, 24 (1): 199–226.

Klaidman, D. (2012) *Kill or Capture: The War on Terror and the Soul of the Obama Presidency*. New York: Harcourt.

Krasmann, S. (2012) Targeted killing and its law. On a mutually constitutive relationship. *Leiden Journal of International Law*, 25 (3): 665–82.

Krasmann, S. (2014) Der Aufstieg der Drohnen. Über das Zusammenspiel von Ethik und Ökonomie in der Praxis des gezielten Tötens. *Westend*, 11 (1): 25–43.

Kreps, S. and Kaag, J. (2012) The use of unmanned aerial vehicles in contemporary conflict: A legal and ethical analysis. *Polity*, 44 (2): 260–85.

Lash, S. (2007) Power after hegemony: Cultural studies in mutation? *Theory Culture Society*, 24 (3): 55–78.

Law, J. and Ruppert, E. (2013) The social life of methods: Devices. *Journal of Cultural Economy*, 6 (3): 229–40.

Law, J. and Urry, J. (2004) Enacting the social. *Economy and Society*, 33 (3): 390–410.

Leander, A. (2013) Technological agency in the co-constitution of legal expertise and the US drone program. *Leiden Journal of International Law*, 26 (4): 811–31.

Lemke, T. (2015) New materialisms: Foucault and the 'government of things'. *Theory, Culture & Society*, 32 (4): 3–25.

Lentzos, F. and Rose, N. (2009) Governing insecurity: Contingency planning, protection, resilience. *Economy and Society*, 38 (2): 230–54.

Marcuse, H. (1982) "Some Social Implications of Modern Technology," in Andrew Arato and Eike Gebhardt (eds.), *The Essential Frankfurt School Reader*. New York: Continuum, pp. 138–62.

Maurer, P. (2013) "The Use of Armed Drones Must Comply with Laws," Interview, 10 May. Available at: www.icrc.org/eng/resources/documents/interview/2013/05-10-drone-weapons-ihl.htm (Accessed 10 April 2016).

Mayer, J. (2009) "The Predator War. What are the risks of the C.I.A.'s covert drone program?," *The New Yorker*, 26 October. Available at: www.newyorker.com/reporting/2009/10/26/091026fa_fact_mayer (Accessed 10 April 2016).

Mendel, J. (2010) Afghanistan, Networks and Connectivity. *Geopolitics*, 15 (4), 726–51.

Muenkler, H. (2013) "Aufklärungs- und Kampfdrohnen: Waffen zwischen Krieg und Frieden," Available at: www.sicherheitspolitik-blog.de/2013/03/13/ethik-der-drohnen-muenkler/ (Accessed 10 April 2016).

Niva, S. (2013) Disappearing violence: JSOC and the Pentagon's new cartography of networked warfare. *Security Dialogue*, 44 (3): 185–202.

O'Grady, N. (2013) Adopting the position of error: Space and speculation in the exploratory significance of milieu formulations. *Environment and Planning D: Society and Space*, 31: 245–58.

Petraeus, D.H. and Mattis, J.N. (2006) *Counterinsurgency. Field Manual 3–24, Fleet Marine Force Manual 3–24*. 16 June (Final Draft). Available at: http://fas.org/irp/doddir/army/fm3-24fd.pdf (Accessed 10 April 2016).

Pugliese, J. (2013) *State Violence and the Execution of Law. Biopolitical Caesurae of Torture, Black Sites, Drones*. New York: Routledge.

Rajkovic, N.M. (2012) "Global law" and governmentality: Reconceptualizing the "rule of law" as rule 'through' law. *European Journal of International Relations*, 18 (1): 29–52.

Reid, J. (2013) Interrogating the neoliberal biopolitics of the sustainable development–resilience nexus. *International Political Sociology*, 7: 353–67.

Rosén, F. (2014) Extremely stealthy and incredibly close: Drones, control and legal responsibility. *Journal of Conflict & Security Law*, 19 (1): 113–31.

Rosenow, D. (2012) Dancing life into being: Genetics, resilience and the challenge of complexity theory. *Security Dialogue*, 43 (6): 531–47.

Sandvik, K.B. and Lohne, K. (2014) The rise of the humanitarian drone: Giving content to an emerging concept. *Millennium: Journal of International Studies* (Online First), 1–20.

Sauer, F. and Schörnig, N. (2012) Killer drones: The 'silver bullet' of democratic warfare? *Security Dialogue*, 43 (4): 363–80.

Schmidt, J. (2013) The empirical falsity of the human subject: New materialism, climate change and the shared critique of artifice. *Resilience: International Policies, Practices and Discourses*, 1 (3): 174–92.

Schüttpelz, E. (2008) "Der Punkt des Archimedes. Einige Schwierigkeiten des Denkens in Operationsketten," in Georg Kneer, Markus Schroer and Erhard Schüttpelz (eds.), *Bruno Latour's Kollektive*. Frankfurt am Maine: Suhrkamp, pp. 234–58.

Shaw, I.G.R. (2012) "The Historical Rise of the Predator Drone." Available at: http://understandingempire.wordpress.com/2012/10/28/essay-the-historical-rise-of-the-predator-drone-2/ (Accessed 10 April 2016).

Shaw, I.G.R. (2013) Predator empire: The geopolitics of US drone warfare. *Geopolitics*, 18 (3): 536–59.

Shaw, I.G.R. and Akhter, M. (2012) The unbearable humanness of drone warfare in FATA, Pakistan. *Antipode*, 44 (4): 1490–509.

Sniderman, A.S. and Hanis, M. (2013) "Drones for Human Rights," *The New York Times*, 13 January. Available at: www.nytimes.com/2012/01/31/opinion/drones-for-human-rights.html?_r=0 (Accessed 10 April 2016).

Stanford International Human Rights & Conflict Resolution Clinic (Stanford Law School) and Global Justice Clinic (NYU School of Law) (2012) *Living Under Drones: Death, Injury, and Trauma to Civilians. From US Drone Practices in Pakistan*. September. Available at: http://chrgj.org/wp-content/uploads/2012/10/Living-Under-Drones.pdf (Accessed 10 April 2016).

Tams, C.J. (2009) The use of force against terrorists. *The European Journal of International Law*, 20 (2): 359–97.

Thacker, E. (2013) "Nekros, or: The Poetics of Biopolitics," *Foucault Blog*. Available at: www.fsw.uzh.ch/foucaultblog/blog/20/nekros-or-the-poetics-of-biopolitics (Accessed 10 April 2016).

The White House (2013) "Remarks by the President at the National Defense University," 23 May. Available at: www.whitehouse.gov/the-press-office/2013/05/23/remarks-president-national-defense-university (Accessed 10 April 2016).

The White House (2014) "President Barack Obama's State of the Union Address," 28 January. Available at: www.whitehouse.gov/the-press-office/2014/01/28/president-barack-obamas-state-union-address (Accessed 10 April 2016).

Ulrich, J. (2005) The gloves were never on: Defining the President's authority to order targeted killing in the war against terrorism. *Virginia Journal of International Law*, 45 (4): 1029–63.

United Nations (2005) *Hyogo Framework for Action 2005–2015: Building the Resilience of Nations and Communities to Disasters. Extract from the Final Report of the World*

Conference on Disaster Reduction (A/CONF.206/6), Geneva. Available at: www. unisdr.org/2005/wcdr/intergover/official-doc/L-docs/Hyogo-framework-for-action-english.pdf (Accessed 10 April 2016).

Urry, J. (2005) The complexity turn. *Theory Culture Society*, 22 (5): 1–14.

Valverde, M. and Mopas, M. (2004) "Insecurity and the dream of targeted governance," in Wendy Larner and William Walters (eds.), *Global Governmentality. Governing International Spaces*. London, New York: Routledge, pp. 233–50.

Van Veeren, E. (2013) "On the Limits of the Visual to 'Speak Security' or: There is More than One Way to Imagine a Drone," Paper presented at ISA Annual Conventions, San Francisco, April. Available at: www.academia.edu/2905784/ Drone_Imaginaries_There_is_more_than_one_way_to_imagine_a_drone (Accessed 10 April 2016).

Walters, W. (2014) Drone strikes, *dingpolitik* and beyond: Furthering the debate on materiality and security. *Security Dialogue*, 45 (2): 101–18.

Weber, S. (2005) *Targets of Opportunity. On the Militarization of Thinking*. New York: Fordham University Press.

Weizman, E. (2011) *The Least of All Possible Evils. Humanitarian Violence from Arendt to Gaza*. London, New York: Verso.

Zehfuss, M. (2011) Targeting: Precision and the production of ethics. *European Journal of International Relations*, 17 (3): 543–66.

Zenko, M. and Kreps, S. (2014) *Limiting Armed Drone Proliferation*. New York: Council on Foreign Relations.

Zoche, P., Kaufmann, S. and Haverkamp, R. (eds.) (2011) *Zivile Sicherheit. Gesellschaftliche Dimensionen gegenwärtiger Sicherheitspolitiken*. Bielefeld: Transcript.

2 Lifting the fog of war?

Opportunities and challenges of drones in UN peace operations

John Karlsrud and Frederik Rosén

Introduction[1]

In 2013, United Nations (UN) peacekeeping entered the "age of the drone." On December 3, 2013, surveillance drones were for the first time officially included and made operational in the eastern Democratic Republic of the Congo (DRC) by the UN peacekeeping mission MONUSCO. At the launch event for the UN Unarmed Aerial Vehicles (UAVs),[2] Hervé Ladsous, UN Under-Secretary-General (USG) for peacekeeping operations declared that "[t]his is a first in the history of the United Nations that such an advanced technological tool has been used in a peacekeeping mission" (UN News Centre 2013a). He added that with the inclusion of the surveillance drone capability, UN peacekeeping finally "entered the 21st century" (UN Office of the Spokesperson 2013a). Permission for the deployment of surveillance drones in MONUSCO was given by the UN Security Council on a case-by-case basis. In June 2014, the UN Department of Peacekeeping Operations (DPKO) assessed that the inclusion of the surveillance drones in MONUSCO had been successful, and asked to move on to also include a drone capability in the UN mission MINUSMA in Mali (UN News Centre 2014). The DPKO also contemplated the inclusion of drones for other missions as well.

Concurrently with the introduction of surveillance drones, the UN Security Council started to equip UN missions with more robust mandates. In March 2013, the UN Security Council included a Force Intervention Brigade in MONUSCO in the DRC, mandated to "take all necessary measures" to "neutralize" and "disarm" groups that pose a threat to "state authority and civilian security" (UNSC 2013a: 7–8). The inclusion of the Intervention Brigade in MONUSCO, composed of troops from South Africa, Tanzania and Malawi, have been seen by many commentators as a turn from peacekeeping to peace enforcement, violating the traditional UN peacekeeping principles of impartiality, limited use of force and consent of the main parties (Kulish and Sengupta 2013; Karlsrud 2015). In April 2013, the Council authorized MINUSMA in Mali "in support of the transitional authorities of Mali, to stabilise the key population centres, especially in the north of Mali and, in this context, to deter threats and take active steps to prevent the return of armed elements to those areas" (UNSC 2013b: 7). In 2014, the UN also gave a robust mandate to a stabilization mission, MINUSCA, in the Central African Republic (UNSC 2014).

So far, the introduction of peacekeeping drones has been subjected to limited academic scrutiny with respect to the opportunities and challenges of introducing unmanned technology in peace operations (Karlsrud and Rosén 2013; Rosén 2014; Rosén and Karlsrud 2014), with some discussion in news reports and policy blogs. To begin to bridge this knowledge gap, this chapter seeks to further open the debate about how the "lifting of the fog of war" from certain aspects of UN peacekeeping operations may affect these, particularly in the context of increasingly robust peacekeeping operations. To that end, we proceed in three main parts. In the first section we describe previous instances of surveillance drones in the UN, and present the discussion around the surveillance drones in MONUSCO. This section also includes a brief overview of the latest developments, including the process of including drones in MINUSMA. Section 2 explores the main issues, such as the perceptions of drones by various stakeholders and various pros and cons of including drones in UN peacekeeping. In this section we also detail the perspectives of member states, how the discussion on drones is inscribed in a larger discussion about what level of force UN peacekeeping can use, and the relationship with humanitarian actors, which is closely related to this matter. Lastly in this section we look at issues concerning the management of the data gathered by surveillance drones.

Finally, based on these discussions, we conclude the chapter by suggesting that the UN's inclusion of a drone surveillance capability is a natural and necessary upgrade in an age where surveillance drones have become conventional tools of the police and the military. Drones can help the UN to better protect civilians, and implement mandated tasks. However, the inclusion of drones can also be seen as the first step toward weaponized drones also in the UN. This converges with a trend toward more robust missions and stronger participation by Western member states in peacekeeping (Karlsrud and Smith 2015). At the same time, we want to point out that surveillance drones present UN peacekeeping with a sudden new technological, operational and also legal reality. Hence UN peacekeeping urgently needs to develop thorough guidelines and tools for how the drone capability should be included and operated by missions, and how the acquired information should be disseminated and managed.

Surveillance drones in UN peacekeeping operations

The UN has for a long time wanted to deploy surveillance drones to increase the situational awareness capability of peacekeeping missions and improve the ability to protect their own forces and civilian populations. However, the deployment of surveillance drones in the eastern DRC is not the first instance in a UN context. Although mostly overlooked, there are two instances where the UN itself deployed a surveillance drone capability.

The first instance of surveillance drones deployed under a UN mandate was in 2006 in the peacekeeping mission in the DRC. MONUC was supported for a period of time by a European force (EUFOR) and Belgian troops brought with them surveillance drones.[3] Both MONUC and EUFOR operated under a UN mandate. Although the deployment of drones in MONUC in some instances was a success, detecting illegal shipments of arms and enabling UN officials to confront the perpetrators (Dorn 2011: 65), the deployment came to a rather abrupt end. One of the drones was shot down and the other crashed, killing one person and injuring several others in Kinshasa, bringing to an end that particular effort to employ drones (Isango 2006).

The second instance was in Chad in 2009 to 2010. This was rather ad hoc and not planned for, but due to the rehatting of Irish troops who were deployed as part of the European force EUFOR that operated alongside a civilian UN mission. When the UN took responsibility also for the military component on March 31, 2009, Irish troops were rehatted and included in the UN force. These troops had brought with them surveillance drones as part of the force (UNSC 2009), and continued to use these after being part of the UN mission MINURCAT. As the UN Security Council had issued a mandate to use aerial surveillance "to monitor transborder activities of armed groups along the Sudanese borders with Chad and the Central African Republic in particular through regular ground and aerial reconnaissance activities" (UNSC 2006: 4), there was also legal backing for the use of surveillance drones in this instance. The drone capability proved very useful to the mission during a cross-border attack by opposition forces based in Darfur during the spring of 2009. UN forces could closely monitor the movement of the opposition forces and enhance the protection of refugees, IDPs, and humanitarian aid workers accordingly, thereby living up to the mandate of the mission (Karlsrud 2014a; Karlsrud 2014b).

Of course, the absence of surveillance drones in UN peacekeeping until now does not mean that the UN has not been making use of aerial surveillance. In the DRC, the peacekeepers have made extensive use of heliborne reconnaissance, and in 2011, MONUC had four observation helicopters and eight attack helicopters equipped with advanced observation equipment (Dorn 2011: 75). Furthermore, individual force-contributing countries frequently bring their own, typically smaller-sized drones.[4] However, the UN has never had an airborne drone surveillance program with larger drones, centralized drafted rules and procedures such as the one we see advancing with the current UAV program.

MONUSCO

The UN started a bidding process to contract surveillance drones for the MONUC mission in the DRC in 2006 after being allocated $5.83 million for an "airborne surveillance system" by UN headquarters (Dorn 2011: 125). However, after several years of back and forth, the process of contracting the company Airscan was aborted (ibid.: 126) due to concerns that the company had been involved in human rights abuses in South America (ibid.: 151–152; International Labor Rights Forum 2003). Seeing that it was likely that a broad member state discussion on the possible inclusion of surveillance drones could be protracted with a significant risk of a negative response, the UN Secretariat refrained from approaching the GA committee dealing with peacekeeping issues (commonly known as the C-34).[5] Instead the Secretary-General sent a letter to the Security Council noting with concern the situation in the eastern DRC and suggested that the inclusion of monitoring and surveillance equipment such as surveillance drones (or unmanned aerial systems in UN parlance) could support the implementation of the MONUSCO mandate, enhance force protection and staff security and reduce the dependency on helicopters. The UN Security Council held two closed sessions to discuss the proposal, being briefed by the USG for peacekeeping, Hérve Ladsous, and technical experts, and the Security Council was subsequently given one week to submit questions in writing before the Secretary-General issued a note stating that it intended to deploy UAVs in the eastern DRC. The Security Council took note of this and approved it on "a case-by-case basis and without prejudice to the ongoing consideration by relevant United Nations bodies of legal, financial and technical implications of the use of unmanned aerial systems" (UNSC 2013c). The contract was valued at approximately €10 million per year (UN Office of the Spokesperson 2013b).

In the case of the DRC, UN HQ and the UN mission MONUSCO chose to contract a private company to supply surveillance drones. The Italian company Selex, a subsidiary of Finmeccanica, has delivered one system consisting of four drones, worth US$13.25 million per year for three years, with two optional years (*Global Times* 2013). The UN chose the Falco UAV system, consisting of several drones in each system with medium altitude long endurance, able to stay in the air for up to 72 hours and with night-flight capability (Selex ES 2013). The Falco UAVs can be airborne night and day, in all types of weather. They are equipped with a high-resolution camera for stills and video, a thermal camera and an infrared camera for night operations and bad weather.[6] They also have a synthetic aperture radar on board meaning that they can look through foliage, although not the triple foliage canopy that is common in the areas covered with rainforest in the eastern DRC, and they are thus able to provide good data even through several layers of vegetation. The drones are large enough to also include other payloads such as signals intelligence equipment, distance measuring equipment, GPS and altimeter. The UN emphasizes strongly that their drones will not be armed, yet the Falco is, in principle, large enough to carry light weapons systems.

As there is no air traffic control over the eastern DRC, the UN operates the drones at a height of 15,000 feet, which is the space above unpressurized aircrafts such as helicopters and small planes operate in below pressurized aircrafts.

The drones take off from the airport in Goma, circle up to the right altitude and then fly to the operations area.

The UN argues that the drones can enable the UN to radically improve their situational awareness by surveying large areas for troop and population movements, zoom in on emerging situations and track the movement of particular groups, also at night and in deep forest (UNSC 2013c; UN Office of the Spokesperson 2013a). The conflict-affected areas in the DRC mostly have dense jungles, rough landscape and poor infrastructure. UAVs may thus improve the security and safety of UN troops, civilian personnel and the civilian population, and allow for the pursuit of belligerent groups while avoiding unexpected confrontations and ambushes. The Force Commander for MONUSCO informed the Security Council that the mission would use the drones to:

> identify armed groups headquarters, logistics hubs, troop movements, convoys, clandestine air strips and roadblocks; to obtain early warning of armed groups' movements and intentions; and to monitor camps for internally displaced persons. The ability to fly over sensitive areas for extended periods of hours and days will provide timely information. Those UAVs will help to deter hostile action by the armed groups and to trigger the use of rapid reaction forces.
>
> (UNSC 2013c: 2)

The UN expects the drones to have a deterrent effect as the mere possibility of being under surveillance may well change the behavior of individuals and groups. The effect may thus extend beyond the actual presence of drones. Studies in regions where drones have been used demonstrate how the presence of drones affects life on the ground in a substantial manner – an effect which in principle is no different from the effects induced on citizen behavior by CCTV in western cities. What kind of deterrent effect the UAVs may achieve will probably depend on the ability of the UN to follow up the presence of drones with a presence on the ground in due time.

The UAVs can also be used for less urgent tactical purposes, like collecting information that may indicate emerging situations and potential violence, thereby enabling peacekeeping troops to position themselves in ample time between potentially conflicting groups or prevent attacks on civilian populations.[7] Compared to previous airborne surveillance platforms such as the helicopters used in the DRC, drones are likely to be much more cost-effective than helicopters and planes. Furthermore, helicopters and planes that before were needed for surveillance may now be used for other purposes.[8]

MINUSMA

MINUSMA was declared operational on September 1, 2013. Alongside MINUSMA, the French Opération Serval was conducting offensive operations under the same UN Security Council mandate until July 15, 2014, when it was replaced by Operation Barkhane launched in August 2014 to fight Islamist fighters in the Sahel (Barluet 2014). Operation Barkhane covers Burkina Faso, Chad, Mali, Mauritania and Niger and led from Chad, but is maintaining a sizeable presence in Mali and also includes two Reaper drones that became operational on January 16, 2014 (ibid.: Defense-Unmanned. com 2014). In Mali, the Dutch and Swedish contingents in MINUSMA have employed short- to medium-range drones (Boeing Scaneagle and Swedish-made Örnen (Eagle)). These are lightweight, easy to operate, and able to stay in the air for 15 hours. They can transfer live video streams and are also equipped with infrared and other sensor capabilities (Boeing 2014). The UN is also in the process of including a surveillance drone capability in Mali, similar to Selex ES drones in MONUSCO (UN News Centre 2014). However, neither of these types of drones will enable the mission to have eyes on the north of the country, due to their limited range (Karlsrud and Smith 2015).

The mission in Mali is in a challenging position. By April 2016, the UN had suffered 55 casualties after attacks by armed groups. Within MINUSMA an All Sources Information Fusion Unit (ASIFU) has been established, and tactical intelligence teams, provided by the Netherlands, have been inserted at the field level.[9] With the confluence of a robust mandate, tactical intelligence, surveillance drones and asymmetrical threats, MINUSMA is facing similar challenges to MONUSCO.

Opportunities and challenges of including surveillance drones in UN peacekeeping

Compared to the military powers that have pioneered the use of drones in armed conflict, namely the US and the UK, UN peacekeeping's "entering the age of the drone" happened more suddenly. For instance, the armed forces of the UK and the US, the key developers of military surveillance technology, "lived" the progress in technology and developed institutional capabilities accordingly. In contrast, UN peacekeeping troops have been severely under-equipped in terms of technology (see e.g. Dorn 2011). They have struggled with low, if not absent surveillance and communication capabilities, due to factors ranging from budget restraint to member states' reluctance toward equipping peacekeeping operations with intelligence tools and capabilities.

Hence, on the one hand, the range of surveillance options enabled by UAVs creates a momentum for UN peacekeeping. If managed and used properly, the UN UAVs may have game-changing effects for UN peacekeeping. On the other hand, the many and various implications flowing from the availability and operation of such equipment must be addressed. Solid experiences and expertise with drones in armed conflicts are readily available in UN member states, but the challenge for the UN is to erect relatively instantly an institutionalized UN UAV program that dovetails with UN peacekeeping capacities. These challenges are not just about flying the drones and translating the enhanced situational awareness into force advantages. Rather, DPKO faces a very wide range of issues flowing from the availability and operation of such equipment, including contract management, with the private contractor providing the drones; norm developments regarding what the drones should and should not be used for; ownership and management issues related to the information collected by drones; to the broader political, legal and moral questions attached to the availability and operation of such equipment. One critical aspect is how the additional surveillance capacity triggers the legal obligation to use this capacity to take due precaution in the conduct of armed force (Rosén 2014). As there has been little time to prepare for the inclusion of surveillance drones in UN peacekeeping, institutional functions need to urgently be provided for. To be sure, inclusion of drones puts UN peacekeeping on a steep learning curve.

In addition, the challenge of constructing the culturally, discursively and politically "good UAVs" and convincing member states that they are not "killer drones" or "spy drones" has been a key challenge. Against the backdrop of years of controversial use of "killer drones" by the US and UK, the UN drone program expectedly stirred up tense debate among UN member states. The planning unit for the UN UAV program at UN HQ thus spent considerable time engaging with member states to clarify for them the aims and the scope of the program (Interview with UN official, New York, October 11, 2013). In this regard the team has insisted on the UAV concept to distance their program semantically from the image of the killer drone, and has used every opportunity to emphasize that UN UAVs will stay unarmed – in fact, the chosen UAV, the Selex Falcon cannot, according to the producer, be equipped with weapons (Selex ES 2013). Troop contributing countries (TCCs) have also been concerned with the UN collecting information that could potentially incriminate their troops or violate the core principles of sovereignty and consent (Lynch 2013; Charbonneau 2014).

To address concerns, the UN has used this very opportunity to demystify the drones. For instance, in the DRC they flew the drones without mufflers to make the local populations aware of the "bird" in the sky (the local population has described the drones as "loud mosquitos" (*IRIN* 2014)).[10] And after the UN drones in the DRC during the spring of 2014 were used to detect a capsized boat, which led to a successful rescue operation, the episode was used to provide positive press coverage of the UN and their new drone capability (Rosén and Karlsrud 2014). Indicating the extent of the public attention the UN UAVs have drawn, when one of the UAVs suffered a damaging hard landing in mid-January 2014, this comparatively minor event drew quite a few headlines in the international media (see e.g. *The Guardian* 2014; *MONUSCO NEWS* 2014). It must however also be noted that some of the UN member state reluctance toward procuring UAVs has been purely economic: Some TCCs are simply concerned that the UAVs would mean a reduction in the need for boots on the ground and thus a loss of jobs and reimbursements for their troops provided to the UN (Lynch 2013). In the following we will look

more closely at some of the key issues that emerge with the inclusion of surveillance drones in UN peacekeeping operations.

Helpful tool or band-aid for a political problem?

The inclusion of drones has primarily been motivated by the UN with
arguments about improving the ability of UN peacekeeping missions to
protect civilians and UN peacekeeping troops (also see Lidén and Sandvik,
Chapter 3). Unfortunately, we have seen how the failure to provide effective
protection of civilians may not always have been a result of weak situational
awareness. Constrained mobility or even a reluctance to act has also
contributed to missions failures, such as the inaction of MONUC during
the Kisangani massacre in May 2002 (Marks 2007: 71) or the inaction of
MONUC in Ituri in 2003, resulting in a scathing report by MONUC's first
Force Commander:

> [the contingent] refused to react by opening fire after proper challenge and
> in accordance with the mandate to protect the population and in accord-
> ance with quite unambiguous rules of engagement. Instead, they persisted
> in only firing in the air, declaring that they could only act under Chapter
> VII and engage in combat with prior authority of [their parliament].
> (UN 2003 quoted in Holt and Taylor 2009: 251–252,
> inclusions in brackets in original)

These are not the only examples, in May 2004, the Uruguayan battalion
commander gave control of the airport in Bukavu to the rebel leader Laurent
Nkunda and the UN failed to protect the city (ibid.: 257–259). Enhanced
awareness may not therefore necessarily create better protection for civilians.
However, the combined "live streaming of events," which makes it very
difficult for commanders to claim they lack information, combined with
better situational awareness, which makes it safer for UN troops to leave their
bases, could create a peacekeeping environment where civilians may enjoy
more efficient protection and where peacekeeping missions will be obliged
to act (Karlsrud and Rosén 2013; Better World Campaign 2013: 5–6). In
this light, the inclusion of drones could be seen as a "force activator," giving
information that obliges the UN to strengthen its efforts to protect civilians.

UN surveillance drones and the Force Intervention Brigade

It is of significant importance that the surveillance drones in MONUSCO
were included concurrently with the mandate for the Force Intervention
Brigade (FIB), with the mandate being issued in March 2013, soon after the
green light was given to contract the drones in January 2013. The Intervention
Brigade consisted of troops from South Africa, Tanzania and Malawi. The
Security Council authorized MONUSCO, with clear reference to the Force

Intervention Brigade, to "take all necessary measures" to "neutralize" and "disarm" groups that pose a threat to "state authority and civilian security" (UNSC 2013a: 7–8). The FIB was deployed prior to the surveillance drones, and during the autumn of 2013 the FIB, together with the national army, the FARDC, defeated the M23 rebel group. After the fighting had subsided, the government of the DRC stated that political negotiations with M23 were no longer necessary. It seems as if the military victory has, for the time being, quelled the wish to achieve political and long-term solutions (Karlsrud 2015).

The inclusion of the drones and the Force Intervention Brigade in MONUSCO was, by most commentators, considered to "constitute a turning point in UN peace missions" (Gberie 2013), and the defeat of the M23 could be seen to substantiate this argument. However, as detailed above, there is a long history of MONUSCO having significant military capabilities on the ground, only to not take action when push comes to shove. The difference this time is that (as admittedly was also the case in 2006 under the leadership of General Cammaert) the Force Intervention Brigade has been able and willing to use significant amounts of force to pursue the M23. The Force Intervention Brigade originally planned to continue its operations in 2014 against other groups such as the Patriotic Resistance Front in Ituri (FRPI) and the Congolese People's Liberation Army (ALPCU), aided by the surveillance drones. However, Council has shown the FDLR has been singled out as a main spoiler, and the UN Security Council showed increasing frustration with little action being taken against the group. In January 2015, the UN Security Council "stresses the importance of neutralizing all armed groups, including, among others, the Democratic Forces for the Liberation of Rwanda (FDLR)" (UNSC 2015: 1). In our view, the inclusion of the Intervention Brigade and surveillance drones against the backdrop of the ongoing war fighting against armed groups, can increase the perception that the UN is taking sides and increase the risk of attacks against civilian and humanitarian components of the UN (*IRINNews* 2013).

In Mali, the UN mission MINUSMA took over from the African Union mission AFISMA on July 1, 2013. In April 2013, the Council authorized MINUSMA in Mali "[i]n support of the transitional authorities of Mali, to stabilize the key population centers, especially in the north of Mali and, in this context, to deter threats and take active steps to prevent the return of armed elements to those areas" (UN 2013c: 7). This operation operates alongside the French Barkhane force that deployed its first Reaper drones in January 2014 (*Reuters* 2013). Ladsous has indicated his willingness to also include an armed intervention brigade in other missions, including in Mali (Crossette 2014).

Member state divisions on UN peacekeeping

The go-ahead to include the Force Intervention Brigade into a UN peacekeeping mission, effectively turning it into a peace enforcement mission, was given with great reluctance by some of the members of the UN Security

Council. The resolution noted that the Intervention Brigade was established "on an exceptional basis and without creating a precedent or any prejudice to the agreed principles of peacekeeping" (UNSC 2013a: 6). Russia was the most vocal of the critics, emphasizing that "what was once the exception now threatens to become unacknowledged standard practice" (Security Council Report 2014).

The surveillance drones in MONUSCO also come at the confluence of several important and ongoing debates at the UN. At the member state level, the drones were discussed at length, and permission was given to MONUSCO on a case-by-case basis, but the practice has now been extended to MINUSMA as detailed previously in this chapter. To better understand the discussions about surveillance drones at the UN, it is useful to take a look at how peacekeeping operations, and the key actors, are decided upon. The mandates are issued by the UN Security Council, which although including ten nonpermanent members, is dominated by the five permanent veto members. Of these, France and the UK are the most active penholders (drafting resolutions) with the US closely consulted (the permanent three or P3). China is the largest troop contributor of the five, and while Russia does not hold the pen nor contribute with many troops, it has its veto power and also has a significant, albeit indirect economic interest as Russian companies inter alia provide a lot of the airlifting capacity of UN peacekeeping: "In 2011, Russian companies held contracts from the UN worth $382 million, which composed 14% of UN peacekeeping services. Almost all of this is comprised of aviation transportation services provided by Russian aviation and cargo companies" (Nikitin 2013: 163).

Among the TCCs, Bangladesh, India and Pakistan are among the biggest contributors, but also several African, Asian and Middle Eastern countries provide significant numbers of troops (UN 2013a). For some of these contributors there is a concern that if the UN is making use of surveillance drones and other high-tech equipment, this can reduce the need for actual boots on the ground (see e.g. Lynch 2013). The inclusion of surveillance drones also signifies a Western influence on the actual implementation of peacekeeping operations on the ground that some of the traditional TCCs may find irksome – insinuating that they are not capable enough to perform their tasks without these technological aides and that they cannot afford to include them in the standard equipment of their troops. However, there are diverging views among the traditional TCCs, as many are also starting to include drones in their national capabilities and see them as a useful tool that can help them better protect their troops.

On a regional level Russia has voiced concern that the presence of the surveillance drones "could become an irritant, hindering the establishment of an atmosphere of trust among neighbours and even the very process of Congolese peacebuilding" (UNSC 2013c: 9). Rwanda has only reluctantly accepted the presence of the drones in the DRC. However, while the UN in this round has asked for permission from neighboring countries to deploy drones in the eastern DRC, they will change their tactic and only ask for permission from the host country, going forward (Interview with UN official, New York, October 11, 2013).

There is also uncertainty in how the surveillance drones will be received by local populations. So far, NGOs in the eastern DRC argue that the local population has dubbed the drones "loud mosquitos" and that they have not been sufficiently informed about the function and purpose of the drones – not even knowing if they are armed or not (*IRIN* 2014). The drones are intended to have a preventive effect by hovering in the air – the flipside of this is that the "eye in the sky" may be frightening to some. Local perceptions will also be strongly affected by perceived inaction – if surveillance drones hover above while attacks are taking place and the UN still does not intervene. Conversely, if the presence of drones can make belligerents halt attacks or is followed by the presence of UN troops on the ground they can bolster positive local perceptions.

UN drones and humanitarian actors

MONUSCO and the Force Intervention Brigade have managed to conquer the M23. At the same time, there are many more rebel groups residing in the eastern DRC, and without political solutions more conflicts are likely to erupt. In this context, some of the humanitarian community is watching, with growing scepticism, the increasing will of the UN to use force. As the UN is becoming a party to the conflict, what are the implications for the humanitarian parts of the UN? Will they be targeted by rebel groups and is the inclusion of a drone capability adding to the tension between the parties? We look at the consequences of including surveillance drones – perceived to be an offensive military capability by humanitarian and other actors – in this context.

The UN Humanitarian Country Team stated its position on its relationship with armed actors in 2013, where they expressed their strong disapproval of armed escorts and emphasized that the relationship between humanitarian and military actors should be based on co-existence (IASC 2004; OCHA 2013a, 2013b).[11] This, however, has not been the case and there are reports of armed escorts being furnished as the only option, as MINUSMA is not able to deploy sufficient troops to provide area security (NUPI 2013). In this context, we suggest that the use of drones could be put forward as a solution that navigates the dilemma of the lack of peacekeeping troops vs. access to beneficiaries.

As mission mandates have grown more complex, the UN has developed its policies for the relationship between military, political and humanitarian actors under the integrated mission framework (UNSG 2000; Eide et al. 2005; UN 2010; OCHA 2011, 2012), tailored to maximize the impact of the UN response.

In 2013, new guidance for joint UN planning was released (UN 2013b), moving the UN away from a "mission-centric" focus (UN 2013c). According to an influential middle-of-the-road approach, the more force the UN is mandated and willing to use, the less integration there should be between the humanitarian and political/military pillars of the UN (Egeland et al. 2011). However, current mandate developments in the DRC and Mali represent a departure from this approach by suggesting more force but no alterations in the level of integration between peacekeeping and humanitarian operations.

While it is possible to identify valid arguments voiced for the inclusion of surveillance drones, it remains difficult to discern a comprehensive strategic vision for the long-term impact of these missions for the UN more generally, and for the humanitarian enterprise more specifically.

The drone capability has deliberately been included under the support pillar of the UN mission, and not in the military component, and is under the direct tasking command of the Head of the mission, the Special Representative of the Secretary-General. This is also to enable tasking of the drone capability by the civilian components and it is envisaged that the drone capability will enable the mission to track militia movements and IDP movements, in support of humanitarian action by UN agencies and others (Interview with UN official, October 11, 2013). How will this be perceived by humanitarian actors – are they going to make use of the services of surveillance drones to ensure access to beneficiaries or are they going to resist them? Some concerns have been uttered. In the eastern DRC, NGOs reacted to the UN's offer to use drones for humanitarian information gathering, saying that this "would compromise the core principles of relief organizations: neutrality, impartiality and operational independence" and that accepting MONUSCO's offer would be akin "to handing out food aid from the back of a tank" (*IRIN* 2014; see also *ReliefWeb* 2014a; World Vision 2014). Yet the concerns were not about the UAVs as such, but more about using a tool (the UAVs), which belonged to a part of the conflict (MONUSCU), thus risking a "blur of the lines" between humanitarian and military work. However, there has already been at least one clear case where the drones have been used for a humanitarian purpose, the above-mentioned rescue mission on Lake Kivu in the DRC in May 2014 (*MONUSCO NEWS* 2014).[12] In 2014, the mission and the humanitarian community was in the process of revising the guidelines for coordination between humanitarians and MONUSCO, but the issue of information stemming from drones was not directly addressed in the draft document at that stage (ibid.).

Although the instinctive reaction of humanitarian actors is to have very clear divides between military and humanitarian actors in the field, asking military actors to respect the "humanitarian space" (Metcalfe et al. 2011; Collinson and Elhawary 2012; Karlsrud and Felix da Costa 2013), the potential benefits of surveillance drones may be so tempting that some may silently accept them or even outright ask the UN to make use of surveillance drones to ensure that safe passage is possible to populations in need. It is also increasingly difficult to deny that drones are literally everywhere and used for any purpose.

Managing the data

The surveillance drones will gather massive amounts of data that will be stored on the ground by the mission. The issue of intelligence gathering and potential breaches of sovereignty is central, and host and neighboring countries where drones are deployed fear that intelligence could be gathered by the drones that is either not central to the implementation of the mandate, or could incriminate the actions of these countries. Adding to this, they fear that the intelligence is controlled by Western states (Lynch 2013), by way of contracting or through the mission personnel. The contractor, Selex ES, will "deploy a highly experienced team of pilots, maintenance engineers and information analysts using the most sophisticated sensors and data exploitation tools available" (Selex ES 2013). This means that the contractor will be managing and analyzing the data and the information that is being collected by the drones. This has been noticed by Azerbaijan, a member of the Security Council, who asked what arrangements have been "put in place to ensure that the information provided by the UAVs is properly handled for United Nations' use, particularly when we all know that the operators are non-United Nations personnel" (UNSC 2013c: 15). Transparency about what information is being collected, who has access to it and how it will be used will thus be of continuing concern to member states (see also McDuffee 2013), particularly taking into consideration what the UN is doing elsewhere in this regard, with two UN Special Rapporteurs looking at the potential illegal use of armed UAVs (UN News Centre 2013b).

A critical question is whether we will see the use of information that is gathered by drones, used in courts as evidence in cases of war crimes. As confirmed by Hervé Ladsous: "I suppose it might. I don't know what degree of detail we shall be getting on the pictures but certainly for mass incidents that would get a much better knowledge, and of course we will have to see how to share this appropriately" (France 24 2013). The Force Commander of MONUSCO has also indicated that the drones can enable the UN to "provide real evidence of events on the ground" (UN 2013a; UNSC 2013c). It must thus be asked just what kind of criminal behavior may the drones be used to investigate? Are we only talking about human rights abuses or will we also see a focus on organized crime, transborder activities and other serious illegal activities known to impact on peacekeeping (Kemp et al. 2013)?

There is also a need to determine how long the UN will store the data. Can the ICC request the UN to share the data at a later date? How long should data be stored for, and who can require access post facto? These are among some of the challenging questions the UN must address when further developing the institutional framework for the inclusion of a drone capability in UN peacekeeping operations.

Conclusion

The inclusion of peace enforcement mandates alongside new tools and technologies in UN peace operations will have consequences that may not yet be foreseen (Friis and Karlsrud 2013). The UN expects that the drones will help them obtain early warning of movements of armed groups and their intentions, deter these from attacks, record evidence of various illegal activities and in general strengthen the intelligence gathering capabilities and situational awareness of UN peacekeeping missions. We concur with this aspiration, but we would also caution that surveillance drones will not be a panacea for UN peacekeeping operations – they will only provide more information to the missions. However, in the past it has not been the lack of information that has limited the ability of the mission to protect civilians, but the willingness to risk the lives of the MONUSCO troops in actively engaging those who are committing atrocities. Adding equipment will thus not automatically lead to action on the ground. The inclusion of surveillance drones and the Force Intervention Brigade can, in this light, be seen as a continuation of a long trend of trying to solve essentially political and social issues with more troops and more equipment, turning the attention away from more sustainable and long-term solutions. MONUSCO has long been a significant challenge for UN peacekeeping – furnished with a mandate pivoting around the protection of civilians and covering a very large area where there is little peace to keep. With the inclusion of the Force Intervention Brigade and surveillance drones the mission has taken another turn toward peace enforcement, with the hope that military prowess will deter rebel groups from further attacks. However, there is a risk that the focus on strengthening the military capabilities of MONUSCO detracts attention from reaching long-term political and social solutions for the various populations of the eastern DRC.

At the UN, neither should the possibility of turfism and hoarding of information be underestimated. Although drones may collect valuable information, it may very well be that the information is not shared with those who may need it, even internally in the UN, or with humanitarian actors to make sure that they assist those in need, irrespective of whether these civilians are affiliated with groups such as the M23, FRPI or the ALPCU, all considered to be the enemy of the UN peacekeeping/enforcement mission (UNSC 2013a). Thus, the combination of a peace enforcement mandate, the Force Intervention Brigade and surveillance drones in the DRC unfortunately creates fertile ground for those opposing the inclusion of a drone capability in UN peacekeeping.

However, on balance, we think that the inclusion of surveillance drones in UN peacekeeping is a timely, necessary, natural and altogether good step forward for UN peacekeeping, but we would urge member states to consider the implications of the confluence of the factors noted above. At the level of member states, traditional TCCs may be skeptical to the inclusion of drones as these could imply that their militaries are less advanced than Western ones. These opposing trends make it difficult to predict whether traditional TCCs will start to acquire surveillance drones, but if they do, we can expect that surveillance drones might be more commonly included in the standard equipment of contingents provided to the UN. Cheaper types of surveillance drones may also be included in the support programs that states such as the US direct toward troop contributing countries, particularly in Africa. In these programs, African troops are provided with their contingent owned equipment and training, and light surveillance drones may well be included in these support packages going forward.

We have so far seen a positive assessment by the UN of the inclusion of surveillance drones in MONUSCO (UN 2014). This has led to the UN Secretariat asking for support to include drones in MINUSMA, and we expect other missions to follow. As the discussion matures, we hope to see more policy discussion on this topic at the UN, in particular around questions of the increase in precautionary obligations of UN peacekeepers when having access to surveillance drones, the tasking of drones to support humanitarian action, and the use of evidence gathered by surveillance drones by the ICC and other courts.

Further research in this area should look more closely at how surveillance drones are put to use by UN missions and how humanitarians and local populations perceive them. There is also a need for greater understanding of the long-term implications of the contractual arrangements of the drones, for example, with regards to the storing and sharing of information. Finally, there is a need to look at the longer-term impact on the ability of UN peacekeeping operations to implement their mandate and protect local populations.

Notes

1 The authors would like to acknowledge the many valuable comments and input received from the editors, as well as the participants and co-authors of this volume at the writer's workshop "The Rise of the Good Drone," organized by the Norwegian Centre for Humanitarian Studies and the Peace Research Institute of Oslo (PRIO), Oslo, September 5, 2013.
2 We will use the terms "drones" and "UAVs" interchangeably throughout this chapter.
3 The United Nations Organization Mission in the Democratic Republic of the Congo (MONUC) was established with UN Security Council Resolution 1279 on November 30, 1999, and renamed MONUSCO with UN SCR 1925 on May 28, 2010. See UNSC (1999) *S/RES/1279*, November 30, 1999. New York: United Nations; UNSC (2010) *S/RES/1925*, May 28, 2010. New York: United Nations.
4 For example, the Dutch troops in Mali who have brought Boeing ScanEagle drones, see below for more information.
5 UN official, New York, October 11, 2013.
6 The rest of this paragraph is based on an interview with a UN official, New York, October 11, 2013.
7 In 2006, heliborne surveillance identified militia fighters from the Cobra Matata group approaching UN forces in the eastern DRC, allowing UN troops "to avoid a surprise attack and to respond appropriately" (Dorn 2011: 66).

8   Ibid.
9   The ASIFU is also a new element in UN peacekeeping. It is supposed to fuse information from tactical intelligence officers with signal intelligence and other information, providing a real-time understanding of the challenges on the ground to tactical and operational decision-makers.
10   According to UN Staff, August 21, 2014, Berlin.
11   "Where cooperation between the humanitarian and military actors is not appropriate, opportune or possible, or if there are no common goals to pursue, then these actors merely operate side-by-side. Such a relationship may be best described as one of co-existence, in which case civil–military coordination should focus on minimizing competition and conflict in order to enable the different actors to work in the same geographical area with minimum disruption to each other's activities." (IASC 2004).
12   For a full analysis of the event, see Rosén and Karlsrud (2014).

References

Barluet, A. (2014) "Au Sahel, l'opération 'Barkhane' remplace 'Serval,'" *Le Figaro*, July 13. Available at: www.lefigaro.fr/international/2014/07/13/01003-20140713ARTFIG00097-au-sahel-l-operation-barkhane-remplace-serval.php (Accessed January 7, 2015).

Better World Campaign (2013) "The UN's Use of Unmanned Aerial Vehicles in the Democratic Republic of the Congo: U.S. Support and Potential Foreign Policy Advantages," Better World Campaign. Available at: www.betterworldcampaign.org/assets/pdf/bwc-white-paper-the-uns-use-of-uavs-in-th-drc-may-2013.pdf (Accessed January 29, 2014).

Boeing (2014) "Scaneagle: Overview." Available at: www.boeing.com/boeing/defense-space/military/scaneagle/ (Accessed April 16, 2014).

Charbonneau, L. (2014) "Rwanda Opposes Use of Drones by the UN in Eastern Congo," *Reuters*, January 9. Available at: www.reuters.com/article/2013/01/09/us-congo-democratic-un-rwanda-idUSBRE90802720130109 (Accessed January 27, 2014).

Collinson, S. and Elhawary, S. (2012) "Humanitarian space: a review of trends and issues." *HPG Reports 32*. London: Overseas Development Institute.

Crossette, B. (2014) "UN Peacekeeping Upgrades Its Reactions to Conflicts and Adds Surveillance Tools" *PassBlue*, November 11. Available at:http://passblue.com/2014/11/11/un-peacekeeping-upgrades-its-reactions-to-conflicts-and-adds-surveillance-tools/ (Accessed April 1, 2016).

Defense-Unmanned.com (2014) "Barkhane: French Air Force's Reaper UAVs Pass 2,000 Flight Hours." Available at: www.defense-unmanned.com/article/1616/french-reaper-uavs-pass-2,000-flight-hours.html (Accessed January 7, 2015).

Dorn, W.A. (2011) *Keeping Watch: Monitoring, Technology & Innovation in UN Peace Operations*. Tokyo: United Nations University Press.

Egeland, J., Harmer, A. and Stoddard, A. (2011) *To Stay and Deliver: Good Practice for Humanitarians in Complex Security Environments*. Geneva and New York: UN OCHA.

Eide, E.B., Kaspersen, A.T., Kent, R. and von Hippel, K. (2005) *Report on Integrated Missions: Practical Perspectives and Recommendations*. New York: UN ECHA Core Group.

France 24 (2013) "Hervé Ladsous, UN Under-Secretary-General for Peacekeeping Operations," France24 [Interview December 4]. Available at: www.france24.com/en/20131203-interview-herve-ladsous-dr-congo-drones-peacekeeping-goma-m23-rebels-rwanda-uganda/ (Accessed January 27, 2014).

Friis, K. and Karlsrud, J. (2012) "FN går til krig," *NRK Ytring*, May 10. Available at: www.nrk.no/ytring/fn-gar-til-krig-1.11015310 (Accessed October 28, 2013).

Gberie, L. (2013) "Will Drones and International Military Offensive Bring Stability to DRC?," *The Africa Report*, August 21. Available at: www.theafricareport.com/East-Horn-Africa/will-drones-and-international-military-offensive-bring-stability-to-drc.html (Accessed January 29, 2014).

Global Times (2013) "UAV Deployment in DRC to Cost over $13m Annually," *Global Times*, August 6. Available at: www.globaltimes.cn/content/801784.shtml#.UqBTB8TuJqU (Accessed December 5, 2013).

Holt, V. and Taylor, G. (2009) *Protecting Civilians in the Context of UN Peacekeeping Operations: Successes, Setbacks and Remaining Challenges*. New York: United Nations.

IASC (2004) *Civil–Military Relationship in Complex Emergencies: An IASC Reference Paper 2004*. Geneva: IASC.

International Labor Rights Forum (2003) "Lawsuit Filed Against Occidental Petroleum for Involvement in Colombian Massacre," International Labor Rights Forum, April 24. Available at: www.laborrights.org/end-violence-against-trade-unions/colombia/news/11403 (Accessed January 28, 2014).

IRIN (2014) "NGOs Against MONUSCO Drones for Humanitarian Work," *IRIN*, July 23. Available at: www.irinnews.org/report/100391/ngos-against-monusco-drones-for-humanitarian-work (Accessed November 19, 2014).

IRINNews (2013) "After North Kivu, UN, DRC Forces Set Sights on Orientale," *IRINNews*. Available at: www.irinnews.org/report/99330/after-north-kivu-un-drc-forces-set-sights-on-orientale (Accessed December 16, 2013).

Isango, E. (2006) "Drone Crash in Congo Kills 1, Injures 2," *Washington Post*, October 3. Available at: www.washingtonpost.com/wp-dyn/content/article/2006/10/03/AR2006100300778.html (Accessed January 16, 2014).

Karlsrud, J. (2014a) "Peacekeeping 4.0: Harnessing the Potential of Big Data, Social Media and Cyber Technology," in Kremer, J.F. and Müller, B. (eds.), *Cyber Space and International Relations. Theory, Prospects and Challenges*. Berlin: Springer, pp. 141–160.

Karlsrud, J. (2014b) "United Nations Mission in the Central African Republic and Chad (MINURCAT I + II)," in Koops, J.A., MacQueen, N., Tardy, T. and Williams, P.D. (eds.), *Oxford Handbook on United Nations Peacekeeping Operations*. Oxford: Oxford University Press, pp. 1–20. DOI: 10.1093/oxfordhb/9780199686049.013.70.

Karlsrud, J. (2015) The UN at war: Examining the consequences of peace enforcement mandates for the UN peacekeeping operations in the CAR, the DRC and Mali. *Third World Quarterly*, 36 (1): 40–54.

Karlsrud, J. and da Costa, D.F. (2013) Invitation withdrawn: Humanitarian action, UN peacekeeping and state sovereignty in Chad. *Disasters*, 37 (4): 171–187.

Karlsrud, J. and Rosén, F. (2013) In the eye of the beholder? UN and the use of drones to protect civilians. *Stability of Security and Development*, 2 (2): 1–10.

Karlsrud, J. and Smith, A. (2015) "Europe's Return to UN Peacekeeping in Africa?: Lessons-Learned from Mali," *Providing for Peacekeeping*, No. 10. New York: International Peace Institute.

Kemp, W., Shaw, M. and Boutellis, A. (2013) *The Elephant in the Room: How Can Peace Operations Deal with Organized Crime?* New York: International Peace Institute.

Kulish, N. and Sengupta, S. (2013) "New U.N. Brigade's Aggressive Stance in Africa Brings Success, and Risks," *The New York Times*, November 12. Available at: www.nytimes.com/2013/11/13/world/africa/new-un-brigades-aggressive-stance-in-africa-brings-success-and-risks.html?_r=2& (Accessed January 14, 2015).

Lynch, C. (2013) "U.N. Wants to Use Drones for Peacekeeping Missions," *The Washington Post*, January 8. Available at: www.washingtonpost.com/world/national-security/un-seeks-drones-for-peacekeeping-missions/2013/01/08/39575660-599e-11e2-88d0-c4cf65c3ad15_story.html (Accessed January 29, 2014).

Marks, J. (2007) The pitfalls of action and inaction: Civilian protection in MONUC's peacekeeping operations. *African Security Review*, 16 (3): 67–80.

McDuffee, A. (2013) "The UN Launches Its Own Spy Drone Program," *Wired*, December 4. Available at: www.wired.com/dangerroom/2013/12/un-drones/ (Accessed January 29, 2014).

Metcalfe, V., Giffen, A. and Elhawary, S. (2011) *UN Integration and Humanitarian space*. London: Overseas Development Institute.

MONUSCO NEWS (2014) "MONUSCO Peacekeepers Rescue 14 People from a Sinking Boat on Lake Kivu." Available at: http://monusco.unmissions.org/Default.aspx?ctl=Details&tabid=10927&mid=14594&ItemID=20526 (Accessed November 9, 2014).

Nikitin, A. (2013) "The Russian Federation," in Alex Bellamy and Paul Williams (eds.), *Providing Peacekeepers. The Politics, Challenges, and Future of United Nations Peacekeeping Contributions*. Oxford: Oxford University Press.

NUPI (2013) *Post-Election Mali: Challenges and Opportunities*. [Seminar, December 9].

OCHA (2011) *Policy Instruction: OCHA's Structural Relationships Within An Integrated UN Presence*. Geneva: OCHA.

OCHA (2012) *OCHA on Message: Integration: Structural Arrangements*. Geneva: OCHA.

OCHA (2013a) *Humanitarian Country Team Position on the Interaction Between the Humanitarian Community and Armed Forces Present in Mali*. Bamako: OCHA.

OCHA (2013b) *Guidance on the Use of Foreign Military and Civil Defence Assets (MCDA) to Support Humanitarian Operations in the Context of the Current Military Intervention in Mali*. Bamako: OCHA.

ReliefWeb (2014) "U.N. Says Drone Crashes in DR Congo," *ReliefWeb*, January 15. Available at: http://reliefweb.int/report/democratic-republic-congo/un-says-drone-crashes-dr-congo (Accessed November 19, 2014).

Reuters (2013) "France to Use Unarmed U.S.-made Drones to Hunt al Qaeda in Mali," *Reuters*, December 19. Available at: www.reuters.com/article/2013/12/19/us-mali-france-drones-idUSBRE9BI0VY20131219 (Accessed January 16, 2014).

Rosén, F. (2014) Extremely stealthy and incredibly close. Drones, control and responsibility. *Journal of Conflict and Security Law*, 19 (1): 113–131.

Rosén, F. and Karlsrud, J. (2014) The MONUSCO UAVs: The implications for actions and omissions. *Conflict Trends*, 2014 (4): 42–48.

Security Council Report (2014) "In Hindsight: Changes to U.N. Peacekeeping in 2013," Security Council Report. Available at: www.securitycouncilreport.org/monthly-forecast/2014-02/in_hindsight_changes_to_un_peacekeeping_in_2013.php (Accessed November 18, 2014).

Selex ES (2013) *Selex ES to Deliver Unmanned Aerial Surveillance to the United Nations for Peace Keeping.* Available at: www.finmeccanica.co.uk/-/un-falco (Accessed April 10, 2016).

The Guardian (2014) "UN Surveillance Drone Crashes in Congo," *The Guardian,* January 15. Available at: www.theguardian.com/world/2014/jan/15/united-nations-surveillance-drone-crashes-congo (Accessed January 29, 2014).

UN (2010) *Integrated Planning for UN Field Presences.* Available at: www.ccopab. eb.mil.br/biblioteca/documentos/DPKO_DFS_IMPP_Jan2010_GdL.pdf (Accessed April 10, 2016).

UN (2013a) "Security Council 6987th Meeting. Force Commanders Dwell on New Technology, Pre-Deployment Training, Inter-Mission Cooperation in Briefing Security-Council on Peacekeeping Operations," United Nations. Available at: www. un.org/News/Press/docs//2013/sc11047.doc.htm (Accessed January 29, 2014).

UN (2013b) *Policy on Integrated Assessment and Planning.* New York: United Nations.

UN (2013c) *Letter from Helen Clark and Valerie Amos – IAPP Endorsement from UNDG.* New York: United Nations.

UN (2014) "Delegates Argue Merits of Unmanned Arial Vehicles, Other Technologies as Security Council Considers New Trends in Peacekeeping," June 11. Available at: www.un.org/press/en/2014/sc11434.doc.htm (Accessed January 7, 2015).

UN News Centre (2013a) "UN Launches Unmanned Surveillance Aircraft to Better Protect Civilians in Vast DR Congo," UN News Centre. Available at: www. un.org/apps/news/story.asp?NewsID=46650&Cr=democratic&Cr1=congo#. UtPgZieMk0F (Accessed January 13, 2014).

UN News Centre (2013b) "UN Rights Experts Call For Transparency in the Use of Armed Drones, Citing Risks of Illegal Use," UN News Centre. Available at: www.un.org/apps/news/story.asp?NewsID=46338&Cr=terror&Cr1=drone#. Uukb6FOMk0G (Accessed January 29, 2014).

UN News Centre (2014) "Mali: UN Peacekeeping Chief Cites Progress on Political Track as Key to Stability," UN News Centre. Available at: www.un.org/apps/news/ story.asp?NewsID=48077#.VGnrGVd0bDw (Accessed November 17, 2014).

UN Office of the Spokesperson (2013a) "Highlights of the Noon Briefing. By Martin Nesirky, Spokesperson for Secretary-General Ban Ki-Moon. Tuesday, December 3, 2013," United Nations. Available at: www.un.org/sg/spokesperson/highlights/ index.asp?HighD=12/3/2013&d_month=12&d_year=2013 (Accessed January 14, 2014).

UN Office of the Spokesperson (2013b) "Highlights of the Noon Briefing. By Martin Nesirky, Spokesperson for Secretary-General Ban Ki-Moon. Monday, August 5, 2013," United Nations. Available at: www.un.org/sg/spokesperson/highlights/ index.asp?HighD=8/5/2013&d_month=8&d_year=2013 (Accessed January 29, 2014).

UNSC (1999) *S/RES/1279,* November 30. New York: United Nations.

UNSC (2006) *S/RES/1706,* August 31, 2006. New York: United Nations.

UNSC (2009) *S/2009/214,* April 23, 2009. New York: United Nations.

UNSC (2010) *S/RES/1925,* May 28, 2010. New York: United Nations.

UNSC (2013a) *S/RES/2098.* March 28, 2013. New York: United Nations.

UNSC (2013b) *S/RES/2100,* April 25, 2013. New York: United Nations.

UNSC (2013c) *S/PV.6987,* June 26, 2013. New York: United Nations.

UNSC (2014) *S/RES/2149,* April 10, 2014. New York: United Nations.

UNSC (2015) *S/PRST/2015/1*, January 8, 2015. New York: United Nations.

UNSG (2000) "Note of Guidance on Relations Between Representatives of the Secretary-General, Resident Coordinators and Humanitarian Coordinators," United Nations. Available at: http://reliefweb.int/node/22011 (Accessed August 17, 2011).

World Vision (2014) "Unmanned Drones Used by UN Peacekeepers in the DRC," World Vision, July 15. Available at: www.worldvision.org.uk/news-and-views/latest-news/2014/july/unmanned-drones-used-un-peacekeepers-drc/ (Accessed January 14, 2015).

3 Poison pill or cure-all?

Drones and the protection of civilians

Kristoffer Lidén and Kristin Bergtora Sandvik[1]

Introduction

This chapter has a twofold starting point. First, there is a widespread concern that the protection of civilians (PoC) agenda is facing a crisis of unrealistic pretentions, as well as inadequate implementation. Second, that the uses of drones in the global battlespace, the humanitarian emergency zone and everyday risk society are often explicitly or implicitly motivated and legitimated by references to protection. In carving out an analytical context that allows us to present a more comprehensive account of this relationship, we ask whether drones are a poison pill or a cure-all for PoC.

Following the large-scale atrocities in Rwanda and the Balkans, PoC emerged as a key concern for the international community. From the mid-2000s, it has entered the spheres of military interventions, peacekeeping and humanitarian assistance. Today, the PoC agenda faces multiple challenges and is often portrayed as falling abysmally short. Still, PoC is intensively used as a frame to shape and legitimate different "regimes of intervention" (Marcus 2010). PoC is both a strategic label and a qualifier that can be filled with a range of contents. This duality has transformed PoC into a politically, technically and normatively amorphous agenda.

Because the mechanisms of PoC – peacekeeping, humanitarian relief and the conduct of combatants in war – are also key coordinates of the moral map of global governance, the notion of the protection of civilians is particularly liable to strategic "frame appropriation." Jon Harald Sande Lie (2012) describes PoC as a "battlefield of knowledge" where the concept is worked and reworked in practice as actors compete to infuse the discourse with meaning, while borrowing from its moral supremacy. Lie suggests that, rather than being the prerogative of peacekeepers and humanitarians, PoC represents an ideational discursive framework open to other actors, even if their mandate and institutional culture diverge from the protection discourse (Lie 2012). Borrowing from Jutta Joachim and Andrea Schneiker (2012), in this chapter we understand PoC as a frame that can be appropriated or transformed as actors appropriate the language and elements of PoC that best fit their interests or needs. Framing is here understood as a conscious strategic effort by actors to fashion shared understandings of the world and of themselves that legitimate and motivate collective action (McAdam, McCarthy and Zald 1996). The question of frame appropriation is important with respect to the deployment of drones because various aspects of the PoC agenda are at play in the rationales for ongoing and emergent use of drones in combat, peace-keeping and humanitarian action.

So far, there has been some academic focus on what the actors hope that the humanitarian aspects of the PoC agenda "can do" for "their" drones. To legitimate the use of force, states have attempted to promulgate views of combat drones as humanitarian weapons based on their ability to perform surgically precise targeting (Brunstetter and Braun 2011; Kreps and Kaag 2012). The UN peacekeeping mission in DR Congo, MONUSCO, promotes its own humanitarian, life-saving use of the new surveillance drone cap-acity, much to the consternation of the NGO community (*IRINNews* 2014; D'Onofrio 2014). To lessen the stigma engendered by the killer drone label, military manufacturers have made considerable efforts to craft "humanitar-ian purposes" for their drones. The strategic objective of these efforts has been to enable technology transfers from military to civil use, to identify new humanitarian usages and potential customers, and enhance support for opening civil airspace to drones (Sandvik and Lohne 2014). Civilian drone manufacturers and volunteer and technological communities have tried to carve out a role for themselves as protection actors by promoting drones that can "save lives," while traditional humanitarian actors have started to embrace drones to realise unfulfilled ambitions of effectiveness and knowledge-based decision-making in their protection efforts (Sandvik and Jumbert 2015).

Beyond this, little systematic attention has been given to the relationship between drones and the PoC agenda.[2] Specific references to PoC in the con-text of drones have often been descriptive (Sharkey 2011), and are primar-ily associated with *violations* of PoC in the context of the War on Terror. These issues include the targeting and killing of civilians due to mistaken identities, technical mishaps or human error, or the controversial targeting of rescue parties. Consequences for survivors include mental problems, limited access to health care and education, financial ruin and the undermining of local political life and cultural fabric (Stanford Law School Human Rights and Conflict Resolution Clinic and NYU School of Law Global Justice Clinic 2012). Conversely, in the most optimistic scenarios, drones for target-ing, surveillance, or relief drops are presented as a response to fundamental challenges that are currently facing the international PoC agenda. These chal-lenges include the insecurity of humanitarian workers, and the inadequate capacity of peacekeepers to offer effective military protection to civilians in the midst of armed conflict.

Yet, in the broader context of international efforts to promote the PoC through legal, humanitarian, peacekeeping and military measures, the con-nections between drones and PoC are complex. Protection is a key task of states and international organisations. Protection activities are associated with public services and civilian policing, as well as military action. As noted in the introduction to this volume by Jumbert and Sandvik, the domains of these activities – the global battlespace, the humanitarian emergency field and the everyday risk society – are sites of drone controversies, including the Drone Wars and the opening of civil airspace to drones. To that end, the ambition and approach of this chapter is largely conceptual. To begin to untangle the complex linkages between PoC and drones we critically review what drones "can do for PoC," bracketing the related question of "what PoC can do for drones."

The chapter is structured around a set of ideational versions of PoC actors and concerns that, despite their distinct institutional trajectories, build on each other (Lie 2012). In a helpful conceptual contribution, Hugh Breakey (2012) proposes a PoC matrix structured according to the actors involved: *combatants, humanitarian organisations, peacekeepers* and the *Security Council*. Because current practices of PoC reflect the actual competences and priorities of these actors, this matrix leaves us with a concrete starting point for the consideration of the use of drones for the purpose of PoC. The following exposition adapts Breakey's typology to provide a careful but non-exhaustive overview of PoC-related functions that drones could be imagined to assume (due to space constraints, we will not discuss the impact of drones on the PoC related work of the Security Council). We also outline a number of debates that might arise in the context of such usages.

The chapter proceeds as follows. The first section introduces PoC as a political concept. The following sections consider current or likely uses of drones within the fields of combat, peacekeeping and humanitarianism. We identify the perils and promises of these uses for the protection of civilians, as a basis for further research and debate. In the conclusion, the analysis of the potential impact of drones on PoC is summed up and related to the overarching question of how drones may affect the very concept and strategies of PoC, reflecting the opportunities presented by the technology itself. We suggest that the deployment of drones to enhance the efficiency of current practices associated with PoC tends to be a response to indefinite objectives – a problem that the drones cannot themselves resolve.

The protection of civilians

The principle of PoC stems from international humanitarian law (IHL), particularly as a reaction to the massive targeting of civilians during WWII (Ferris 2011: 6–16). The category of civilians originally developed to exclude non-combatants from protection afforded to belligerents. As an attempt at mitigating war, the legal status of the term changed with the 1949 IV Geneva convention, which banned traditional military practices such as collective punishments, inhumane internment, deportations etc. While civilians were no longer a legitimate target, civilian deaths were still permissible if the targeting was based on military necessity and if civilian casualties were proportional to the military advantage gained.

When picked up in reaction to the civilian suffering in civil wars and genocide throughout the 1990s, PoC was transformed from a doctrine pertaining to the conduct of the military into an organising principle for international engagement in conflict-ridden countries (Ferris 2011). Reflecting a frustration in the UN with its reliance on the norms of state security and non-intervention in countries where civilians were the main victims of war, the notion of PoC was redefined in order to mandate international actors with the protection of *individuals* rather than *states*. It represented a "third way" for humanitarianism between a "Dunantian" emphasis on neutrality and impartiality and a "Wilsonian" emphasis on integrating humanitarianism in the political promotion of human rights and democracy across borders (Rieff 2002; also Barnett 2011).

In this respect, the new conception of PoC was closely related to the development of the doctrine of the "Responsibility to Protect" (RtoP). RtoP emerged from a concern with the distribution of responsibility for protection, essentially placing a responsibility on international actors to react if a state does not fulfil its responsibility to protect its own citizens. When the version of the RtoP doctrine which was adopted by the UN General Assembly in 2005 was confirmed by the Security Council in *Resolution 1674*, it happened under the heading of the protection of civilians (UN Security Council, 2006). Furthermore, the principle of PoC was invoked as a justification for coercive interference à la RtoP in UN Security Council debates and mandates leading up to the NATO operation in Libya in 2011 (Bellamy and Williams, 2011).[3]

The specific concerns currently associated with the protection of civilians in armed conflict are spelled out in the OCHA Aide Memoire, which since 2002 has defined the scope of PoC for the Security Council. In the Memoire, the overarching objective of PoC is defined as "protection of, and assistance to, the conflict-affected population" (OCHA, 2014: 7–10). While supposedly narrowing the scope of the widely adopted ICRC definition of protection as "all activities aimed at obtaining full respect for the rights of the individual in accordance with the letter and spirit of relevant bodies of international law," the Memoire's definition of PoC merely relates the objective of protection to conflict-affected populations. The Aide Memoire then narrows this general concern down to a set of "protection concerns," as well as a range of more specific concerns related to the protection of children and women in armed conflict. While listing specific measures under each area of concern, the Memoire is still wide open for interpretation at the operational level. This openness, combined with the array of areas of protection, invites the introduction and contestation of new actors, strategies and techniques.[4] The introduction of drones for protection is such a contested novelty, as analysed below along the dimensions of combat, peacekeeping and humanitarian aid.

Combatant PoC

Combatant PoC is the original domain of PoC, revolving around the conduct of armed forces in war. It concerns their general responsibility towards the civilian population within their control, including the protection of displaced persons and humanitarian workers. The central elements of combatant PoC relate to the core principles of international humanitarian law, including the principles of using means that are proportionate to their ends, and of discriminating between civilians and combatants. Public debate on the use of drones in warfare usually centres on the alleged failure to uphold these principles (or that they are the wrong principles and that a human rights framework should apply instead); on civilian casualties; and on the detrimental social consequences of targeted killings by armed drones.

However, drones have a wider scope of functions for combatants than targeted killings. Frederic Mégret (2013) notes that the challenge is to find out what is *specifically* problematic about drones: following this line of reasoning, we set out to take the possibility that drones can also be an effective tool to protect civilians seriously. Hence, in the following, we start out by considering arguments for how drones may have a positive effect on PoC in combat, without thereby denying that the current use of weaponised drones in "the Global War on Terror" casts a dark shadow over the arguments. Furthermore, the challenge is to single out the difference that drones make to combat while recognising the fundamental impact of context on their efficiency and legitimacy.[5]

In a certain respect, the debate on the connection between drones and PoC is a battle of contextual imagination. While critics tend to concentrate on civilian casualties in controversial campaigns like the US use of drones in Pakistan or Yemen, proponents take a militaristic perspective on how the lives of good soldiers may be spared, how effectively enemies can be targeted, or on the use of drones for humanitarian and peacekeeping purposes as intrinsically ethical. In the following, we concentrate on two functions of drones: surveillance (broadly defined), and targeted killings.[6]

Intelligence, surveillance, reconnaissance and target selection

Compared to satellites, drones can provide more detailed and immediately available footage, and change flight paths according to need. The oldest and most prevalent use of medium altitude and long endurance (MALE) drones is for surveillance (the monitoring of behaviour and activities over a large part of the battlefield) and reconnaissance (the process of getting information about enemy forces or positions, including target selection) to improve situational awareness in combat, and military strategic decision-making. The first use of drones for intelligence, surveillance and reconnaissance (ISR) that may in some way be termed a PoC use, was the US deployment of the Gnat 750, a predecessor to the Predator, over Bosnia in 1994 (*The*

Economist 2012). Since then, the use of larger and more sophisticated high altitude long endurance (HALE) (Global Hawk by Northrop Grumman) and MALE drones like the Heron (IAI) or the Predator (General Atomics) for ISR have become commonplace in conflict. Handheld micro and nano drones such as Raven B (Aerovironment) and Black Hornet (Prox Dynamics) are also increasingly common in combat. These function as "binoculars in the air" to enhance force protection and combat effectiveness. Non-state armed groups have also acquired surveillance drones, including the Hezbollah, Hamas and the Islamic State (Zwijnenburg, 2014).

The primary rationale for using drones for ISR in war is to increase the efficiency of operations and reduce the risks for military personnel. However, if combined with a sincere commitment to PoC, improved ISR capabilities may also reduce the accidental killing of civilians and other collateral damage. This includes an improved ability to identify permissible military targets, and make more accurate determinations of proportionality – better balancing military gain against civilian harm. Rosén (2014) suggests that drone technology offers an effective precautionary measure, which may trigger precautionary obligation across all weapons systems. If a state possesses drone technology, and if the deployment of this technology may potentially reduce unnecessary harm from armed attacks, including shelling, the state is obliged under IHL to employ this technology for precaution.

The use of drones by armed forces for ISR can also be related to the broader PoC norm: that armed groups are responsible for protecting civilians within the territory under their control. This responsibility entails the integration of PoC concerns in military planning, including protection of people on the run, of humanitarian workers, and of wounded civilians. Increasing the situational awareness of armed groups through the use of drones might support such efforts and increase their responsibility towards civilians within their control.

On the other hand, surveillance information can also be used for the very purpose of harming civilians. Deliberate attacks on certain groups of civilians are frequent in war, generally when they are seen as supporting the enemy (Slim 2008). In civil war settings, even very basic hobby drones may be used by militants to track down people fleeing from an attack. There are many examples of state regimes deliberately targeting their own civilian citizens by way of airpower, for example, with the al Bashir government in Sudan (aerial bombing in Darfur and along the South Sudan border) and the Assad regime in Syria (aerial bombing and chemical attacks on civilians in strongholds of opposition forces). In both of these cases, drones were reportedly used for reconnaissance and target identification (Zwijnenburg, 2014). An example in the grey zone between internal and external use is attacks by Israeli forces on political leaders of Hamas in Gaza (controversially defined as legitimate "non-civilian" targets because Hamas is defined as a terrorist organisation). In this case, drones are used for ISR purposes, as well as for assassinations (HRW 2009).

Even if the analysis is limited to forces committed to IHL, the net effect of drones used for ISR is not necessarily positive for PoC. In increasing the effectiveness of ISR and reducing the costs of warfare, drones reduce the threshold for resorting to armed force. Although causing less harm to civilians on average, more war generally means more civilian suffering. While this assertion is far too general and abstract to be made as an argument against military drones *per se*, it points to the need to question the equally simplistic assumption that the use of drones for ISR will necessarily result in a reduction of harm to civilians.

Targeting civilians, targeting for civilians?

Armed combat drones come with a host of promises to protect civilians, to "clean up combat" and make war more humane. Generally, proponents of combat drones cite their potential for improving *jus in bello* compliance: by offering "surgically precise targeting," armed drones are presented as a humane weapon, in the sense that collateral damage is reduced compared to previous attempts at precision bombing from fighter planes. Such precision is assumed to have a positive effect not only on discrimination but on proportionality. For instance, when the objective is to reduce the threat from an enemy force, key commanders and weaponry can be targeted instead of engaging in a conventional battle against the whole army. A well-known argument in defense of combat drones is that they are deployed instead of "boots on the ground" and therefore save lives on both sides. Drones promise to limit the geographical scope for the use of force to sites where targets, just the most wanted dangerous enemies, are located (Krasmann, Chapter 1). This is taken to benefit the host populations, but also one's own soldiers, their families and communities. Furthermore, drones are supposed to increase the efficiency and shorten the time span of military activity, through achieving strategic and tactical objectives more quickly (and cheaply). It is even claimed that drones minimise the risk of a conflict escalating into full-scale war by selectively eliminating targets (for a critique, see Brunstetter and Braun 2011: 346).

However, these arguments can also be inverted. In particular, the role of armed drones as a vehicle for the use of force, and the practice of signature strikes are deeply problematic from a PoC perspective. According to critics, armed drones have become a push factor for military action: it becomes the number of targets drones *can* select and eliminate that determines the overall strategy. Drones may then contribute to dragging nations into war without any clear purpose, ethnical rationale or exit strategy (Cronin 2013; *National Public Radio (NPR)* 2015). Signature strikes target not specific individuals but groups engaged in suspicious activities. The term is used to distinguish strikes conducted against individuals who match a pre-determined "signature" pattern of behaviour linked to militant activity, rather than targeting a specific person. As extensively documented, this practice has resulted in significant civilian casualties. More generally, it has also contributed to the continued blurring of categories between protected civilians and individuals who can be defined as legitimate targets under international law.

The problem is not only collateral damage whereby civilians are mistakenly targeted, or that they are killed because they are in the wrong place at the wrong time or due to technical mishaps: the drone wars have also engendered significant socio-economic and psycho-social problems for surviving civilians, including individual injuries or traumas, poverty resulting from the loss of breadwinners, limitations in the access to health care or education, financial ruin, or the weakening of local political life and the cultural fabric (Stanford Law School Human Rights and Conflict Resolution Clinic and NYU School of Law Global Justice Clinic 2012). For instance, in interviews with *The Guardian* in 2014, thirteen-year-old Mohammed Tuaiman described a short life spent in fear of "death machines," which had killed his father and brother in 2011, when they were out herding camels: "I see them every day and we are scared of them ... They turned our area into hell and continuous horror, day and night, we even dream of them in our sleep." January 2015, Mohammed Tuaiman himself was killed by a drone strike (Madlena, Patchett, and Shamsan 2015).

In an analysis of the war on terror paradigm, Sarah Kreps and John Kaag argue that the defenders of armed drones overstate the ability of technology to answer the difficult ethical, legal, and political questions posed by the principles of distinction and proportionality. They observe that "technology, even when it is sophisticated and precise, cannot determine the proportionality of strikes when nearly everything counts as a military objective" (Kreps and Kaag 2012: 261). They voice concern that there is a risk of conflating technological ability with increasingly sophisticated individual judgment (Kreps and Kaag 2012). Thus, as noted above, the perceived technical ability to effectively target designated individuals runs the risk of becoming the rationale for doing so. This criticism still presupposes a general commitment to PoC among the actors operating armed drones. Again, we should also consider the effects of drones on PoC when in the hands of forces with little or no respect for IHL. The promise of armed drones is to be able to engage an observed target immediately. With their ISR capacity, armed drones would be a useful tool for totalitarian regimes fighting a resistance movement, or for terrorists, insurgents or guerilla groups.

So far, the debate on the legitimacy of armed drones has centred on the three countries that are known to have them, namely the US, and to a more limited extent, Israel and the UK. In 2015, the export ban on US produced armed drones was lifted, although under conditions of governmental control and guarantees. As noted by several commentators (Prupis 2015; Zenko 2015), history tells us that once the US transfers a weapon to another nation it is nonetheless difficult to control how it is used, regardless of what guidelines are established for their use. Armed drones will enable countries to engage more easily in military strikes against neighboring nations or attacks on their own people. Justified as a way of supporting allied countries, the new US policy will probably set a precedent for countries that are already exporting unarmed drones (see Knuckey 2015). The near-future likelihood of a global proliferation of combat drone platforms, reinforced by the strong economic incentives to enter this new market, is a disconcerting development for the future of PoC.[7]

Peacekeeping PoC

While combatant PoC centres on the conduct of armed groups in war – including when increasingly robust peacekeeping missions engage in warfare (Karlsrud 2015) – peacekeeping PoC centres on PoC as a distinct *objective* of peacekeeping beyond limiting the civilian casualties of combat conducted by peacekeeping forces. Nearly all current peacekeeping operations include PoC as a central part of their mandate. The most obvious PoC aspect of peacekeeping is the direct protection of civilians against attacks by armed groups – and against mass atrocities in particular. In addition to intervening militarily, this task involves the prevention of attacks, reporting on violations, and supporting political and military parties in providing physical protection to civilians within their control. All of these activities require extensive collection and analysis of information on combatants and civilians in volatile areas. Such surveillance capability has often been seen as a weakness of peacekeeping operations, especially for operations undertaken in countries with limited infrastructure and a risky environment (Dorn 2011). Over the past few years, surveillance drones have been introduced as a remedy to this problem. While previously relying on the drone capabilities of troop contributing countries, the UN has started acquiring surveillance drones of its own. In addition to the physical protection of civilians in areas of combat, peacekeeping relates to other PoC concerns identified in the Aide Memoire, including the provision of security for displaced persons and humanitarian relief workers; and creating the right security environment for demobilisation, material reconstruction, political and security reforms and reconciliation processes. Hence, the impact of drones in peacekeeping should be analysed broadly, beyond the scope of direct military protection.

Surveillance, reconnaissance, documentation and deterrence

The key promise of drones in the peacekeeping context is to allow for rapid *response* to suspicious movements of military troops and material, to actual attacks, or to refugee streams. The ideal would be to detect and *prevent* looming atrocities and provide information for *early warning* systems. Furthermore, when used in connection with a military operation, drones can be used for *reconnaissance* and *target selection*, as described in the previous section on combatant PoC (on these functions, see Karlsrud and Rosén, Chapter 2).

In addition to supporting the operations of peacekeeping forces, the potential role for surveillance drones in *documenting* atrocities has been highlighted by several observers (e.g. Whetham 2015). Such documentation can be used for reporting to headquarters, and serves as a basis for adequate international responses. It can also potentially be used as evidence in court. The documentation of war crimes and mass atrocities is part of peacekeeping mandates, both as information that may feed into international political debate, including in the UN Security Council, and as evidence for the International Criminal Court.[8] If potential perpetrators expect that information obtained by drones about violence against civilians will entail a military response, or at least have political or legal consequences, then surveillance drones may have a *deterrent* effect as well.

There are several contentious issues to consider before a conclusion can be drawn on the impact of drones on PoC in peacekeeping, however. Firstly, reflecting the widespread scepticism against "killer drones," there is the concern that drones operated by peacekeepers or humanitarians in conflict settings may be spreading fear and confusion among the host populations. This concern is most relevant in theatres where armies have previously used drones for target selection or targeting, and where the sight of a drone therefore is associated with an imminent attack. If operating in parallel with combat drones, peacekeeping drones would not only possibly create panic but reduce the predictability of attacks.

A more mundane concern, which is also shared with humanitarian PoC, is the question of resource management. Are drones a sound investment in a situation where resources already fall short, especially considering the transactions costs of learning to operate the drones, analysing the collected data and using it in the right ways? The argument in favour of drones for surveillance is that they enhance the efficiency of operations, and they are cost effective compared, for example, to surveillance by manned aircraft. However, as Karlsrud and Rosén warn in the conclusion of their contribution to this volume, the main problem for current peacekeeping efforts is not a lack of information but of the capacity and will to react. Hence, the investment in drones must be combined with enhanced reaction capabilities and extra resources to compensate for the transaction costs.

Furthermore, we have to ask how drones affect the character of peacekeeping, and whether this development is desirable. It is possible that the demands that would justify the investment in surveillance drones are of the wrong kind. As we will discuss further in the section on humanitarian PoC, Mark Duffield argues that there is a tendency in peacekeeping and humanitarianism towards "bunkerisation" and distancing – a withdrawal from the host-population due to risk aversion and a failure to address the causes of the insecurity (Duffield, 2013). According to Duffield, this tendency undermines the very role of peacekeeping, of being present, visible and establishing relations of trust across the sides of the conflict. Karlsrud and Rosén (2013) reject the argument that drones exacerbate this development. To the contrary, they argue, surveillance drones allow peacekeepers to "lift the fog of war," reducing the risk to the troops and facilitating more effective operations. Yet, the very premise of an argument by Caroline Kennedy and James Rogers that will be further discussed below, is that peacekeeping has become too dangerous, and that drones *should* be deployed as a form of peacekeeping by remote. They argue that "one virtue of drones would be to reduce the number of ground-based monitoring, observing, reporting and peace enforcement personnel needed in high-risk regions" (Kennedy and Rogers, 2015: 216).

The operation in South Sudan (UNMISS) in 2014 may be taken as an example, where the PoC mandate was reduced to documenting and reporting violations in response to a deteriorated security environment.[9] As peacekeepers were intimidated on several occasions, the mission did not have the force necessary for protecting civilians beyond the walls of their own military compounds (Oudenaren 2014). In response, permission was requested from the authorities to deploy UN surveillance drones of the kind used in DR Congo and Mali. However, permission was allegedly denied (Sengupta 2014). If it had been accepted, the ability of drones to monitor the movements of armed groups would potentially have allowed the peacekeepers to leave their bases more freely (drone surveillance would also have allowed peacekeepers to *remain* at their bases while doing the monitoring). Images transmitted by drones cannot replace intelligence provided by contacts on the ground. Yet, as a tool for investigating and verifying reports emerging from around the country, the drone could be an important contribution to peacekeeping in a setting like South Sudan.

The fact that permission was denied by the authorities – supposedly the very wardens of the peace process – may nonetheless be an even more fundamental concern regarding the operational and strategic implications of drone deployment. Why would a government that is reliant on international goodwill and support reject their deployment? Probably because controlling the information on military and political developments is key to the power and legitimacy of the authorities. Furthermore, if information on the movements of the government forces and friendly militias was obtained by the opposition forces, accidentally or on purpose, it would be a serious disadvantage for the government forces. In South Sudan, the UN peacekeeping operation did not side with the government to the same degree as the UN has done in DR Congo and Mali since the outbreak of civil war in 2013. Instead it pushed for a negotiated solution. The UN would therefore probably not be willing to share surveillance information with the authorities. Doing so would be a major asset for the authorities, and also make the peacekeepers even more of a target for militias siding with the opposition.

Despite the introduction of PoC as a key principle, the core task of peacekeeping remains to be the implementation of a ceasefire or peace agreement. Arguably, this is also the most essential contribution peacekeeping can make to PoC, as it has a more fundamental bearing on the security of a population than the direct protection that a peacekeeping force can provide during conflict. If the use of drones for protection purposes in any way would undermine the role of peacekeeping missions in supporting a peace process, it would therefore be counterproductive also from a PoC perspective. The case of South Sudan illustrates how balancing a protection mandate with neutrality can be a contentious issue, and how the proposed use of drones for protection may endanger the balance.

Monitoring without peacekeeping

Before we turn to an argument for using *armed* drones in peacekeeping, we will consider a proposition of employing surveillance drones for documentation and deterrence *in the absence of a peacekeeping mission*. In a controversial 2012 op-ed piece in *The New York Times*, Andrew Sniderman and Mark Hanis, representing the Genocide Intervention Network, called for the use of surveillance drones to monitor and collect evidence of human rights abuses in Syria, stating that "it's time we used the revolution in military affairs to serve human rights advocacy" and that "if human rights organizations can spy on evil, they should." Sniderman and Hanis further suggested that the evidence could be broadcast to a global audience, including prosecutors at the International Criminal Court (Sniderman and Hanis 2012).

Following a similar logic, David Whetham argues that sending in a fleet of unarmed drones into situations where the option of a full-scale peacekeeping operation is ruled out would be preferable to inaction. He proposes that drones with surveillance capabilities could be deployed under a relatively uncontroversial resolution by the United Nations Security Council "in a matter of days or even hours to nearly anywhere on the planet to stand witness and record events on the ground as they happen" (Whetham, 2015: 203). In addition to providing neutral evidence for political decision-making, "all footage of violations of human rights could then be passed to the ICC for culpable individuals to be identified, prosecution cases to be built, and indictments handed out when possible" (ibid.). Later, when the situation allows, the evidence could be used in court, also for cross-referencing with eyewitness accounts, he suggests. The main purpose would not be the indictments, however, but prevention by reducing the incentives for committing atrocities: "If this could be done in a suitably public way, thus deploying them with as much fanfare as possible to ensure that belligerents are aware of what is going to happen, the fear of being observed may be enough to modify behaviour" (ibid.). Whetham recognises the many hurdles to such deployment. In an environment like Syria, the authorities would surely oppose the arrangement, and with the support from Russia, a Security Council resolution might be barred. Furthermore, belligerents might simply respond by shooting the drones down.[10] While there are other weaknesses to the argument as well, including a highly optimistic view of the role and capacity of the ICC, the proposition deserves serious attention.

Could this approach even replace boots on the ground in contexts where drone deployment would be more practical but where peacekeeping would also be an option? If so, it would tie-in to the rationale for remote peacekeeping advanced by Kennedy and Rogers (2015). Here, we enter the seriously contentious domain of drones replacing soldiers in order to eliminate risk and reduce costs, where the road is short to including armed drones in peacekeeping.

Targeting in peace enforcement missions

Proponents of surveillance drones in peacekeeping have struggled with distancing themselves from the image of the "killer drone" and the prospects for employing it. Lamenting this averseness, Kennedy and Rogers (2015) make the case for integrating armed drones in peacekeeping for the sake of rapid response in environments that are hard to access and/or would pose significant risks to the lives of peacekeepers (see also McNeal 2012). Against developments in DR Congo, Mali, CAR and Sierra Leone, and the history of shortcomings in Rwanda and Srebrenica, they draw a picture of peacekeeping as getting more dangerous and ambitious, and with resources falling dramatically short. Neutrality, they argue, is no longer central to peacekeeping, nor is the role of ceasefires or the consent of all parties. Instead, peacekeeping has become a matter of taking sides, generally by fighting alongside government forces (ibid. 219). Their argument is partly motivated by a critique of the prospects for surveillance drones:

> It would appear that such unarmed drones would only be able to ensure the UN as a reactive monitor of abuses with little increase in its ability to actively prevent them. In essence, a better picture may be available but unarmed drones do little to proactively address the manifest shortfalls and risks which we have outlined. They do even less to reduce the need for peacekeepers on the ground in high-risk regions, and, if deployed as a sole entity ... they are unable to directly intervene to protect vulnerable populations from genocide or human rights abuses.
>
> (ibid. 221)

This is not only a sobering account of the prospects of surveillance drones. It also indicates how the deployment of unarmed drones entails an argument for arming them. Kennedy and Rogers then put forward the view that armed drones would be a far more effective source of deterrence, as well as being used to halt rebel and militia advances (ibid. 223). Beyond this, they provide no examples of how exactly armed drones would be used, which prevents a critical consideration of negative effects. Instead, they concentrate on past failures and imply that armed drones would have solved the problem.

Against the backdrop of the "Global War on Terror," we may presume that the introduction of armed drones would radically change the nature of peacekeeping. Even in comparison with the rather aggressive peacekeeping mandates on DR Congo, Mali and Sierra Leone that, after all, are exceptions to the general character of peacekeeping, attacks by drones would be something different. As mentioned in the section on combatant PoC, it is well documented how living under the continuous possibility of bombardment from "a blue sky" may have serious mental and social consequences. It would surely have a negative effect on the perception of the peacekeeping endeavour – and it is well established how local legitimacy is key to the success of any such effort (Donais 2012). Kennedy and Rogers, to the contrary, expect effective use of armed drones for the protection of civilians to entail a new image of drones as "virtuous."

Among the many drawbacks, we would highlight how the arming of drones would undermine efforts at reducing fears of "peacekeeping drones" among the host population. This problem of perception is a recurrent theme in the literature, and it seems that the positive effects of surveillance drones for PoC would be outweighed if they themselves were a source of insecurity. In response, Kennedy and Rogers would probably refer to the potential for halting ongoing atrocities around the world as outweighing such fears. Yet, the question is whether armed drones for peacekeeping would have the positive effects they foresee. Indeed, the scenario they propose would represent exactly the kind of development that could be undermining the essential virtues of peacekeeping – virtues that they consider a lost case.

Furthermore, the contentious issue of extrajudicial killings in the War on Terror would also apply here: the promise of the ICC and transitional justice mechanisms is to hold perpetrators accountable. Targeted killings based on evidence obtained by surveillance drones would be a clear deviation from this approach of "policing" rather than "fighting." While we cannot rule out that extraordinary situations will arise where there is a clear rationale for the use of armed drones as part of a peacekeeping or peace enforcement operation, introducing it as a general component of peacekeeping seems counterproductive for PoC.

Humanitarian PoC

International humanitarian organisations have taken on a central role in the PoC agenda. Their classic roles in the context of armed conflict have been to provide relief to victims of war (increasingly civilians), and to promote international humanitarian law (including "combatant PoC"). Assistance to displaced persons (refugees and IDPs) is also a central PoC-related activity by humanitarian organisations. In recent years, humanitarian actors have also focused on how to better protect civilians against urban violence (Reid-Henry and Sending 2014).

Drones have been used for surveying the impact of natural disasters, locating survivors and assessing infrastructure damages; to monitor population movements; conduct needs assessments to determine where, and how many people are in need and what their needs are; and build better short-term strategies for handling humanitarian logistics and distributing relief. Drones are expected to improve factors such as access and the scale of assistance, also by enabling surveillance and information gathering over geographically large areas, or areas that are difficult to enter due to lack of roads or security threats against humanitarian workers. Moreover, efforts are made at developing systems that would allow fleets of drones to distribute payloads of medical supplies, food and other humanitarian goods (Sandvik and Lohne 2013). So far, the focus on drones for humanitarian purposes has centred on natural disasters. The question for PoC, then, is what the potential is for deploying drones in support of humanitarian efforts in conflict settings. Due to the military connotations of drones, humanitarian organisations have been wary of entering this domain, except for humanitarian demining.

Crisis mapping and cargo

While drones were used to survey damage and reconstruction after the 2010 Haiti earthquake, Typhoon Hayan is generally seen as the "breakthrough" for the use of small, handheld drones in humanitarian operations. At present, there is a proliferation of private sector and non-profit initiatives to develop drones for humanitarian purposes in response to natural disasters. A subset of the new breed of "techie humanitarians" has entered the race to fill the concept "humanitarian drones" with meaning. Their aim is to develop and deploy small drones to conduct search and rescue (SAR), or to provide early-onset or post-disaster data (Clark 2012).

In addition to using drones for crisis mapping, hopes are high that drones can contribute to the demanding logistics of humanitarian operations. In a Foreign Policy article from 2012, Jack Chow pondered about the potential of drones to deliver HIV/AIDS medication. According to Chow, cargo drones could be a "game changer" for aid distribution, which could eliminate or reduce the type of corruption, theft and insecurity (as well as the consequences of difficult weather conditions and problems caused by disasters) which frequently undermines current efforts (Chow 2012). A number of commercial startups have emerged, that want to use drones to carry relief: for example, Matternet, one of a group of Silicon Valley UAV entrepreneurs, has described its plans for a network of UAVs that will create "the next paradigm for transportation" of goods and medicines to remote settlements (Gibb 2012). Moreover, established humanitarian actors are also embracing drones, usually in collaboration with either or both of the communities above. The World Food Program started experimenting with drones almost a decade ago (Meier 2014). MSF collaborates with Matternet in Papua New Guinea to set up a tuberculosis diagnostic station (Smedley 2015). The Danish firm Sky-Watch, in cooperation with DanChurch Aid, has used airborne thermal imagery to spot people stranded amongst storm debris (Smedley 2015).

The potential for transfer to conflict settings

What is the potential for transferring these capabilities to conflict settings? Breakey lists a range of strategies that humanitarian agencies use for the sake of protecting conflict-affected populations, including: protection through *presence* of humanitarian personnel; *empowering local populations* in self-protection; *creation of safe areas*, for example, through negotiations with belligerents; creation and dissemination of *information*; *transport or evacuation* of civilians; *engagement with all parties* to the conflict, at all levels of authority, in order to advance civilian protection; and *structuring and designing* aid facilities and programmes in ways that enhance civilian safety (Breakey 2012: 56). From our previous analysis of peacekeeping, we see how some of these strategies may be reinforced by surveillance drones, like the collection and dissemination of information on civilian suffering. The impact on the strategy of presence is ambiguous, as drones on the one hand can support presence in exposed areas, but where they could also facilitate the withdrawal of aid workers from risky environments. Invoking the argument of Whetham (2015) discussed above, the presence of surveillance drones might inherit the deterrent effect of the physical presence of humanitarian workers, but this would arguably be a bleak replacement.[11]

Regarding the designing of aid programmes according to protection needs, both drones for surveillance and cargo could have a role. Monitoring the movements of displaced people would be an example. And if cargo drones could effectively distribute aid to deprived areas, preventing people from leaving their homes, it might have a positive effect on protection as well.

As regards the protection concern in the Aide Memoire of small arms and light weapons, mines and explosive remnants of war, there is already extensive experience with humanitarian demining with drones. Drones can help in producing detailed, up-to-date maps of an area before de-miners enter with their instruments. For example, in response to the flooding in the Balkans in spring 2014, the UN deployed drones on-site in collaboration with traditional relief workers, to support them not only with damage assessment and area mapping but visual inspection and re-localising of the many explosive remnants of war which had been moved due to the flooding and landslides (De Cubber et al. 2014).

On the other hand, drones have so far had little to contribute to the above-mentioned strategies of safe areas, evacuation and local engagement. If replacing humanitarian personnel, drones could even directly undermine such efforts. Furthermore, while some humanitarian organisations take an active role in reporting from the field, others rely on the trust of all parties as a means of humanitarian access. If humanitarian surveillance drones boosted the information strategy of some organisations, it could exacerbate tensions with groups that become the subject of negative reporting.

Another dimension of humanitarian PoC is to design programmes in ways that do not *undermine* PoC. A classic example of such adverse effects is the provision of a safe harbour and supply chain for militias in refugee camps and through the distribution of aid. If drones were to replace personnel in gathering intelligence of local belligerents or in distributing food and medicine, the ability to avoid such harmful effects would probably be reduced. Again, we are back to the crucial distinction between deploying drones in *support* of personnel on the ground or as their *replacement* for the sake of rationalisation and risk management.

The 2011 OCHA study on good practice in risk and security management, *To Stay and Deliver*, emphasises that "The objective for humanitarian actors in complex security environments … is not to avoid risk, but to manage risk in a way that allows them to remain present and effective in their work." Remote management of hard-to-reach areas has been greatly facilitated through information technology and social media, such as the use of SMS-surveys to map basic needs or the reliance on Skype for day-to-day management. Evidently, drones fit perfectly into this picture in conflict-ridden countries. In parallel to remote management, there is also a concerted focus on resilience, and on how humanitarian information can help beneficiaries make life-saving decisions and better "protect themselves" (Sandvik et al. 2014). Surveillance and cargo drones are clearly a part of this "turn to technology" in humanitarian action, with the attendant dangers of technological utopianism: that drones can both save humanitarian action and save civilians. While humanitarians speak about the "protection gap" or that PoC is "falling off the agenda," there is rarely talk about the PoC overreach of the burgeoning humanitarian enterprise as it is continuously doing more things in more battlefields; or the notion that PoC might be falling off the agenda due to declining understanding of context and ever increasing risk averseness (for the last point, see MSF 2014).

While achieving limited objectives like crisis mapping and the distribution of aid, the deployment of drones fails to address the underlying causes of the insecurity or inaccessibility that they "resolve." As such, relying on drones as a solution would further distance the humanitarian enterprises from the broader social and political landscapes that they operate within. With the crisis of efficiency and legitimacy outlined by Duffield, drones may come to represent the wrong end at which to begin, although they may still be a part of the solution.

Targeting in humanitarian interventions

Citing UNSC Resolution 1973, on Libya, which was passed on 6 February 2011, President Obama approved the use of armed drones, justifying their use as tools of humanitarian assistance for the protection of civilians (*CBS News* 2011). According to the principle of "the responsibility to protect" (RtoP), states are collectively responsible for reacting when a state does not take the necessary measures to protect civilians under its jurisdiction. Controversially, such reaction may involve the resort to military force, or "humanitarian intervention." The most prominent recent examples of operations that were justified by this purpose are the NATO bombing campaigns in Bosnia and Herzegovina (1995), the Federal Republic of Yugoslavia (1999) and Libya

(2011) (where armed drones were used as part of the larger air campaign). Through high altitude aerial bombardment that posed minimal risk to the pilots, these operations set the stage for the deployment of armed drones for the same purpose.

While the use of weaponised drones for humanitarian intervention is highly controversial (both the usage of armed drones *and* humanitarian intervention are among the most controversial issues in world politics), it can still be argued that enhancing the efficiency of military action for the protection of civilians is the least problematic context for the use of armed drones. Along the lines of targeted killings in the war on terror where the operation is not part of a larger military campaign, and parallel to the argument of Kennedy and Rogers (2015) for armed drones in peacekeeping, a case can even be made for expanding the scope of "humanitarian intervention" by deploying armed drones alone. This would introduce another chapter in the story of humanitarian intervention, possibly lowering the threshold for such intervention.

With the controversial standing of humanitarian intervention against the will of state authorities, combined with the widespread scepticism towards "killer drones," this seems like an unlikely scenario at present. It is more likely that armed drones would be used in support of state authorities when they have lost military control over a region where militias are responsible for mass atrocities. Boko Haram in Nigeria has now become an example of such a potential target. With the future spread of armed drones to ever more countries, the general rule would probably rather be that states themselves turn to targeted killings by drones as an alternative to deploying ground troops against militias within their territory. As with the rhetoric of counterterrorism, the highly imprecise norm of protecting civilians would provide authorities with exactly the kind of justification they need for doing so.

This would be the kind of militarisation of humanitarian politics that critics of humanitarian intervention and the responsibility to protect warn against. It is also not granted that the effect of more effective humanitarian intervention would be less civilian suffering. From recent experiences in Libya and the War on Terror, it appears that it rather could exacerbate domestic and international tensions, and perpetrators of mass atrocities could easily turn to forms of atrocities that are hard to detect or halt "from above." Yet, while unlikely at present, it seems very probable that calls for such use of armed drones for the protection of civilians will come up in response to future atrocities, redefining the scope of the PoC and RtoP agendas.

Conclusion

While drones may support efforts of PoC along a series of dimensions, branding drones as generally "PoC friendly" would be misleading. The title of this chapter is in some ways rhetorical: Drones are certainly not a cure-all for PoC, and if relied upon as a source of PoC, it may indeed be a political poison pill for protection. However, to chart a path between these two positions, we have engaged in a deliberate, yet tentative effort to map out what drones can and cannot do for PoC across the domains of armed combat, peacekeeping and humanitarianism. We observe that drones partly support existing PoC efforts, but also offer solutions that lead warfare, peacekeeping and humanitarianism in new directions. Regarding combatant PoC, drones contribute to creating a new worldwide battlefield by lowering both the risks and costs of engagement. By improving intelligence, surveillance, reconnaissance, target selection and precision in targeting, drones can be presented as expedient to PoC. Yet, with the global spread of military drones, such improvement may also be used for the frequent purpose of targeting civilians, and their offensive use can spark more conventional warfare.

Peacekeeping and humanitarianism are faced with a context where there appear to be insurmountable challenges to protecting an unprecedented number of civilians against atrocities, and where resources are perceived as falling dramatically short. We have observed how drones offer significant promises in mitigating this situation. For peacekeeping, the key contributions relate to surveillance, reconnaissance, documentation and, potentially, deterrence. The use of armed drones in peacekeeping was also considered, and it was suggested that such use would be undermining the potential of peacekeeping in protecting civilians if introduced as a general measure. For humanitarianism, the promises for PoC relate to improved crisis mapping and transportation. If facilitating the presence of humanitarian personnel in volatile areas and more effective distribution of aid, the dividend for PoC could be significant. However, drones are likely to exacerbate the tendency of remote management in peacekeeping and humanitarianism, where international personnel are withdrawn from the field.

In sum, we may conclude that while serving functions with significant advantages for PoC, these functions tend to reinforce policies that may eventually undermine PoC in the longer run: as a tool of combat, drones lower the threshold for resorting to military force; as a tool of peacekeeping, they exacerbate an unrealistic promise of protecting all civilians from violence; and as a tool of humanitarian assistance they facilitate a withdrawal of humanitarian personnel from dangerous environments.

Against this backdrop, it is necessary to consider how drones may affect the very concept and strategies of PoC. While all the surveyed uses of drones involve explicit assumptions that they operate with surgical precision and slash costs, there is also a set of underlying assumptions about functionality at work – namely that drones are inherently efficient, appropriate and practical. Drones currently exist in a context of technological optimism with respect to how unmanning and automating technology can create more effective, accountable, measurable and safer societies. Notions of functionality are paired with assumptions about relevance and purpose: beyond technological optimism, there is what the introduction to this volume labels "drone utopianism," where technology – fashioned in a deeply depoliticised manner – becomes the answer to political problems.

Accordingly, if branded as "PoC-friendly," drones may be a driver for more interventionist policies across the domains of warfare, peacekeeping and humanitarian aid. If drones are construed as the answer to the troubles of protection, more or less disjointed from practical scenarios, the resulting policies may fail to address the real insecurities or grievances experienced by civilian populations. As argued by Ferris, (2011) protection is too broad, unfocused and ambitious an objective for guiding peacekeeping and humanitarian assistance. Protection presupposes a state-like capacity to prevent and alleviate suffering for whole populations – generally exceeding the capacities of peacekeepers or humanitarian agencies by far. By striving to fill this role, international organisations divert power and initiative from local political actors and their host-states. Ascribing the responsibility for protection to international institutions, without devising them with the power to fulfil it, undermines the very objective of protection and institutes a sense of crisis of protection – a state of exception that justifies the introduction of extraordinary measures like the extensive reliance on drone technology. The scenario proposed by Kennedy and Rogers for drones in peacekeeping exemplifies this logic.

As an alternative to a general optimism or pessimism concerning the impact of drones on PoC, we have attempted to begin to elaborate on a more comprehensive and nuanced framework for considering this connection. We hope that this framework can be useful for future research on specific-use cases, as well as for policy development.

Notes

1 This chapter is an output of the "Protection of Civilians: From Principle to Practice" project funded by the Norwegian Research Council under the HUMPOL programme 2012–2016.
2 The exception is a recent literature on drones for peacekeeping, which is discussed in this chapter as well as in Chapter 2 by Karlsrud and Rosén.
3 Because of the controversies surrounding this operation and its aftermath, the Libya resolutions were a blow to the international consensus on PoC. Today, the two principles are generally presented as separate doctrines in order not to taint PoC with the contentious case of the RtoP for armed humanitarian intervention (e.g. Breakey 2012).
4 For example private security companies presenting themselves as humanitarians (Joachim and Schneiker 2012).
5 On the tendency in the drone debate to generalize from unattainable assumptions on effects and across disparate contexts, see Carvin (2015).
6 Cargo drones (the Kaman K-Max) have also been used for military logistics, but will not be discussed here. See Sandvik and Lohne (2014).
7 The year 2015 saw several important developments in this regard. Pakistan reported the use of a domestically produced combat drone (Ansari 2015). The South African company Denel Dynamics debuted an armed version of its Seeker 400 drone called "the Snyper" which came with four Impi-S missiles (Defenceweb 2015). China was also reported to have exported five armed drones (China Aerospace Science and Technology Corporation CH-3) to Nigeria to boost its efforts in fighting a war on terror against Boko-Haram (Mccarthy 2015; Maughan 2015).

8 Whereas humanitarian actors will tend to be deeply uneasy with any direct or indirect linkage with international criminal justice and how their drone footage might be used for such purposes.

9 The evolution and latest versions of the mandate are documented on the website of UNMISS: www.un.org/en/peacekeeping/missions/unmiss/mandate.shtml. (Accessed 7 October 2015).

10 Among the solutions, Whetham suggests that cheap or outdated drones could be used. This solution nonetheless seems to ignore the very limited reach and battery time of small drones of the cheaper kinds.

11 Humanitarian action is currently shaped by the metanarrative of a "shrinking humanitarian space." There is concern about the lack of respect for humanitarian principles and increased humanitarian worker insecurity. At the same time, both increasing donor funding and growing competition within the sector for those funds have created powerful incentives for aid agencies to be present and operational in conflict-affected countries (Collinson and Elhawary 2012). Remote management is an operational response to this challenge, which involves transferring greater programme responsibility and risk to local staff or local partner organizations, and overseeing activities from a different location (Stoddard, Harmer and Renouf 2010).

References

Ansari, U. (2015) Pakistan Surprises Many With First Use of Armed Drone. 10 September. Available at: www.defensenews.com/story/defense/air-space/strike/2015/09/08/pakistan-surprises-many-first-use-armed-drone/71881768/ (Accessed 10 April 2016).

Barnett, M. (2011) *Empire of Humanity: A History of Humanitarianism*. Ithaca: Cornell University Press.

Bellamy, A.J. and Williams, P.D. (2011) The new politics of protection? Côte d'Ivoire, Libya and the responsibility to protect. *International Affairs*, 87 (4): 825–850.

Breakey, H. (2012) The Protection of Civilians in Armed Conflict: Four concepts, in A. Francis, V. Popovski and C. Sampford (eds.), *Norms of Protection: Responsibility to Protect, Protection of Civilians and their Interconnection*. New York: UN University Press, 40–61.

Brunstetter, D. and Braun, M. (2011) The implications of drones on the Just War tradition. *Ethics and International Affairs*, 25 (3): 337–358.

Carvin, S. (2015) Getting drones wrong. *The International Journal of Human Rights*, 19 (2): 127–141.

CBS News (2011) Obama Oks Use of Armed Drone Aircraft in Libya. *CBS News*, 24 April. Available at: www.cbsnews.com/news/obama-oks-use-of-armed-drone-aircraft-in-libya/ (Accessed 10 April 2016).

Chow, J. (2012) Predators for Peace. *Foreign Policy*. Available at: http://foreignpolicy.com/2012/04/27/predators-for-peace/ (Accessed 10 April 2016).

Clark, L. (2012) Openrelief Launches Open Source Disaster Relief Drone. The Linux Foundation, 7 June 2012. Available at: www.linux.com/news/featured-blogs/200-libby-clark/586942-openrelief-launches-open-source-disaster-relief-drone (Accessed 10 April 2016).

Collinson, S. and Elhawary, S. (2012) Humanitarian Space: A Review of Trends and Issues. *HPG Report 32: ODI – Overseas Development Institute*.

Cronin, A.K. (2013) Why drones fail. When tactics drive strategy. *Foreign Affairs*, 94: 44–54.

De Cubber, G., Balta, H., Doroftei, D. and Baudoin, Y. (2014) UAS deployment and data processing during the Balkans flooding. *Safety, Security, and Rescue Robotics (SSRR), 2014 IEEE International Symposium on Safety, Security and Rescue*.

Defenceweb (2015) Weaponised Seeker 400 debuts at IDEX. 24 February. Available at: www.defenceweb.co.za/index.php?option=com_content&view=article&id=381 29:weaponised-seeker-400-debuts-at-idex&catid=35:Aerospace (Accessed 10 April 2016).

Donais, T. (2012) *Peacebuilding and Local Ownership: Post-Conflict Consensus Building*. New York: Routledge.

D'Onofrio, A. (2014) Drones 'R' Us? Reflections on the Use of UAVs in Humanitarian Interventions. International Rescue Committee, 4 September. Available at: www. rescue.org/blog/drones-r-us-reflections-use-uavs-humanitarian-interventions (Accessed 10 April 2016).

Dorn, W.A. (2011) *Keeping Watch: Monitoring, Technology and Innovation in UN Peace Operations*. New York: United Nations Press.

Duffield, M. (2013) Risk-management and the fortified aid compound: Everyday life in post-interventionary society. *Journal of Intervention and Statebuilding*, 4 (4): 453–457.

Ferris, E.G. (2011) *The Politics of Protection: The Limits of Humanitarian Action*. Washington DC: Brookings Institution Press.

Gibb, A. (2012) Drones in the Field. *OpenCanada.org*, 10 December 2012.

HRW (2009) Precisely Wrong, Gaza Civilians Killed by Israeli Drone-Launched Missiles. Human Rights Watch, 30 June. Available at: www.hrw.org/report/2009/06/ 30/precisely-wrong/gaza-civilians-killed-israeli-drone-launched-missiles (Accessed 10 April 2016).

IRINNews (2014) NGOs Against MONUSCU Drones for Humanitarian Work. *IRIN*, 23 July. Available at: www.irinnews.org/report/100391/ngos-against-monusco-drones-for-humanitarian-work (Accessed 10 April 2016).

Joachim, J. and Schneiker, A. (2012) New humanitarians? Frame appropriation through private military and security companies. *Millennium: Journal of International Studies*, 40 (2): 365–388.

Karlsrud, J. (2015) The UN at war: Examining the consequences of peace enforcement mandates for the UN peacekeeping operations in the CAR, the DRC and Mali. *Third World Quarterly*, 36 (1): 40–54.

Karlsrud, J. and Rosén, F. (2013) In the eye of the beholder? UN and the use of drones to protect civilians. *Stability: International Journal of Security and Development*, 2 (2).

Kennedy, C. and Rogers, J.I. (2015) Virtuous drones? *International Journal of Human Rights*, 19 (2): 211–227.

Knuckey, S. (2015) Washington's New Drone Sales Policy Could Export US-Style Drone War. *Just Security*, 20 February. Available at: http://justsecurity.org/20223/ washingtons-drone-export-policy-expand-us-style-drone-warfare/ (Accessed 10 April 2016).

Kreps, S. and Kaag, J. (2012) The use of unmanned aerial vehicles in contemporary conflict: A legal and ethical analysis. *Polity*, 44 (2): 260–285.

Lie, J.H.S. (2012) The knowledge battlefield of protection. *African Security*, 5 (3–4): 142–159.

Madlena, C., Patchett, H. and Shamsan, A. (2015) We Dream About Drones, said 13-year-old Yemeni Before His Death in a CIA Strike. *The Guardian*, 10 February. Available at: www.theguardian.com/world/2015/feb/10/drones-dream-yemeni-teenager-mohammed-tuaiman-death-cia-strike (Accessed 10 April 2016).

Marcus, G. (2010) Experts, reporters, witnesses: the making of anthropologists in States of Emergency, in D. Fassin and M. Pandolfi (eds.), *Contemporary States of Emergency: The Politics of Military and Humanitarian Intervention*. New York: Zone Books.

Maughan, T. (2015) China's Drone Army Is Beginning to Look a Lot Like the US's, *VICE*, 17 September. Available at: http://motherboard.vice.com/read/china-drone-army-war-us (Accessed 10 April 2016).

McAdam, D., McCarthy, J.D. and Zald, M.N. (eds.) (1996) *Comparative Perspectives on Social Movements: Political Opportunities, Mobilizing Structures, and Cultural Framings*. New York: Cambridge University Press.

McCarthy, N. (2015) The Countries Importing The Most Drones [Infographic]. *Forbes*, 18 March. Available at: www.forbes.com/sites/niallmccarthy/2015/03/18/the-countries-importing-the-most-drones-infographic/ (Accessed 10 April 2016).

McNeal, G. (2012) United Nations Wants to Use Drones in Africa, Could Legally Be Armed. *Forbes*, 24 November. Available at: www.forbes.com/sites/gregorymcneal/2012/11/24/united-nations-wants-to-use-drones-in-africa/ (Accessed 10 April 2016).

Mégret, F. (2013) The humanitarian problem with drones. *Utah Law Review*, (5): 1283–1319.

Meier, P. (2014) On UAVs for Peacebuilding and Conflict Prevention. 14 September. Available at: http://irevolution.net/2014/09/14/uavs-peacebuilding-and-conflict-prevention/ (Accessed 10 April 2016).

MSF (2014) Where is Everyone? Available at: www.msf.org/article/msf-report-where-everyone (Accessed 10 April 2016).

NPR (2015) The Drone War's Bottleneck: Too Many Targets, Not Enough Pilots. *NPR*, 24 January. Available at: www.npr.org/2015/01/24/379550383/the-drone-war-hits-a-bottleneck-too-many-targets-not-enough-pilots (Accessed 10 April 2016).

OCHA (2014) Aide Memoire: For the Consideration of Issues Pertaining to the Protection of Civilians in Armed Conflict, 5th edn (United Nations, 2014). Available at: https://docs.unocha.org/sites/dms/Documents/aide%20memoire%202014%20-%20English.pdf (Accessed 10 April 2016).

Oudenaren, D.V (2014) Peacekeeping Under Attack in South Sudan. *Radio Tamazuj*. 27 May. Available at: https://radiotamazuj.org/en/article/peacekeeping-under-attack-south-sudan-i (Accessed 10 April 2016).

Prupis, N. (2015) In 'Disastrous Decision', US Prepares to Widen Exports of Armed Drones. *Common Dreams*, 17 February. Available at: www.commondreams.org/news/2015/02/17/disastrous-decision-us-prepares-widen-exports-armed-drones (Accessed 10 April 2016).

Reid-Henry, S. and Sending, O.J. (2014) The 'humanitarianization' of urban violence. *Environment and Urbanization*, 26 (2): 427–442.

Rieff, D. (2002) *A Bed for the Night: Humanitarianism in Crisis*. New York: Simon & Schuster.

Rosén, F. (2014) Extremely stealthy and incredibly close: Drones, control and legal responsibility. *Journal of Conflict and Security Law*, 19 (1): 113–131.

Sandvik, K.B. and Jumbert, M.G. (2015) Les drones humanitaires. *Revue Internationale et Stratégique*, 2: 139–146.

Sandvik, K.B. and Lohne, K. (2013) The Promise and Perils of 'Disaster Drones', *Humanitarian Exchange Magazine* 58. Available at: http://odihpn.org/magazine/the-promise-and-perils-of-%C2%91disaster-drones%C2%92/ (Accessed 10 April 2016). (2014) The rise of the humanitarian drone: Giving content to an emerging concept. *Millennium: Journal of International Studies*, 43 (1): 145–164.

Sandvik, K.B., Jumbert, M.G., Karlsrud, J. and Kaufmann, M. (2014) Humanitarian technology: A critical research agenda. *International Review of the Red Cross*, 96 (893): 219–242.

Sengupta, S. (2014) Unarmed Drones Aid UN Peacekeeping Missions in Africa. *The New York Times*, 2 July. Available at: www.nytimes.com/2014/07/03/world/africa/unarmed-drones-aid-un-peacekeepers-in-africa.html?_r=2&mtrref=undefi ned&gwh=EE5F032C6A5A0AA073EC94C78BBD4A04&gwt=pay (Accessed 10 April 2016).

Sharkey, N. (2011) The automation and proliferation of military drones and the protection of civilians. *Law, Innovation and Technology*, 3 (2): 229–240.

Slim, H. (2008) *Killing Civilians: Method, Madness and Morality in War*. London: Hurst & Co.

Smedley, T. (2015) Drones' New Mission: Saving Lives in Developing Countries. *The Guardian*, 9 January. Available at: www.theguardian.com/sustainable-business/2015/jan/09/drones-tech-natural-disasters-medical-developing-countries?CMP=share_btn_tw (Accessed 10 April 2016).

Sniderman, A.S. and Hanis, M. (2012) Drones for Human Rights. *The New York Times*, 30 January. Available at: www.nytimes.com/2012/01/31/opinion/drones-for-human-rights.html?_r=0 (Accessed 10 April 2016).

Stanford Law School Human Rights and Conflict Resolution Clinic and NYU School of Law Global Justice Clinic (2012) Living under Drones: Death, Injury, and Trauma to Civilians from US Drone Practices in Pakistan. Available at: http://chrgj.org/wp-content/uploads/2012/10/Living-Under-Drones.pdf (Accessed 10 April 2016).

Stoddard, A., Harmer, A. and Renouf, J.S. (2010) *Once Removed: Lessons and Challenges in Remote Management of Humanitarian Operations for Insecure Areas*. New York: Humanitarian Outcomes.

The Economist (2012) The Dronefather. Technology Quarterly, *The Economist*, 1 December 2012.

UN Security Council (2006) *Resolution 1674*.

Whetham, D. (2015) Drones to protect. *The International Journal of Human Rights*, 19 (2): 199–210.

Zenko, M. (2015) The Great Drone Contradiction. *Foreign Policy*, 19 February. Available at: http://foreignpolicy.com/2015/02/19/the-great-drone-contradiction-unmanned-aircraft-systems/ (Accessed 10 April 2016).

Zwijnenburg, W. (2014) Drone-tocracy? Mapping the Proliferation of Unmanned Systems. *Sustainablesecurity.org*, 8 October. Available at: http://sustainablesecurity.org/2014/10/08/drone-tocracy-mapping-the-proliferation-of-unmanned-systems/ (Accessed 10 April 2016).

4   Creating the EU drone
Control, sorting, and search and rescue at sea

Maria Gabrielsen Jumbert

Introduction

This chapter will analyze the "good" drone in the context of border control as imagined, acquired and foreseen to be deployed in the EU. In recent years, there has been a growing interest in the use of drones for border control over land and at sea. Drones have been deployed along the border between Ecuador and Colombia, to prevent armed confrontations (*The Jerusalem Post* 2008), along Ecuador's coastline, as well as by Brazilian Federal police along its northwestern border, against drug traffickers and smugglers (Higuer 2014). Israel deploys drones over its border with Egypt, for border contro and counterterrorism (*The Jerusalem Post* 2014), and China has develope its own drones for border surveillance (Lin and Singer 2014). In 2013, the US and Japan promised to assist Kenya in purchasing drones for border security and to prevent arms trafficking (Bergenas and Stohl 2013). India recently purchased 49 drones from Israel for border patrolling (*The Nation* 2014). Many of these examples of drone deployment are for national security purposes, either as part of the broader global war on terror, or as part of a war on drugs. Drones have also been deployed along the US–Mexico border since March 2013 (*The Guardian* 2014), both to prevent drug smuggling and unauthorized migration. The European Union and Australia appear to have followed suit: Australia has already purchased drones from the US for border patrolling (*BBC News* 2014a) and the EU Border Agency Frontex, in January 2013, expressed its interest in acquiring drones (Nielsen 2013). In both of these cases, the prevention of unwanted migration is the central aim, although objectives of fighting cross-border crime, terrorism, or simply "illegal migration" are frequently also listed to increase the security stakes (EUROSUR Regulation 2013). However, central to the EU discourse and arguing for the benefits of drones for border surveillance is the argument that drones will enable a better detection of the many migrants in distress at sea. In 2013–2014, the Italian Navy, under its operation Mare Nostrum, deployed drones to detect migrants in distress (Kington 2014).

According to a report by the International Organization for Migration (IOM), more than 14,600 migrants died in perilous attempts to cross the

Mediterranean between 1993 and 2012 (Brian and Laczko 2014). The number of people crossing the sea began to decrease towards the end of the last decade, often imputed to the increased border controls and improved surveillance mechanisms, especially by the Spanish Guardia Civil around the main passing point across the strait of Gibraltar. These efforts however also led to a shift in the flows of migrants to other crossing points, notably the Italian island of Lampedusa or through Greece (Carling 2007a, 2007b; de Haas 2008). A new increase in migrants crossing the sea followed in the wake of the Arab spring, nourishing fears of an "exodus of biblical proportions" in the words of the Italian Interior Minister Roberto Maroni (Pop 2011). However, the highest predictions never materialized and the numbers fell again the following year, but the intensification of a series of crises and conflicts in various neighboring regions, notably in Syria, led to a new increase in 2013. Following two major shipwrecks outside Lampedusa and Sicily in October 2013 (Brian and Laczko 2014), where several hundred people lost their lives, new political attention has been devoted to the issue. An estimated number of 700 died in 2013, more than tripling to 3072 in 2014. And 2015 quickly became a new record year with close to 250,000 arrivals and at least 2,300 deaths, as of August 2015 (IOM 2015).

Unmanned Aerial Vehicles (UAVs), popularly known as drones, and their real and imagined functionalities fit into an already existing narrative of a need to control borders through better "situational awareness." This awareness is perceived to be best achieved through surveillance – ideally from the air, achieving the so-called "God's Eye" vision, the imagined see-all vision from above. Drones are presented as the latest (and most suited) complement in a long trend of increased technologization of border control. Drones can see more, for a longer period of time and at a lower cost. Able to fill the "dull" job of simply watching over remote areas, for hours on end, in search of any movement or minor change, the drones come with a narrative that they will both see more (larger areas, better sensors, more flexibility than manned airplanes or satellites), and do so in a more cost-efficient way than manned border patrols. Drones are able to detect so-called abnormal movement across borders, but potentially also to detect people in distress in need of rescue: as such it answers to the central concerns along the EU external border in the Mediterranean as expressed in the policy documents preparing the establishment of a EU Border Surveillance System, EUROSUR (European Commission 2008 and 2009; EUROSUR regulation 2013; see also Wolff 2008). As smaller drones have already been deployed as part of the Italian Mare Nostrum operation between 2013 and 2014, and briefly as part of the MSF-MOAS Search and Rescue (SAR) operation, this is a crucial moment to critically examine the real functionalities, and limits, of a possibly extended use of border drones in the Mediterranean.

I suggest in this chapter to home in on two specific meanings of "good" in drone deployment at the borders. Firstly, in the sense of *control*; whereby the drone represents the ideal tool to increase control over the difficulties in managing maritime border zones, supposedly overwhelmed by boat migrants. Technologized surveillance, with drones at the fore, is represented as the solution needed to reclaim control over areas perceived to be "out of control." As such, it can also be understood as a form of political disavowal on behalf of EU policymakers in the field of immigration; amid a series of complex and sensitive issues, drones are imagined as able to handle the issues outside or at Europe's external borders, and in line with the "public order drone" (Hayes, Jones and Töpfer 2014; see also Sandvik, Chapter 5) to reinstate order where there is disorder. With the introduction of drones, political issues are transformed into a technical matter, as the drone capabilities reduce larger and complex political issues into matters of functionalities, of what the drone can and cannot do. Secondly, the meaning of "good" is in part both a complement and a counter-weight to the first meaning of the term, insofar as that "good" draws on the drone's potential to provide rescue, or at least to facilitate rescue operations, by providing crucial information about people in distress (sharing alerts, locating the vessels, etc.). During the preparations of the EUROSUR regulation, there was a tug-of-war between the EU Council and the EU Parliament (European Commission 2011), regarding whether or not to include "save more lives at sea" as one of the objectives of the new EU Border Surveillance System (EUROSUR Regulation 2013). The "rescue" side of maritime surveillance has been either advanced as an indispensable legal and moral obligation (i.e. there cannot be reinforced means of border control without them also contributing to saving more lives), or as a complementary and legitimating aspect (i.e. recognizing that surveillance for border control might also gather information that is relevant for rescue purposes, and putting this forward can also reinforce the general legitimacy of the border control system). In this chapter I address the question of how these two ideas of the "good" border patrolling drone play out and interact, and what ground it creates for a future larger deployment of border drones at the EU external borders.

The chapter is divided into three parts. In the first part, I place drones in the broader context of increased political efforts to control the EU external borders, through new surveillance technologies and the interconnection of surveillance systems. In this context, the drone is perceived to be the perfect instrument to fulfill the stated need for a better "situational awareness," in addition to being presented as particularly adapted to spot migrant vessels. In the second part, I examine the "border control" drone, and argue that it first and foremost serves to provide a *sense* of control over areas that are hard to reach and hard to manage, rather than actually filling any "social sorting" function at the border, between authorized and unauthorized travelers. In the third part, I examine the "search and rescue" drone, through the role that this aspect of the border control drone plays in justifying its overall deployment, while drawing attention to the legal dilemmas that are raised by the attempts to do both border control and search and rescue. I will draw on some examples from the US deployment of drones along its border with Mexico to illustrate these two last sections.

In order to show how the EU border control drone is presented as the most adapted tool to increase control and improve rescue capacities, this chapter builds on insights from the field of critical security studies, and especially the subfield of surveillance studies (Lyon 2006). More specifically, it draws on contributions dealing specifically with migration, border control and policing (Huysmans 2006; Bigo and Guild 2005; Gammeltoft-Hansen 2011; Lutterbeck 2006; Jeandesboz 2011).[1] My approach also builds on concepts and approaches provided by the framing literature (Finnemore and Sikkink 1998; Marullo, Pagnucco and Smith 1996), and especially recent contributions looking at security measures framed as rescue providers and humanitarian technologies (Joachim and Schneiker 2012; Lemberg-Pedersen 2013; Sandvik and Lohne 2014). These contributions show how different framing strategies are put forward in order to make the security solutions and technologies more publicly acceptable, and as central strategies to open up for legal authorization and further commercial development. Although a series of scholarly contributions has critically examined the ensemble of technology-based surveillance measures taken to control the EU external borders (Bigo and Guild 2005; Jeandesboz 2010, 2011; Marin 2011), fewer have looked at aerial surveillance as such, and even less so the prospected drone deployment. The "smart borders" planned by the EU for several years and based on electronic surveillance, as well as increasingly sophisticated aerial and maritime surveillance over the external borders, have been referred to as a new "Cyber-Fortress Europe" (Guild, Carrera and Geyer 2008) or a "Technological Fortress" (Marin 2011). Drones can in this context be seen as only the latest add-on in a larger attempt to collect more data, earlier on, to control every movement at, or even before, the border in the logic of pre-emptiveness.

The political rationales behind the increasingly technologized border surveillance

The main drivers behind the introduction of drones into the efforts to build up a European Border Surveillance System (EUROSUR) are threefold: (1) they are perceived to provide better surveillance over larger areas, and thus improve the so-called "situational awareness"; (2) they are argued to be more cost-effective (than manned patrols for example); and (3) they are best adapted to spot migrants. This first section considers these justifications as political rationales creating the ground for a border-patrolling drone that could eventually also extend the areas put under surveillance.

The EU project of scaling down its internal borders, within the framework of the Area of Freedom, Security and Justice and the establishment of the Schengen area has been counter-balanced by the scaling up of external border controls. The Schengen project presupposes a mutual trust in effective control at the external borders. This combined opening of internal borders and strengthening of external borders is in many ways illustrative of the way Western liberal states view and want to portray themselves: they depend on a political and de facto demarcation of their sovereign borders, all the while insisting that their porous nature is in line with modern understandings of globalization and progress. Along with an increased technologization of security management in general, the control of our external borders has followed suit with investments, R&D projects and new technological inventions to control movement across our borders (Ceyhan 2008; Guittet and Jeandesboz 2010; Rijpma and Vermeulen 2015). Technologies for border surveillance changes the way borders are conceived and experienced, yet allow a combined fluidity with control where deemed necessary. However, concerns are frequently raised with regards to the extent of democratic governance over the introduction of new security technologies affecting our daily lives. This has, in particular, been raised in connection with an increased technologization and militarization of European border control, where the security industry plays a central role. As Lemberg-Pedersen (2013: 152–153) observes, European private security companies (PSCs) have been central in framing, formulating and shaping the day-to-day governance of the European borders, raising "serious questions regarding the opaqueness of borderscape budgets, lock-in effects making it difficult for public actors to reverse PSC militarization of borders and the humanitarian consequences of this for migrants." Further, Hayes, Jones and Töpfer (2014: 7) describe an "emerging EU drone policy," based on the two perceptions that drones (for a range of unspecified uses) must be developed, and that the barriers (mainly regulatory and technical) must be overcome. They further show how this is a policy developed almost entirely outside of public scrutiny. The interesting paradox in this opaque form of policymaking is the inherent message that better, more transparent and more widely shared information represents the way forward to approach a series of security issues. The idea of a see-all device with a perfect vision, epitomized by the drone, is arguably a form of the neoliberal definition of ethics, based on the premise that a "complete picture" will lead to the best decisions, ethically speaking (see for example Lyon 2002; Sewell and Barker 2001).

The EU Border Surveillance system EUROSUR was proposed in 2008, became operational in December 2013, and is intended to improve Member States', authorities' and Frontex's situational awareness with the "purpose of detecting, preventing and combating illegal immigration and cross-border crime and contributing to ensuring the protection and saving the lives of migrants" (EUROSUR Regulation 2013). The idea of improving EU border authorities' "situational awareness," through increasingly interconnected information systems and more performant surveillance devices, is also among the core aims of the EU Border Agency Frontex as such.[2] The ambitious project of building an EU Border Surveillance system not only means building "interoperability" between existing systems, but also investing considerably in upgrading and modernizing existing capabilities. The European Commission estimated the costs at €338 million before its launch, but according to Hayes and Vermeulen (2012: 8), "its methods do not stand up to scrutiny" and the total amount could end up being two or three times higher.

More specifically, the drones are seen as useful to feed into what Frontex calls the "Common Pre-Frontier Intelligence Picture" (CPIP). Frontex's Director refers to this CPIP as areas "beyond the border," and "international borders or some further areas" (quoted in Nielsen 2013). In a Commission staff working paper on the progress made to develop EUROSUR, the stated aim behind "Step 4: The research and development to improve the performance of surveillance tools" is to "improve the performance and use of surveillance tools in order to *increase the area covered and the number of suspicious activities* detected as well as to improve the identification and tracking of potentially suspicious targets and the access to high-resolution observation satellite data" (European Commission 2009: 7).[3] Surveillance of the pre-frontier area is mainly for intelligence purposes, and is seen as important for the aims of preventing "irregular migration and cross-border crime" (Seiffarth 2011: 146). The subsequent chapter in the Commission staff working paper, "The common application of surveillance tools," explains that "FRONTEX could act as a facilitator in this regard, e.g. via the procurement of satellite imagery on behalf of Member States and coordinating the sharing of surveillance equipment such as unmanned aerial vehicles (UAV)" (ibid.: 8).

More than at any terrestrial border, there is a manifested interest along the maritime borders to stop migrants before they reach the territorial waters, and if possible to stop them before they even depart. When the territorial waters are formally entered, it appears as legally more difficult to prevent the migrant vessels from reaching land, and as I will show below, actually returning them would amount to an expulsion and a potential violation of the obligation of non-refoulement if any person on board is entitled to international protection (Convention Relating to the Status of Refugees (1951). This supports the idea that EU border guards "need" to be aware and collect information about what happens beyond the border in order to best adapt their control measures at the border. However, the legal constraint is not circumvented by pushing the border control further out, as established by the case of Hirsi Jamaa and others vs. Italy. Before the recent Mare Nostrum operation, Italy was rather known for its practice of conducting so-called "push-back operations," starting in May 2009 and continuing until the beginning of the Arab spring in 2011 (Human Rights Watch 2012). Under the umbrella of a "Friendship Pact" between Italy and Libya, signed in August 2008, Italian coast guards would forcibly return migrants intercepted at sea to Libya (Human Rights Watch 2009). The practice was firmly condemned by human rights organizations. In 2009, a group of Somali and Eritrean nationals brought their case to the European Court of Human Rights (ECtHR). They were onboard a vessel that was stopped before it reached Italian waters, and they were then brought back to Libya onboard an Italian navy vessel before being handed over to the Libyan authorities. The ECtHR found that the migrants, when on board the Italian vessel, were under Italian *de jure* and *de facto* jurisdiction, and their "push-back" operation in practice amounted to a collective expulsion and a breach of the non-refoulement principle (ECRE 2012). This Italian practice effectively stopped as the civil uprisings began in Libya in 2011, were not re-established with the Transitional government and have thus not taken place since the ECtHR judgment either. There have been recent reports of Greek border guards pushing back migrants into Turkish waters (Frenzen 2014). The prospect of adding drones to the surveillance toolkit, however, nourishes fears that they will be used mainly to enable the stopping of migrants earlier on and further away from our sight. As stated in an International Peace Institute (IPI) Global Observatory analysis (Ó Súilleabháin 2013) of Frontex's expression of interest in acquiring drones:

> European Union member states participating in Frontex fall short of their human rights commitments when operations prevent the arrival of refugees to European land. Already, migrants intercepted at sea near Europe's coast are not screened for possible refugee status. The addition of drones and unmanned aircraft to Frontex's surveillance toolkit would compound this legal problem, with the interception of potential refugees occurring more often and even further from European land.

In the following sections, I will detail the limited screening capacities of the drones, and draw attention in the last section to the fact that the modus operandi of Mare Nostrum has rather shown that, although migrants were intercepted earlier on, they were then taken to the Italian mainland. This does not preclude the operation from a series of critical questions raised in the above quote, but requires an assessment that is founded on the actual current practices.

The next step foreseen in the Commission staff working paper from 2009, step 6, describes the objectives for the CPIP, which are to "provide the national coordination centers in a frequent, reliable and cost-efficient manner with effective, accurate and timely intelligence on the pre-frontier area, which is of relevance for the prevention of illegal immigration and related cross-border crime" (European Commission 2009: 8). The next section will now focus on two aspects of this statement: the cost-efficiency argument, and the idea that drones are the best vehicle for gathering information relevant to preventing so-called illegal immigration and cross-border crime.

First, a well-known argument in defense of the deployment of surveillance drones, whether for military reconnaissance, policing or other civilian purposes, is that the drone is more cost-efficient than any other means of surveillance, as it can (at least partly) replace other human forms of patrolling, for longer stretches of time without consideration of eight hour shifts or the need to refuel (Sandvik and Lohne 2014). As Frontex Director Ilka Laitinen states in an interview with *EU Observer* in early 2013, "traditional surveillance methods rely on patrols and manned aircraft," and adds that drones would be "much more cost-effective" (Nielsen 2013). The idea here is not only that drones replace manned patrols, but also that they will provide intelligence to border guards about which stretches of the border needs closer monitoring, so as to rationalize their efforts. This point can be illuminated by an example from the US Customs and Border Protection (CBP) patrol, where an officer argues that drones are the best response to the agency's restricted resources, as he explains: "You want to deploy your resources to where you have a greater risk, a greater threat" (*BBC News* 2014b). Although drone intelligence may help to rationalize manned border patrolling efforts, the deployment of drones as such, however, has a significant cost. These spendings were criticized in a Department of Homeland Security report from January 2015, revealing that the CBP has vastly underreported the costs of the drone program, as they have claimed they cost US$2,468 per hour of flight time, at least five times less than the actual estimated cost (Nicas 2015).

Further, the argument that drones have the benefit of being able to do the "dull, dirty and dangerous" jobs better than humans is applied in the context of border surveillance as well. While the Mediterranean is not a battlefield of any kind, border patrolling drones still come with the promise of reaching or continuing to provide crucial information in different weather conditions (provided the drones are made to resist such conditions), and able to conduct the "dull" job of watching over large areas searching for small changes or movements. While it may be more cost-efficient to have drones doing this job, it is again not simply about *replacing* human patrols that would otherwise have taken place; the existence of the border control drone in itself provides new opportunities and is likely to extend the areas put under almost constant surveillance. As argued by Hayes, Jones and Töpfer, just as with the combat drones, "surveillance drones will lower the threshold for launching overt and covert surveillance operations" (2014: 9).

Second, the idea that drones are the most adapted tool to gather information about migrant boats is supported by arguments that the smallest rubber boats used for irregular migration across the Mediterranean are usually too hard to spot on any coastal radar or through regular satellites (Seiffarth 2011). Frontex was, in 2006, tasked by the European Council to assess feasibility of establishing a surveillance system over the Mediterranean, and the first report "Feasibility study on Mediterranean coastal patrols network – MEDSEA" stated that: "the big challenge and the decisive function are to discover those vessels and small boats which are not obliged to or avoid to, transmit the information" (Frontex 2006: 10, cited in Rijpma and Vermeulen 2015: 458). Drones are able to stay for longer stretches of time in the air (for most types), they can also provide an overview of larger geographical areas (as opposed to manned airplanes for example), and they are more flexible and can zoom in on certain detected events (more than satellites can, see Romeo, Pacino and Borello 2009). The Medium Altitude Long Endurance (MALE) drones or other larger Predator type surveillance drones also come with the advantage of being more discreet than the manned border patrolling airplanes (because they fly at higher altitudes).

A central question to assess the drones' capacity to contribute to the stated aims of preventing so-called illegal migration or cross-border crime is what the drones can actually see. More specifically, will the border control drones, from the larger surveillance drones to the smaller ones deployed over a specific area, at some point have cameras providing enough detail so as to enable the identification of individuals onboard these boats? At a demonstration event organized by the Hellenic Coast Guard (HCG) as part of the EU-funded project PERSEUS, in October 2014, a newly developed Remotely Piloted Airplane (RPA) was a central part of the simulation.[4] The RPA would fly high enough to not be visible from "the ground" or by people at sea, while the imagery on the screens in the HCG control room revealed shadows and movement on deck, although they were too blurry to give any sense of physical features. Looking at the drone industry more broadly, new imagery systems for surveillance drones may soon be on the market. The ARGUS Camera, for example, can open up to 65 windows at the same time and see objects as small as six inches square on the ground and provide pictures of 1.8 billion pixels from 17,500 feet, making it the highest resolution camera to date (Szoldra 2013). It would still not reveal details of physical attributes but it would, for example, impart the color of a person's t-shirt. However, as I will describe in the next section, even with this level of detail and even if future cameras are able to recognize individual physical features, the camera will not enable operators to fill the aim of *sorting* migrants, between those who are so-called legitimate (with a right to asylum and international protection) and those who are illegitimate (without any right to stay in the EU). This sorting requires a personal examination of each individual case on land (Gammeltoft-Hansen 2011). On another level, seeking to develop more sophisticated cameras for a potential recognition will raise a series of questions relating to privacy and the protection of personal data.

Sorting, control and order

In surveillance studies, "surveillance" is described as a process of social sorting (Lyon 2003, 2007), sorting out abnormal or suspicious behavior, whether through CCTV cameras in defined public spaces, or through electronic surveillance of various digital footprints. Such sorting, also referred to as "triage" in the critical security literature, supposes the pre-definition of what normal behavior looks like, and which movements or other signals given away might indicate abnormal or suspicious behavior (Bigo 2006). Border surveillance distinguishes itself from other forms of societal surveillance, as it is not about distinguishing elements within a crowd, but rather to keep certain elements out in order to protect the inside (Bellanova and González Fuster 2013; Jeandesboz 2011). It is for this kind of surveillance the border control drones will be put to use: to sort out unauthorized border-crossings from authorized ones and spot abnormal behavior. In this section I will first examine the "social sorting" role of border surveillance, in order to show that the drone itself cannot fill this function. I then argue that the drone rather serves to give a *sense* of control over the border areas, by virtue of its aerial surveillance of an area perceived to be hard to control and to manage.

There are mainly three reasons why drones, or image-based aerial surveillance, are limited to conducting social sorting at the border. First, in order for a social sorting process to be possible through the drone gaze, there needs to be clear-cut criteria which justify placing the subjects, in this case the migrants, in one category or the other (of "potentially allowed to enter/stay in the EU," or "not allowed to enter/stay"). Independent of the imagery, creating such neat categories of migrants crossing the Mediterranean is impossible, as each vessel, whether departing from Morocco, Tunisia, Libya or Egypt, may carry migrants from a range of different countries in the region and with a range of different reasons for leaving (from poverty, violent conflict, political instability etc.). A same individual may also fluctuate between different categories, or try several strategies in order to obtain access to their wanted country of destination (Carling 2015). Secondly, another issue raised in connection with increased surveillance of both citizens and population movement across borders in the wake of the global war on terror relates to the automation of sorting processes (Lyon 2007). The EU Data protection directive specifically states that a decision that produces legal effects or significantly affects the subject should not be based solely on automated processing of data (art. 15), and a form of appeal should be provided when automatic decision-making processes are used (Directive 95/46/EC of the European Parliament 1995). Seeking to sort migrants at sea through aerial surveillance would be one such form of automated process, which therefore also needs to be completed with other forms of non-automated, case-by-case processes. Thirdly, despite the EU's attempt to pre-define certain countries as safe, by establishing bilateral return agreements with certain North African and West African countries (Carling 2007b), it is difficult to assess at sea, and even less through surveillance pictures, if the migrants are originally from the country they departed from. Thus, it is also difficult to "sort" migrants at sea between groups ready to be returned, and those who should be taken in to the EU for further examination of their demands – without running the risk of violating the obligation of non-refoulement (1951 Geneva Convention on Refugees).

Hence, despite a recurrent promise, drones cannot and will never be able to conduct this sorting process from above. This is independent from the technological capabilities (e.g. promises of more sophisticated images and better intelligence in the future), as it relates to individual human rights and the blurry lines between the groups of migrants entitled to international protection and those who cannot claim the right to stay in Europe. This assessment, and granting of rights, can only be done on a case-by-case basis. We then need to ask what the social sorting and control function of border surveillance drones will actually be? Drones can contribute to draw attention to certain hotspots, in order for manned patrols to be deployed at those specific locations. It can provide intelligence to border patrols, and indicate that certain migration "routes" are more or less used. Certain types of typical migrant border crossings (i.e. small and overcrowded fishing boats or similar) may probably be detected by future border control drones, yet they will always have to be examined, both by manned patrols and authorities on land, not only to state that they are indeed migrants, but also to "sort out" the ones with a right to protection and a right to stay.

Given the limited capacities to actually trigger interventions to stop migrants before or at the EU external maritime border, I argue here that the border control drone will first and foremost serve the purpose of providing a *sense* of control, as a response to a securitization of the EU border. First of all, a cross-cutting theme in the existing literature on the use of drones, whether in the military field, or in the field of policing, is the power inherent in surveillance and supervision from above (Wall 2013; Neocleous 2013). As Wall and Monahan (2011: 241) write: "it is not technological speed alone that assures control over the enemy, but also the ability to achieve higher elevations in order to gain an observational advantage." In the military field, and especially in the US context, the mastery of the airspace has, since World War II, been seen as key to ensuring general security (DeNicola 2006). Satellites epitomize this ideal overview from above, but drones – by combining an arsenal of larger Predator-type surveillance drones and smaller more flexible drones – push further the perfection of the imagined "God's Eye" vision. This appears to be particularly salient in the maritime geography, as it is hard to have a good overview without this aerial supervision. The sense of an impossibility to control and manage the sea is attempted to be responded to through aerial surveillance (Jumbert 2012), and drones in particular seem to be advanced to (re)claim some of this sense of control. The "need" to control the external borders of the EU rests on a discourse that fundamentally securitizes migration movement across EU borders, by placing threats of cross-border crime and the movement of suspected terrorists into the same box that has to be dealt with through increased border control (Bigo 2005; Huysmans 2000, 2006; Lutterbeck 2006; Ceyhan and Tsoukala 2002). In the US context, the war on drugs, for example, being inherent within any border control effort, has driven forward what is referred to as a paramilitarization of border policing (Correa-Cabrera 2013, 2014). This is, so far, less the case in the EU context, but as several have observed, "the blurring of internal and external security threatens to drive the militarization (or at least paramilitarization) of policing" (Neyroud and Vassilas 2010). It is against the background of this securitizing approach to the EU external borders that the aims of deploying drones must be understood.

The idea that the border patrolling drones are there first and foremost for the general overview, rather than to enable concrete interceptions, is seen also in the context of US surveillance of its border with Mexico, where the efficiency narrative of the border drones has been put to question. The Department of Homeland Security Report (2015) revealed that the border surveillance drones have helped law enforcement agents in making only 2 percent of its border arrests in 2013. A spokesman of the US Customs and

Border Protection reportedly answered to this that the "drones aren't credited with many apprehensions because they typically monitor large stretches of the border to identify hot spots, rather than follow individual targets" (Nicas 2015). Yet he claims, "For the big picture, it's doing great." In other words, it seems to be acknowledged that the drones are not there for actual border *control* (in the sense of assisting actual interceptions), but rather to provide information, intelligence and situational awareness: all elements that increase the *sense* of control over these vast maritime or desert areas. Finally, although the drones deployed in the framework of the Mare Nostrum operation were used to locate vessels in distress with the purpose of bringing search and rescue, and although the Italian navy vessels then proceeded to bring the migrants safely to the nearest Italian port (rather than "keeping them out"), it can nevertheless be argued that it provided Italy with a greater *sense* of control of new arrivals of migrants. It certainly communicated an image of mastering the situation in another way, rather than with images of migrants drowning or stranded on the beaches of Southern Europe. Irrespective of the reasons for the increase in the numbers of refugees and casualties in the year following the closure of Mare Nostrum, the photographic images of these human plights spread across the media, and social media in the late summer of 2015 has increased the pressure on European governments to rethink their policies.

The "search and rescue drone": inherently good or a cover for more control?

Although I argue that the main driving factor behind the deployment of drones along the external maritime border of the EU is to improve existing border control practices, they are generally justified by industry, Frontex and national border agencies first and foremost, with references to their potential for improving rescue capacities. In this third section, I will describe how this potential is often one of the first points brought forward as a strategy to speed up the process of deploying drones along the EU external borders.

The project of establishing a common pre-frontier intelligence picture is easily justified as not only a border control measure, but also as a pre-emptive effort to rescue migrants from unseaworthy vessels *before* they come into a situation of imminent danger. When Frontex, or industry officials, present the benefits of acquiring drones for border surveillance, the key functionalities that are first put forward are the ones relating to rescue. As Ilka Laitinen, then Frontex Director, explains to *EU Observer*: "unmanned aerial vehicles (UAVs) … could be deployed at sea to locate, for instance, migrants in distress" (Nielsen 2013). Further, the same *EU Observer* article reports from a Saab hosted seminar on external borders where the company showcased its Saab 340 maritime security aircraft, equipped with a high-resolution TV camera and electro-optical sensors capable of "detecting debris or people at sea." As Philip Boucher shows (2014), putting forward the less controversial, unquestionably "good" aspects of drones, such as their potential to serve SAR purposes, is part of a dedicated EU "domestication strategy," to make drones in general more acceptable to the wider public. While there have been no public opinion polls realized at EU level yet, polls realized in the US show that about two-thirds support the use of drones for tracking down criminals and to patrol the border for illegal immigration, and overwhelming majorities (80–83 percent) support the use of drones for search and rescue (Monmouth University Poll 2012, 2013).

Although the EUROSUR system is justified partly with the aim of reducing the number of migrant deaths at sea, these aims are not necessarily followed up in the specific border patrol operations. The national Search and Rescue authorities do not have direct access to the data exchanged within the EUROSUR framework, nor do they have a specific mandate provided through the EUROSUR regulation (2013). The legislative framework is rather based on the obligation of *any vessel*, including border patrols, of bringing search and rescue to vessels in distress at sea. The Mare Nostrum operation of the Italian navy had a specific humanitarian and SAR mandate, and with resources allocated accordingly. The Frontex operation, Triton, set up to replace it from November 2014 was, however, presented in these words by the Deputy Director Gil Arias Fernandez: "I would like to underline that operation Triton focuses on border control and surveillance. Having said that saving lives will remain an absolute priority for Frontex" (Frontex 2014). A European Commission press release from October 2014 provides some more details about how Frontex's role is viewed in this respect: "Although Frontex is neither a search and rescue body nor does it take up the functions of a Rescue Coordination Centre, it assists Member States to fulfill their obligation under international maritime law to render assistance to persons in distress" (European Commission 2014). In other words, Frontex is there to support Member States so they can carry out their rescue obligations.

When the possible SAR facilitating function of the drone is invoked there is a sense of it being unquestionably and inherently "good," because it will contribute to rescue people in distress: indeed, how could it at all be controversial? As the framing literature would suggest, the "humanitarian frame" (Joachim and Schneiker 2012), and here more specifically the act of bringing rescue, may be used strategically to legitimize broader practices or policies. There are very few attempts at questioning what the pitfalls of the SAR drone could be, suggesting that the idea of facilitating rescue in itself functions as a guarantee of good, because it contrasts with and acts as a counterweight to the border *control* drone – and the political controversies that come with efforts to keep certain people out. This dual use of the drone technology, as not only a technology that has emerged from the military realm to the civilian sphere, but also the dual migration control vs. search and rescue function, is however not going completely unnoticed by European legislators. Two members of the European Parliament and a Member of the German

Bundestag have enquired into the European Commission-funded projects SUNNY, CLOSEYE and AEROCEPTOR. The projects have involved drone tests in regions of the Mediterranean Sea deemed as "hot spots," where AEROCEPTOR has used aerial police weaponry for the first time (Hunko 2015). MEP Cornelia Ernst recognizes the utility of using drones for search and rescue, stressing that there is nothing preventing these new technologies from being used for maritime rescue, but sees the drones that are being investigated as only a tool to advance EUROSUR's aim of *preventing* migration. MEP Sabine Lösing further denounces the practice of Frontex being involved in the testing of new technologies alongside military authorities, stating: "This adds an inadmissible militarized aspect to migration control (...). We will oppose any use of drones which were originally developed for military purposes in domestic security matters" (ibid.).

While the Frontex Director acknowledges that "there are many legal questions to be solved" (Nielsen 2013), the quest for deploying drones can also be read as an attempt to escape the individual accountability a border agent would have or already has when patrolling outside the EU borders and coming across a situation which requires a (more or less immediate) response. A drone can fly over to "see" and record information, but may perhaps be seen as less accountable for the response that is set forth (or not set forth)? Can the drones see without being seen? According to the Law of the Sea, any vessel coming across another one in distress has a responsibility to bring search and rescue and bring the rescued ones to a safe harbor (UN Convention on the Law of the Sea, and the SAR and Safety of Life at Sea (SOLAS) Conventions). Despite the remoteness, it seems difficult to argue that a drone detecting a situation of distress would not make accountable the agents observing these images, even if they find themselves physically far away.

Conclusion

A central question is, to what extent might preventive rescue operations become a cover for earlier interception and even returning migrants before they have left the territorial waters of the North African state? Following the ruling in the case of Hirsi Jamaa and others vs. Italy, it is hard to imagine how any push-back operations can take place on any consistent scale after that judgment. The general impression from following the situation in the Mediterranean closely, is indeed that there have been no, or close to no, push-back operations since, although there are no comprehensive overviews of patrols conducted at sea and their outcomes. A testimony of this "difficulty" to pursue any form of push-back operations today, is the fact that the Mare Nostrum operation consisted precisely of rescuing earlier, even in Libyan waters, and then bringing the migrants to Italy. The operation thus appears as a de facto recognition of the difficulty to conduct "border control" at the maritime border, if that means refusing entry to some. However, in the lack of other options, this might be precisely the best "controlling" option: if the migrants cannot be turned back, then they will have to be "handled" anyway at some point or another, and hence rescuing them earlier becomes, as stated above, a form of reclaiming control over the border areas. If rescuing in itself is hard to imagine as controversial, then Mare Nostrum has well shown that rescuing on a large scale can be controversial, having been accused of encouraging migration flows, practically acting, as some would put it, as a "ferry service"[5] for migrants into Europe. These are complex questions that are yet to be fully addressed, and whereby a series of factors would need to be taken into account in any future stock-taking, including the various factors that act as push- (crisis, poverty, violence, political or other forms of persecution) or pull- (seeking and believing a better life is possible in Europe) factors for migration. The issue sheds light on the complex territory in which border surveillance drones are entering if they are to be deployed on a larger scale for the monitoring of the EU's external borders.

The border control drone, and the aims given to them of contributing to surveillance beyond national borders, nevertheless appears as a means to keep the "disorder" and "unwanted" elements outside, at least further away from our sight. Any movement of migrants that can be discouraged *outside* the European borders seems also to serve the purpose that it, at the same time, falls outside of "our" line of sight, i.e. of the European public opinion, media, and human rights organizations. Any border and police authority in charge of handling a certain level of migratory pressure is faced with a series of dilemmas and political ambiguities between the advocates of protecting the human lives and their rights, and the advocates of keeping them "out" in order to protect "our territories." In such contexts, the individual border guard may be faced with a lot of ambiguous mandates and obligations on a daily basis. The drone however, by virtue of its dominant position above, in the air, then not only sees large, but can also allow for adopting a certain distance from the individual human destinies on the ground, or in this case at sea.

Notes

1 My observations of the development of EU border surveillance over the recent years draws on my work within the EU FP7-funded project PERSEUS, where I have addressed the legal, ethical and political implications of increased and more coordinated border surveillance at the EU level, and engaged with a series of European political and industry actors seeking to further develop the EU's border surveillance capacities.
2 Frontex, http://frontex.europa.eu/about-frontex/mission-and-tasks (Accessed April 10, 2016).
3 Authors' emphasis.
4 PERSEUS VIP Event, Hellenic Coast Guard headquarters, October 15, 2014.
5 European Day for Border Guards, organized by Frontex, "Migrants at Sea: High Expectations, Limited Solutions," 2014, www.ed4bg.eu/sites/default/files/debates/summaries/Migrants%20at%20sea.%20High%20expectations%20limited%20solutions.pdf (Accessed April 10, 2016).

References

BBC News (2014a) "Australia to Buy US Drones for Border Patrol," March 13. Available at: www.bbc.com/news/world-asia-26541651 (Accessed April 10, 2016).

BBC News (2014b) "US-Mexico Border 'Patrolled by Drones,'" November 13. Available at: www.bbc.com/news/world-us-canada-30044702 (Accessed April 10, 2016).

Bellanova, R. and González Fuster, G. (2013) Politics of disappearance: Scanners and (unobserved) bodies as mediators of security practices. *International Political Sociology*, 7: 188–209.

Bergenas, J. and Stohl, R. (2013) "Unarmed Drones Can Strengthen U.S. and African Security," *International Business Times*, July 16, www.ibtimes.com/unarmed-drones-can-strengthen-us-african-security-1348089.

Bigo, D. (2005) "From foreigners to 'abnormal aliens': how the faces of the enemy have changed following September the 11th," in Elspeth Guild and Joanne van Selm (eds.), *International Migration and Security: Opportunities and Challenges*, London: Routledge, pp. 64–81.

Bigo, D. (2006) "Security, exception, ban and surveillance," in David Lyon (ed.), *Theorizing Surveillance: The Panopticon and Beyond*. Devon, UK: Willan Publishing.

Bigo, D. and Guild, E. (eds.) (2005) *Controlling Frontiers: Free Movement Into and Within Europe*, London: Ashgate.

Boucher, P. (2014) "Domesticating the Drone: The Demilitarisation of Unmanned Aircraft for Civil Markets," *Science Engineering Ethics*, November.

Brian, T. and Laczko, F. (eds.) (2014) "Fatal Journeys: Tracking Lives Lost during Migration," *International Organization for Migration (IOM)*. Available at: www.iom.int/files/live/sites/iom/files/pbn/docs/Fatal-Journeys-Tracking-Lives-Lost-during-Migration-2014.pdf (Accessed April 10, 2016).

Carling, J. (2007a) Migration control and migrant fatalities at the Spanish–African borders. *International Migration Review*, 41 (2): 316–343.

Carling, J. (2007b) "The Merits and Limitations of Spain's High-Tech Border Control," *Migration Policy Institute*, June 7. Available at: www.migrationpolicy.org/article/merits-and-limitations-spains-high-tech-border-control (Accessed April 10, 2016).

Carling, J. (2015) "Refugees Are Also Migrants. And All Migrants Matter," *Border Criminologies* (blog post), September 3. Available at: http://bordercriminologies.law.ox.ac.uk/refugees-are-also-migrants/ (Accessed April 10, 2016).

Ceyhan, A. (2008) Technologization of security: Management of uncertainty and risk in the age of biometrics. *Surveillance & Society*, 5 (2): 102–123.

Ceyhan, A. and Tsoukala, A. (2002) The securitization of migration in Western societies: Ambivalent discourses and policies. *Alternatives: Global, Local, Political*, 27 (1): January–March.

Convention Relating to the Status of Refugees (1951), United Nations High Commissioner for Refugees. Available at: www.unhcr.org/3b66c2aa10.html (Accessed April 10, 2016).

Correa-Cabrera, G. (2013) Security, migration, and the economy in the Texas–Tamaulipas border region: The "real" effects of Mexico's drug war. *Politics & Policy*, 41 (1): February, 65–82.

Correa-Cabrera, G. (2014) Violence on the "forgotten" border: Mexico's drug war, the state and the paramilitarization of organized crime in Tamaulipas in a 'new democratic era. *Journal of Borderland Studies*, 29 (4): 419–433.

de Haas, H. (2008) The myth of invasion: The inconvenient realities of African migration to Europe. *Third World Quarterly*, 29 (7): 1305–1322.

DeNicola, L. (2006) "The Bundling of Geospatial Information with Everyday Experience," in Torin Monahan (ed.), *Surveillance and Security: Technological Politics and Power in Everyday Life*, New York: Routledge, pp. 243–264.

Department of Homeland Security, Office of Inspector General (2015) "CBP Drones are Dubious Achievers," Washington DC, January 6. Available at: www.oig.dhs.gov/assets/pr/2015/oigpr_010615.pdf (Accessed April 10, 2016).

Directive 95/46/EC of the European Parliament and of the Council of October 24, 1995 on the protection of individuals with regard to the processing of personal data and on the free movement of such data, *OJ*, 1995, L281/31.

ECRE (European Council on Refugees and Exiles) (2012) "Push-backs to Libya: Italy condemned by the European Court of Human Rights," February 23, Strasbourg. Available at: www.ecre.org/component/downloads/downloads/432.html (Accessed April 10, 2016).

European Commission (2008) Communication from the Commission to the European Parliament, the Council, the European Social and Economic Committee of the Regions Examining the creation of a European Border Surveillance System (EUROSUR), COM(2008) 68 final.

European Commission (2009) Report on progress made in developing the European Border Surveillance system (EUROSUR), Commission Staff Working Paper, SEC(2009)1265final of September 24.

European Commission (2011) Proposal for a Regulation of the European parliament and of the council establishing the European Border Surveillance System (EUROSUR), COM(2011) 873 final 2011/0427(COD), Brussels, December 12.

European Commission (2014) "Frontex Joint Operation 'Triton' – Concerted efforts to manage migration in the Central Mediterranean," Memo, Press Release Database, Brussels, October 7. Available at: http://europa.eu/rapid/press-release_MEMO-14-566_en.htm (Accessed April 10, 2016).

EUROSUR Regulation (EU) (2013) No 1052/2013 of the European Parliament and of the Council of October 22, 2013, establishing the European Border Surveillance System (EUROSUR), Official Journal of the European Union, L 295/11, 6.11. Available at: http://frontex.europa.eu/assets/Legal_basis/Eurosur_Regulation_2013.pdf (Accessed April 10, 2016).

Finnemore, M. and Sikkink, K. (1998) International norm dynamics and political change. Special Issue: 'International Organization at Fifty: Exploration and Contestation in the Study of World Politics'. *International Organization*, 52 (4): 887–917.

Frenzen, N. (2014) "Turkish Coast Guard Reports Intercepting 12,872 migrants in Aegean Sea in 2014: Some Migrants Pushed Back into Turkish Territorial Waters," *Migrants at Sea* (blogpost), January 5. Available at: http://migrantsatsea.org/2015/01/05/turkish-coast-guard-reports-intercepting-12872-migrants-in-aegean-sea-in-2014-some-migrants-pushed-back-into-turkish-territorial-waters/ (Accessed April 10, 2016).

Frontex (2006) "Feasibility study on Mediterranean coastal patrols network – MEDSEA," Warsaw.

Frontex (2014) "Frontex launches Joint Operation Triton," October 31. Available at: http://frontex.europa.eu/news/frontex-launches-joint-operation-triton-JSYpL7 (Accessed April 10, 2016).

Gammeltoft-Hansen, T. (2011) *Access to Asylum: International Refugee Law and the Globalisation of Migration Control*, Cambridge: Cambridge University Press.

Guild, E., Carrera, S. and Geyer, F. (2008) "The Commission's New Border Package: Does it take us one step closer to a 'Cyber-Fortress Europe'?" CEPS Policy Brief, No. 154, March 2008.

Guittet, E.-P. and Jeandesboz, J. (2010) "Security Technologies," in J. Peter Burgess (ed.), *The Routledge Handbook of New Security Studies*, London: Routledge, pp. 229–239.

Hayes, B. and Vermeulen, M. (2012) "Borderline: The EU's New Border Surveillance Initiatives. Assessing the Costs and Fundamental Rights Implications of EUROSUR and the 'Smart Borders' Proposals," *Heinrich Böll Stiftung and The Greens/European Free Alliance in the European Parliament*, June, 82.

Hayes, B., Jones, C. and Töpfer, E. (2014) *Eurodrones Inc.*, London: Transnational Institute and Statewatch.

Higuera, J. (2014) "Border Control, Internal Security Drive UAV Market," Defense-News, March 25. Available at: http://tealgroup.com/index.php/about-teal-group-corporation/media/item/border-control-internal-security-drive-uav-market (Accessed April 10, 2016).

Human Rights Watch (2009) "Pushed Back, Pushed Around. Italy's Forced Return of Boat Migrants and Asylum Seekers," *Human Rights Watch Report*, 20 September.

Human Rights Watch (2012) "Hidden Emergency: Migrant Deaths in the Mediterranean," August 16. Available at: www.hrw.org/news/2012/08/16/hidden-emergency (Accessed April 10, 2016).

Hunko, A. (2015) Press Release: "Drones for Maritime Rescue Only, Not to Prevent Migration," January 19. Available at: www.andrej-hunko.de/presse/2468-drones-for-maritime-rescue-only-not-to-prevent-migration (Accessed April 10, 2016).

Huysmans, J. (2000) The European Union and the securitization of migration. *Journal of Common Market Studies*, 38 (5): 751–777.

Huysmans, J. (2006) *The Politics of Insecurity: Fear, Migration and Asylum in the EU*. London and New York: Routledge.

International Organization for Migration (IOM) (2014) "Fatal Journeys: Tracking Lives Lost During Migration," Tara Brian and Frank Laczko (eds.). Available at: www.iom.int/files/live/sites/iom/files/pbn/docs/Fatal-Journeys-Tracking-Lives-Lost-during-Migration-2014.pdf (Accessed April 10, 2016).

International Organization for Migration (IOM) (2015) "Mediterranean Migrant Arrivals Approach 250,000," Press Release, August 14. Available at: www.iom.int/news/mediterranean-migrant-arrivals-approach-250000 (Accessed April 10, 2016).

Jeandesboz, J. (2010) "Logiques et pratiques de contrôle et de surveillance des frontières de l'Union européenne" [*Logics and practices of control and surveillance of the borders of the European Union*], in Amandine Scherrer, Emmanuel-Pierre Guittet and Didier Bigo (eds.), *Mobilités sous surveillance: perspectives croisées UE-Canada*, Outremont: Athéna éditions, pp. 149–164.

Jeandesboz, J. (2011) "Beyond the Tartar steppe: EUROSUR and the ethics of European border control practices," in J. Peter Burgess and Serge Gutwirth (eds.), *Europe Under Threat? Security, Migration and Integration*, Brussels: VUB Press, pp. 111–131.

Joachim, J. and Schneiker, A. (2012) New humanitarians? Frame appropriation through private military and security companies. *Millennium: Journal of International Studies*, 40 (2): 365–388.

Jumbert, M.G. (2012) Controlling the Mediterranean space through surveillance. The politics and discourse of surveillance as an all-encompassing solution to EU maritime border management issues. *Espace, Populations, Sociétés*, 3: 35–48.

Kington, T. (2014) "Italy Tailors Rules To Allow UAVs, Military Aircraft in Civil Airspace," *DefenseNews*, May 13. Available at: http://beforeitsnews.com/global-unrest/2014/06/italy-tailors-rules-to-allow-uavs-military-aircraft-in-civil-airspace-2459384.html (Accessed April 10, 2016).

Lemberg-Pedersen, M. (2013) "Private Security Companies and the European Borderscapes," in Thomas Gammeltoft-Hansen and Ninna Nyberg Sørensen (eds.), *The Migration Industry: The Commercialization of International Migration*, Global Institutions Series, Vol. 69, New York: Routledge, pp. 152–172.

Lin, J. and Singer, P.W. (2014) "China Shows Off Its Growing Drone Fleet," *Popular Science*, November 14. Available at: www.popsci.com/china-shows-its-growing-drone-fleet (Accessed April 10, 2016).

Lutterbeck, D. (2006) Policing migration in the Mediterranean. *Mediterranean Politics*, 11 (1): March, 59–82.

Lyon, D. (2002) Everyday surveillance: Personal data and social classifications. *Information, Communication and Society*, 5 (2): 242–257.

Lyon, D. (2003) *Surveillance as Social Sorting: Privacy, Risk, and Digital Discrimination*, London: Routledge.

Lyon, D. (ed.) (2006) *Theorizing Surveillance: The Panopticon and Beyond*, Devon, UK: Willan Publishing.

Lyon, D. (2007) Surveillance, security and social sorting: Emerging research priorities. *International Criminal Justice Review*, 17 (3): 161–170.

Marin, L. (2011) "Is Europe Turning into a 'Technological Fortress'? Innovation and Technology for the Management of EU's External Borders. Reflections on Frontex and Eurosur," September 5, *Criminal Justice, Borders and Citizenship Research Paper* No. 2492058.

Marullo, S., Pagnucco, R. and Smith, J.G. (1996) Frame changes and social movement contraction: US Peace Movement framing after the Cold War. *Sociological Inquiry*, 66 (1): January: 1–28.

Monmouth University Poll (2012 and 2013) "National: U.S. Supports Unarmed Domestic Drones," August 15, 2013; and "U.S. Supports Some Domestic Drone Use," June 12, 2012. Available at: www.monmouth.edu/polling (Accessed April 10, 2016).

Neocleous, M. (2013) Air power as police power. *Environment and Planning D: Society and Space*, 13: 578–593.

Neyroud, P. and Vassilas, P. (2010) The politics of partnership: Challenges to Institution Building in European Policing. *Cahiers Politiestudies*, 3 (16): 75–90.

Nicas, J. (2015) "Drone Patrols on U.S. Border Ineffective, Report Finds," *The Wall Street Journal*, January 6. Available at: www.wsj.com/articles/inspector-general-criticizes-u-s-border-drone-program-1420576272 (Accessed April 10, 2016).

Nielsen, N. (2013) "Frontex Chief Looks Beyond EU Borders," *EU Observer*, January 14, Brussels. Available at: https://euobserver.com/fortress-eu/118471 (Accessed April 10, 2016).

Ó Súilleabháin, A. (2013) "Already Pushing Legal Boundaries, EU's Border Agency Now Seeks Drones," *IPI Global Observatory*, March 27. Available at: http://theglobalobservatory.org/2013/03/already-pushing-legal-boundaries-eus-border-agency-now-seeks-drones/ (Accessed April 10, 2016).

Pop, V. (2011) "Tunisia's 'Biblical Exodus' Pits Rome Against Brussels," *EU Observer*, February 14. Available at: http://euobserver.com/9/31802 (Accessed April 10, 2016).

Rijpma, J. and Vermeulen, M. (2015) EUROSUR: Saving lives or building borders? *European Security*, 24 (3): 454–472.

Romeo, G., Pacino, M. and Borello, F. (2009) First flight of scaled electric solar powered UAV for Mediterranean Sea border surveillance forest and fire monitoring. *Aeorotecnica Missili & Spazio, The Journal of Aerospace Science, Technology and Systems*, 88 (1/2): January–June.

Sandvik, K.B. and Lohne, K. (2014) "The Rise of the Humanitarian Drone: Giving Content to an Emerging Concept," *Millennium: Journal of International Studies*, published online June 27, 2014.

Seiffarth, O. (2011) "The Development of the European Border Surveillance System," in Burgess, J.P. and Gutwirth, S. (eds.), *A Threat Against Europe. Security, Migration and Integration*, Brussels, Belgium: VUB Press and Brussels University Press.

Sewell, G. and Barker, J.R. (2001) Neither good, nor bad, but dangerous: Surveillance as an ethical paradox. *Ethics and Information Technology*, 3 (3): 183–196.

Szoldra, P. (2013) "Drone Spying Capabilities Are About to Take Another Huge Leap," *Business Insider*, January 29. Available at: www.businessinsider.com/darpa-argus-mega-camera-most-detailed-surveillance-camera-in-world-2013-1?op=1 (Accessed April 10, 2016).

The Guardian (2014) "Half of US–Mexico Border Now Patrolled Only by Drone," November 13. Available at: www.theguardian.com/world/2014/nov/13/half-us-mexico-border-patrolled-drone (Accessed April 10, 2016).

The Jerusalem Post (2008), "Ecuador Buying Israeli Drones to Strengthen Troubled Border with Colombia," June 26. Available at: www.jpost.com/International/Ecuador-buying-Israeli-drones-to-strengthen-troubled-border-with-Colombia (Accessed April 10, 2016).

The Jerusalem Post (2014) "Egyptian Militants say Israeli Drone Kills Three Terrorists in Sinai," July 25. Available at: www.jpost.com/Middle-East/Egyptian-militants-say-Israeli-drone-kills-three-terrorists-in-Sinai-368928 (Accessed April 10, 2016).

The Nation (2014) "India Purchases 49 Drones From Israel to Spy Pakistan and Chinese Borders," October 26. Available at: http://nation.com.pk/national/26-Oct-2014/india-purchases-49-drones-from-israel-to-spy-pakistani-and-chinese-borders (Accessed April 10, 2016).

Wall, T. (2013) Unmanning the police manhunt: Vertical security as pacification. *Socialist Studies/Etudes Socialistes*, 9 (2): Winter, 32–56.

Wall, T. and Monahan, T. (2011) Surveillance and violence from afar: The politics of drones and liminal security-scapes. *Theoretical Criminology*, 15 (3): 239–254.

Wolff, S. (2008) Border Management in the Mediterranean: Internal, external and ethical challenges. *Cambridge Review of International Affairs*, 21 (2): 253–271.

5   The public order drone

Proliferation and disorder in civil airspace

Kristin Bergtora Sandvik

The purpose of this chapter is to increase understanding of the relationship between drone proliferation and public order. To that end, it offers an account of the "public order drone," giving particular attention to the types of "drone disorder" that are emerging from the current explosion in recreational drone use.[1]

In realms such as humanitarian assistance or wildlife conservation, discussions of the benefits of drones typically focus on their capacity for "doing good"; in the realm of law enforcement (including both crime fighting and maintaining public order), firefighting and homeland security, discussions of benefits tend to focus on drones' "endless" uses (Sandvik 2015). This chapter focuses mostly on public order policing.

At present, the central project of the drone industry is to gain access to civil airspace in the United States (US) and the European Union (EU).[2] Despite having had considerable success in shaping the political and legislative debates about such access (Hall and Coyne 2014), industry groups continue to face public and government resistance to the integration of drones into civilian airspace. As this volume shows, given the public's skepticism about drone wars, and its concern about the potential threats to privacy associated with domestic drone surveillance, identifying and promoting "good" uses for drones are central to increasing the legitimacy of drone use. What I will here call the "public order drone" (following Hayes, Jones, and Töpfer 2014) has emerged, in recent years, as an important part of industry efforts to achieve legitimacy.

In the popular imagination, the public order drone is typically envisioned as a handheld microdrone (that is, a tiny drone that is electronically tethered to a handheld mobile device);[3] it has functional, appropriate hardware and is flown in an orderly manner by a competent and responsible pilot. In the eyes of the drone industry, the public order drone – through both surveillance and its visible presence – not only maintains order but carries the promise of *increased* order and *improved forms* of order: first because drones make surveillance less costly (and therefore more efficient), and second because they enhance situational awareness by providing increasingly advanced, "God's-eye views" of the ground.

Finally, the industry views the public order drone as having a disciplinary – or even preemptive – impact on behavior in public spaces. And, as surveillance from above will refine the understanding of trespass, the public order drone will also provide a clearer demarcation of the boundaries between public and private property. Thus, the public order drone promises not only a unique vantage point but unique knowledge. Wilcox's (2015, 160) observation about precision warfare is useful here: she argues that the God's-eye view refers not only to the pilots' visual perspective but to a particular epistemology, according to which knowledge is absolute, finite, and attainable.

So far, the drone industry's access-to-airspace efforts have received little attention (for an exception, see Hayes, Jones, and Töpfer [2014]). My objective in this chapter is to position the narrative of the public order drone in the context of the access-to-airspace effort. I take a two-pronged approach: first, I consider public order drones from the perspective of criminology and surveillance studies, where concerns are emerging about the role of drones in the paramilitarization of public order policing. This scholarship is useful for thinking about the tasks public order drones are expected to undertake – in particular, preventing and responding to antisocial behavior and engaging in crowd control. I argue that once drones become accepted as a means of performing these public functions, a question may arise as to how to perform these functions most effectively – which may, in turn, lead to the eventual weaponization of public order drones.

The criminology and surveillance literature does not, however, address the relationship between public order and the disorder produced by drones. Thus, the second dimension of my approach picks up on a contradiction that is currently facing the drone industry: on the one hand, as part of its access-to-airspace project, the industry is encouraging drone proliferation (particularly in the case of public order drones, and with the specific aim of increasing sales to government customers); on the other hand, the proliferation of both commercial and recreational drones may pose a threat to public order, ultimately undermining the industry's access-to-airspace efforts. In other words, the drone industry may be a victim of its own success.

Order and disorder are intimately connected: the endless, public-order uses imagined for drones are mirrored by endless possibilities for disorder. Thus, "drone disorder" – both disorderly drones (those that fly or crash where they should not) and disorder created by drones (panic or suspicion in the face of events such as drone flyovers of nuclear installations) – must be evaluated alongside perceptions and promises of order.

I suggest that drone disorder can be broadly categorized in three ways, all of which must be read against the backdrop of what the industry imagines to be the role of drones in maintaining public order:

- safety issues that may arise in relation to (1) hobbyist piloting and (2) the technical standards of do-it-yourself drones;
- potential risks to air traffic; and
- the possibility of "drone crime" and "drone terrorism."

I also argue that in response to concerns about drone disorder, the narrative of the public order drone is expanding: first, safety concerns are being used as arguments against opening access to civil airspace; second, recreational drone pilots are being labeled as "bad" or "irresponsible"; third, myriad new initiatives are being launched to cope with potential risks to personal and national security.

The chapter includes six principal parts: Section 1 outlines the underlying rationale for the narrative of the public order drone, within the context of the access-to-airspace project. Section 2, which draws on criminology and surveillance literature, examines the public order drone in the context of the paramilitarization of policing. Section 3 describes how monitoring, crowd control, and the prevention of antisocial behavior have emerged as key tasks for the public order drone, and reflects on the ways in which this constellation of tasks may be laying the groundwork for the weaponization of police drones. Section 4 considers the emerging antisociality of drones, particularly as recreational uses proliferate. Section 5 examines how the endless possibilities for creating order are mirrored by endless possibilities for disorder, including crime, threats to national security, and industrial espionage. The chapter concludes with a brief reflection on the meanings that are beginning to accrue around the notion of drones as a mode of maintaining and knowing about public order.

Unlocking access to civil airspace

To offset declining demand from the defense sector, the drone industry is engaging in significant, worldwide marketing efforts (that include emerging markets) to promote the "good" use of drones for purposes other than national security. The industry's overall goal is to open US and European civil airspace to the use of drones outside the context of violent conflict (Sandvik and Lohne 2014; Hayes, Jones, and Töpfer 2014; Boucher 2014). According to drone manufacturers and lobbyists, the lack of general access to civil airspace is the single most important obstacle to the proliferation of commercial and government drones (Presutti 2014; Pilkington 2014a). That lack of access, coupled with deep public skepticism about drone use, has led to squandered economic opportunities domestically, lost market shares globally, and a lag in the cultural acceptance of drones in civil airspace, including for the purpose of maintaining public order. Such claims are accompanied by talk of missed (but vaguely defined) opportunities: according to industry studies, failing to integrate drones into US civil airspace is costing tens of thousands of jobs, and has had significant impact on the US and EU economies.[4]

Despite their expressed intention to be open to "members ... with an active interest in UAVs [unmanned aerial vehicles] and the development of opportunities to use these systems on a routine basis for the overall benefit of mankind" (UAVS 2014), the industry's lobbying organizations perceive themselves as having a "public relations problem," which stems from the industry's failure to properly "educate the public" about the benefits of drone technology in civil airspace (Wolverton 2012). Several issues seem to be behind this failure. Perhaps most important, in the popular perception, the use of drones in civil airspace continues to be associated with the use of weaponized drones in Afghanistan, Pakistan, and Yemen, which has generated massive public controversy, both because of the number of civilian casualties and the fact that US citizens have been targeted.

As part of its effort to reframe how drones are perceived, the drone industry (along with the military) continues to insist on a variety of alternative names, including UAV (unmanned aerial vehicle), RPA (remotely piloted aircraft), RPV (remotely piloted vehicle), and UAS (unmanned aircraft system).[5] The contested nature of the term is well illustrated by Friedenzohn and Mirot (2014), who argue that "the term drone can be counterproductive and the debate over their use (sic) calls for sterile terminology like UAS, which is both correct and free from stigma." In the face of such arguments, even pro-drone observers have accused the industry of failing to recognize the existence of legitimate issues to be debated, and of mistakenly believing that a semantic shift will make the criticisms go away (McNeal 2013).

Another dimension of the industry's "public relations problem" concerns the failure, on the part of manufacturers, to proactively address privacy and data protection. The Federal Aviation Administration (FAA) Modernization and Reform Act of 2012, for example, which was drafted with extensive involvement from the US drone lobby (AUVSI – the Association for Unmanned Vehicle Systems International), made no explicit reference to privacy. To counter the resulting criticisms, AUVSI later issued a code of conduct – which was, in its turn, criticized for ignoring key privacy issues, among other problems (Thalen 2013; Vijayan 2013).

The US public continues to be uneasy about the government's use of surveillance drones: a 2014 poll, for example, showed that the majority of Americans were "extremely" or "very" concerned that private operators could use drones in ways that violate privacy (Associated Press 2014; Cho 2014). With respect to European airspace, a recent study suggests that many industry representatives do not believe that capturing, recording, and storing images of members of the public generates privacy or data protection issues. The study further suggests that the industry's lack of awareness of existing legal obligations indicates that these obligations are not being upheld (Finn et al. 2014).

In sum, despite efforts to "educate the public," the drone industry is facing ongoing challenges in understanding and addressing public and government concerns with respect to privacy, data protection, security, safety and so forth. In response, manufacturers and lobbyists are developing a carefully crafted moral economy of "good" drones, which is designed to help normalize not only various *types* of drones, but a broader range of drone *uses*, whether by government, civil society, or commercial entities; this moral economy is also intended to "make good" many of the uses currently proliferating.

As Graham (2010b) observes, "in the widening deployment of drones, certain key events and deployments are likely to act as shop-windows to showpiece the technology as a means of encouraging further deployments." Border control, policing, and the combination of both are examples of such deployments. For example, in 2012, the US industry group AUVSI launched the Increasing Human Potential website, according to which "unmanned systems increase our human potential. They enable us to execute dangerous and difficult tasks safely and efficiently, saving time, saving money and, most importantly, saving lives." Public order and public safety are specifically within this ambit: "Each year thousands of first responders and military personnel are injured in the line of duty ... Unmanned systems can and will continue to make these jobs safer, more effective and more efficient" (IHP n.d.).

It is important to note that framing drones as a tool for public order both feeds on and reinforces the global normalization of police drones – that is, drones that are deployed to undertake traditional policing tasks. In recent years, the media have reported on numerous uses of drones by US law enforcement for tasks such as general surveillance, evidence collection, crowd control, crime prevention, and arrests. According to one New York Police Department spokesperson, drones "aren't that exotic anymore" (CBS 2012). Police agencies in Alabama, Arkansas, California, Colorado, Florida, Idaho, Maryland, North Dakota, South Carolina, Texas, Utah, and Washington State have requested or received authorization from the FAA to use surveillance drones. Surveillance drones are deployed by police in Australia, Canada, New Zealand, and the United Kingdom, among other countries (Fisher 2013; Fox News 2014; Bohman 2014; Greene 2014; McLeod 2014; Viydo and KREM Staff 2014). In Brazil, surveillance drones have been used in favelas and at sporting events. Drones have been used for counterterrorism in Colombia; to combat rape in India; to control drug trafficking in Mexico; to control drugs, crime, and street protests in Russia; and to track mafia suspects in Italy (Franceschi-Bicchierai 2012; Robbins 2013; Borges 2014; Kington 2014).

The models deployed include the Skyseer, the Skyranger, the T-Hawk, the WASP III, and the Draganflyer X6. Prototypes designed specifically for police use are now also available: Vanguard Industries offers the ShadowHawk to public safety agencies for "military and law enforcement applications" (Conditt 2014). AeroVironment, a US-based military drone contractor that produces the Switchblade, the only armed microdrone in known deployment, also produces the Qube, which it describes as a "rugged and reliable small unmanned aircraft system (UAS) targeting the needs of first responders" (AeroVironment 2011).

As I will discuss in the next section, the trend toward normalization of police drones both stems from and reinforces the paramilitarization of policing. I will argue that, as a result, the deliberate blurring of the boundaries between the military and the civilian is becoming part of how we frame what it means to maintain public order.

Paramilitary policing and technology transfer

In recent years, criminology and surveillance studies have focused on the ways in which military technology, military-style training, and military tactics are being transferred to domestic law enforcement, creating a paramilitary police culture[6] – and, more specifically, driving the paramilitarization of public order policing (Della Porta and Reiter 2006). Particularly in the United States, there has been a significant transfer of big, heavy, and sophisticated (and often free) surplus military equipment – both offensive and defensive – to police departments, including military-grade surveillance equipment capable of obtaining vast amounts of data about citizens. According to a 2013 *New American* article, the US Department of Homeland Security is providing police "with all the gadgets, hardware, and software necessary to keep everybody under surveillance" (Wolverton 2013).

Paramilitary-style public order policing is characterized by the use of intelligence gathering (including surveillance), large-scale planning, specialized units, squad formations, controlled force, riot gear, and strict command-and-control procedures (Waddington 2007). One corollary result is a shift in how law enforcement views the events and behaviors with which it is expected to deal: for example, criminality is redefined as insurgency, and crime control as low-intensity conflict. In a militarized law enforcement environment, both require counterinsurgency tactics and equipment (Kraska 2007). Because of the entirely distinct forms of violence in which the police and the military are supposed to engage – domestic police are trained to use violence only as a last resort, whereas military forces are trained to achieve victory through combat – the paramilitarization of domestic policing is highly problematic (Hall and Coyne 2013).

An emerging critical literature specifically considers the evolving role of drones in domestic law enforcement, as well as the developing capabilities of the drones deployed for policing (from surveillance drones to weaponized platforms) (Wall and Monahan 2011; Finn and Wright 2012; Sandvik 2015). I have argued elsewhere that the drones currently being promoted for civilian uses are, at least in part, a "war dividend" flowing from military spending on the "war on terror." Graham's use of the Foucauldian concept of a "boomerang effect" – whereby the institutions and techniques associated with European colonial power were brought back to the West – is helpful here: as Graham (2010b) observes, military technologies, funded and perfected through the global war on terror (the contemporary incarnation of the colonized frontier), are being imported for use on civilian populations.

Considerable crossover between the military and law enforcement has already occurred: for example, the US Air Force has assisted police in North Dakota with surveillance, and Predator drones belonging to the US Border Patrol have been loaned out to unnamed sheriffs' departments (Fox News 2014). Similarly, the Italian Air Force has allowed the police to use its

Predators and Reapers for crowd monitoring and riot control (Cenciotti 2014; Kington 2014). Such technology transfers, which reflect an underlying belief that only sophisticated military equipment can keep the populace safe, also contribute to a shift in rationalities: the deliberate blurring of the boundary between the military and the civilian becomes a partial precondition for maintaining public order.

In this context, it's useful to take a further look at framing. As noted in the introduction, public order is one drone use among many that are held to be beneficial (other such uses include humanitarian assistance and conservation). But in the realm of law enforcement, the focus is less on the inherent "goodness" of the use and more on the flexibility of the technology – the "endless" opportunities to achieve lower cost and greater ease of operation, for example.

Often, industry and media discussions of public order drones link police work and firefighting under the less controversial "first responder" umbrella. The aforementioned Qube police drone, for example, is designed to give first responders an "immediate eye in the sky so they can find lost kids, they can investigate accidents, they can support disaster recovery for earthquakes in California, tornadoes in the Midwest, hurricanes in the Gulf Coast" (CBS 2013).

With the Qube, AeroVironment is now "zeroing in on a new market – police and fire departments too small to afford their own helicopters, but big enough to have a need for overhead surveillance" (Rieland 2012). Descriptions of the Qube emphasize that it fits easily in the trunk of a car, and can be assembled and ready for flight in less than five minutes (AeroVironment 2011; Pilkington 2014b).

I would argue that this emphasis on infinite possibility as a value in itself is an important part of the constitution of public order drones. Moreover, the notion of infinite possibility is bolstered by implicit connections between public order uses (both stated and hinted at) and past uses of the same or similar technology for military purposes.[7] For example, a representative of AeroVironment observed during a trade show interview that "a lot of law enforcement are familiar with the full line of AeroVironment's unmanned products. Some of them have used them in the military or watched them" (KESQ 2013).

In sum, the public order drone is constituted through the mundane tasks of policing, including general surveillance, evidence collection, crowd control, crime prevention, and arrests; through the systemic blurring of the boundaries between the military and the civilian, with respect to the appropriate fields for the deployment of military technology; and, finally, through the notion of endless uses. In the next section, I suggest that the ways in which the characteristics outlined in this section combine with the specific tasks of public order drones – crowd control and policing antisocial behavior – point beyond surveillance capacities and may be laying the foundation for the weaponization of public order drones.[8]

The evolution of public order policing: from surveillance to weaponization

As used here, public order policing refers to "the use of police authority and capacity to establish a legitimate equilibrium between governmental and societal, collective and individual, rights and interests in a mass demonstration of grievance" (de Lint 2005). More succinctly, public order policing involves regulating behavior with the aim of establishing "good order" (Bachmann 2014: 119). In practical terms, public order is maintained through monitoring, crowd control, and the prevention of antisocial behavior, tasks for which surveillance drones are well suited.

Drones are increasingly the tool of choice for crowd control. In June 2013, for example, police in Northern Ireland purchased and used drones to surveil protests against the G8 summit, explicitly claiming that drones were being used to help maintain public order (Malcolm 2013; Drone Wars UK 2014). Recent news reports suggest that at the behest of the Greek police, the Ministry of Public Order and Citizen Protection has acquired drones for migration management and crowd control; allegedly, the idea of doing so arose during mass protests in Greece in 2011 (The Press Project 2014). Finally, as their deployment in Afghanistan has come to an end, unarmed Predator and Reaper drones are now being used to monitor soccer games and demonstrations, thanks to a deal between Italy's Air Force and its police forces (Kington 2014).

As part of maintaining public order, drones are explicitly tasked with preventing and cracking down on antisocial behavior (Drone Wars UK [2014]; as used here, "antisocial behavior" refers to behavior that is contrary to prevailing norms for social conduct – including arson, panhandling, public drunkenness, reckless driving, loitering, stealing, and vandalism). In the UK in 2007, for example, the antisocial behavior team of the Merseyside police used two drones to "police public order situations and prevent antisocial behavior"; one tactic was to fly the drone over groups of young people who were causing a nuisance in parks (Randerson 2007). In 2011, however, a drone was lost in the river; the Merseyside police subsequently decided to stop using the technology, on account of unforeseen technical and operational challenges and the high costs of associated training (*BBC* 2011).

Unlike crime fighting, public order policing takes place in full view of the public eye; thus, the promise of producing order from above will likely play out through different dynamics than those associated with drone use for crime fighting. Importantly, public order policing of protests is characterized by a moral ambiguity that crime fighting has traditionally lacked: whereas criminals are "outside" the moral community, participants in public assemblies (including protesters) are the moral equals of other citizens (Waddington 2000, 156). At the same time, however, drones can be used to "turn back the gaze" – to monitor police behavior, for example, or to allow visual access to areas that have been closed to journalists (Culver 2014).

Police typically respond to public order disturbances (e.g. antisocial behavior, unruly crowds) by placing restrictions on movement, public assembly, and the use of property – constraints that drones can help implement. But ordering public space through zonal banning – an approach to governing territory that conflates the principles of criminal law with the processes of upholding order, and is implemented through mass surveillance (Palmer and Warren 2014) – inevitably carries racial and class implications (Lemanski 2004). Like other examples of police paramilitarization, drones are likely to have differential impacts on disadvantaged individuals and groups (Salter 2014). And whatever the type or ostensible aims of the unmanned aircraft systems used for surveillance, "the usual suspects" – the poor, people of color, and antigovernment protesters – appear more likely than others to be targeted (Finn and Wright 2012). In Ontario, Canada, for example, police have used drones to monitor First Nations protests against the provincial government's failure to address the murders and disappearances of aboriginal women (Bowman 2014).

Finally, one must ask whether the tasks of the public order drone have a cumulative effect. That is, are armed police drones the logical and inevitable extension of public order drones? According to Graham (2010b), Merseyside was a typical example of technology crossover, whereby "unmanned drones similar to those used to launch lethal raids in Pakistan, Afghanistan might be used to police major events, monitor traffic and address problems of antisocial disorder in Liverpool." The impact of the paramilitarization of policing has already been noted, and industry enthusiasm for the dual-use potential of military drone technology remains strong (Boucher 2014). While arming police drones is a highly contentious issue, legislative provisions against weaponizing drones usually explicitly prohibit only "putting guns" on the drones (Brustein 2013). As I suggest elsewhere (Sandvik 2015), efforts to equip drones with less lethal weapons are already well under way; thus, weaponization should be thought of as an evolving process, not one that is necessarily tied to a single legislative or technological moment.

By the late 1990s, drones were already being proposed as a means of helping law enforcement to "deliver and deploy non-lethal agents" such as smoke canisters (for crowd control) and steel spikes (to destroy tires) (Murphy and Cycon 1999, 1). The drone industry continues to show substantial interest in such uses: the ShadowHawk, for instance – which has already been purchased by local police departments in the United States – is capable of firing rubber bullets and releasing tear-gas canisters and Taser projectiles; reportedly, it also has the capacity to launch grenades and to fire 12-gauge shotguns (Kindynis 2012).

In the realm of weaponization, traditional manufacturers are being joined by a motley group of drone startups – one of which, Chaotic Moon Studios, has developed the CUPID (Chaotic Unmanned Personal Intercept Drone), a "stun-copter" capable of delivering an 80,000-volt shock that, according to the manufacturer, could be used by law enforcement to apprehend fleeing suspects (Aamot 2014). (In 2014, Chaotic Moon Studios provided a live demonstration of the effect of the CUPID on a human.) More controversial is the Skunk Riot Control Copter manufactured by Desert Wolf, a South African company. Designed to be used to "control unruly crowds … without endangering the lives of the protestors or the security staff" (Smith 2014), the drone is equipped with both blinding lasers and on-board speakers to send verbal warnings to a crowd; it also has four high-capacity gun barrels capable of shooting up to 4,000 paintballs, pepper-spray balls, or solid plastic balls at rates of up to eighty balls per second, to be used in an extreme "life threatening situation" (Smith 2014). According to the manufacturer, the Skunk was developed to "assist in preventing another Marikana" – a reference to a 2012 strike in South Africa, in which forty-four miners were killed by police (Smith 2014).

I would argue that improved crowd control and the policing of antisocial behavior, in particular, seem to be central to domesticating the notion of armed drones. I have already observed that the drone industry and other actors appear to be employing the public order drone to improve public acceptance of drones in civil airspace; at the same time, however, a different process is at work: as the notion of using drones to control crowds and manage antisocial behavior becomes normalized, the focus will inevitably shift from the question of *whether drones should be applied to such uses* toward *how to make them as effective as possible*. One potential result is the normalizing of less lethal weapons, as a means of making the public order drone more effective. Thus, the emerging logic of the public order drone is as follows: through its specific contributions to public security, the public order drone is part of the general domestication of drone use; however, the satisfactory completion of such tasks will, over time, require weaponization.

The new drone antisociality: unsafe, untrained, and irresponsible users

Because drones are still an emerging technology, they have been known to collide, fall down, malfunction, or go missing: for example, since 2001, more than 400 large US military UAVs have crashed in major accidents worldwide (Whitlock 2014a). Thus, two of the most persistent challenges facing the drone industry are the creation of safe landing systems (such as parachutes), and the development of sufficiently effective systems for collision warning and avoidance to allow drones to share airspace with other aircraft.[9]

In the view of industry players, both commercial proliferation and the increasingly widespread use of hobbyist drones have the potential to be both disorderly and a source of disorder. This section examines these threats not only to public order, but to the drone industry's efforts to obtain access to civil airspace.

Hobbyist drone use generates a host of safety and security concerns – many of which, as Cho (2014) notes, arise more from the inherent risks of new technology than from the potential for misuse. From the perspective of the commercial drone industry, hobbyists fly too far, too close, too low, and in places they shouldn't, jeopardizing safety, security, and privacy. As one industry representative put it,[10] the current drone environment is "amateur hour," characterized by the emergence of a host of players who want to invent, build, fly, and find new uses for drones. Examples include student competitions focused on building drones for good ("Students Build 3D Printed Search and Rescue Device for LA County Fire Department" [Edwards 2014]; "The Drone That Could Save You From Drowning" [Kumparak 2014]); activist uses of drones to provide relief (e.g. the Syria Airlift Project, which explores "paradigm-changing ways to deliver humanitarian aid in conflict zones inaccessible to traditional aid organizations" [Syria Airlift Project n.d.]); and efforts to save endangered animals from poaching ("Drones for Good: Save the Rhino" [Epema 2014]). Nevertheless, most new drones are owned and flown by hobbyist users for purely recreational purposes.

Among regulators, frequent reports of near misses have created serious concerns about the risk of midair collisions between drones and commercial aircraft (Matishak 2014; Bohman 2014); a 2014 *Washington Post* article, for example, noted that the FAA had reported about "25 episodes in which small drones came within a few seconds or a few feet of crashing into much larger aircraft" (Whitlock 2014b); that same year, a BBC report offered this headline: "Drone Flown 20Ft from Landing Heathrow Jet" (*BBC* 2014). In Australia, amateur drone pilots have been warned to avoid bushfires; according to the Rural Fire Service, drone-related hazards could force firefighters to down their own aircraft (Reilly 2014a). In U____ ____d States, citizens have been fined for crashing drones over police ____ ____ Reilly 2014b); there have also been reports of drone operators ____ ____ ie landing of medical helicopters (WDTN 2014).

As commercial proliferation and th___ ____ in hobbyist use begin to threaten the long-term integration o____ ____o civil airspace, the narrative of the public order drone is s____ ____ esponse. Among the various approaches to dealing with the "an____ ____ of drones, such as voyeurism ("hovering outside bedrooms for whate____ nefarious reasons"; Segar 2014), one is to apportion blame. Pilots' associations, for example, complain about small-drone operators' lack of training (Cho 2014). Another approach is an increasing emphasis, among industry actors, "on abiding by the law." A developer of agricultural drones has noted, for example, that "before the drone industry can thrive in agriculture, search-and-rescue missions or even Amazon.com commercial deliveries ... hobbyists need to abide by the FAA's regulations first ... There are some people messing with the reputation of drone owners" (Ceballos 2014).

Meanwhile, in response to the popularity of drones as Christmas gifts (Hern 2014; Whittle 2014), the FAA and the drone industry launched an awareness campaign called Know Before You Fly, which reminds recreational users that "just because you can buy a UAS, doesn't mean you can fly it anywhere, or for any purpose" (Know Before You Fly 2014).

In another development, safety has become a site of public contestation, with some observers questioning the definition of a "near collision" and claiming that alleged increases in such incidents are being used to justify restrictive regulations (McNeal 2014a, 2014b). And while insurance has so far received little attention in discussions of safety, the Unmanned Aerial Vehicle Systems Association, a UK industry group, has expressed concern "that many UAV operations carried out whether legally or more often illegally have been performed without this appropriate third party liability insurance in place" (UAVS 2015).

In sum, drone proliferation is perceived as engendering various forms of disorder that need to be tackled by apportioning blame, educating users, or distancing the commercial drone industry from the activities of hobbyists. In addition to the privacy, safety, and security issues discussed in this section, drone proliferation in civil airspace is increasingly viewed as presenting a national security risk.

The endless possibilities for future insecurity

In early 2015, a drone crashed on the White House Lawn; in February of that year, mysterious drones were detected flying over Paris at night (Chrisafis 2015). These events highlighted an issue that the drone industry had so far underplayed: while drones are touted as having endless potential to uphold public order, they also offer endless opportunities for criminal or terrorist activities – from stalking to industrial espionage, drug smuggling, airdrops to prison inmates, and terrorism. Moreover, even drones being used for lawful, legitimate purposes are inherently vulnerable: they can be hacked in order to steal, spoof, or destroy information; they can also be compelled to change their flight path. Drones can be used to embarrass or threaten individuals, and can be flown into controlled airspace, in violation of air navigation orders (Segar 2014). Finally, the misuse of drones poses a serious national security threat (Birmingham Policy Commission 2014).

In response to potential risks associated with drone use, there are emerging efforts to resist drone surveillance – not from the perspective of human rights or privacy rights, but out of a desire to protect sensitive industrial or military sites. In an attempt to anticipate and deal with such risks, the French National Research Agency recently put out a call for research and development proposals for technology designed to protect sensitive zones from drone overfly. The request for proposals document noted that in order to anticipate these risks, notably for different scenarios and in different contexts, it is essential to appraise the technical means, which could be available in a mid-term, for the detection, the geolocalisation, the identification and neutralisation of small aerial drones.

(French National Research Agency 2014)

In an innovation call released by a Dutch agency, drones were described as potentially being "used to disrupt the public order and to smuggle forbidden goods" (The Hague Security Delta 2014). Hence, the main focus of the call was on finding ways to "take over control, intercept or redirect, and detect the location of the person in control" of the drone.

The potential of the Fox Drone Catcher (FDC), one of the technologies submitted in response to the Dutch call for proposals, illustrates the paradoxical symmetry of public order and disorder. If developed, the FDC would use vulnerabilities in the wireless protocols to identify the radio signals used by drones, and thereby intervene in their activities or regain control of them (The Hague Security Delta 2014). Thus, technology developed to protect public order (by subverting bad drones) can also create public *disorder* – because it can be used to subvert "good" drones as well as bad. Thus, instead of engendering straightforward results, efforts to grapple with safety and security only add further complexity to the narrative of the public order drone.

Importantly, this complexity suggests that drone use is linked not only to paramilitarization but to bureaucratization. As Hayes, Jones, and Töpfer note, in an effort to gain public support for the use of drones in civilian airspace, the industry invokes scenarios of havoc and mass destruction that are extremely rare in Europe (e.g. terrorist attacks, nuclear meltdowns, high-speed car chases), for which a technological solution – the development and procurement of drones – is proposed. Such scenarios are then "used to justify both substantial public expenditure and the acquisition and use of drones by domestic police forces" (Hayes, Jones, and Töpfer 2014: 9).

The perspective of Hayes, Jones, and Töpfer resonates with the arguments of Monahan and Mokos (2013), who observe that the creation of compelling narratives to justify surveillance is an important element of the securitization process; these narratives are what Crang and Graham (2007) have called "technological fantasies," which posit emerging technologies as necessary and effective responses to dire threats.

Such fantasies are not simply narrative devices used to achieve desired ends; they also actively shape larger security cultures and afford them influence. For example, the EU has structured research and development on the public order drone in such a way as to replace the democratic process with a technocratic one, where elected UK politicians

will not be consulted on the programme or the regulation clearing the development of law enforcement drones that are expected to be cruising the skies in surveillance searches for criminals or to secure public order by the end of the decade.

(Waterfield 2014)

Conclusion

This chapter explores the construction of the public order drone, along with the somewhat ambiguous role that this construction plays in the domestication of drones in civil airspace. As the drone discourse continues to develop, we must continually make sense of new elements of that discourse. Here, I have examined how the meaning accruing around the public order drone is gradually becoming "thicker": to unpack this process, I have considered the perceptions of public disorder that have arisen from the popularization of drones, and the ways in which those perceptions have been incorporated into the narrative of the public order drone. Specifically, the narrative has been expanded to include the notion that hobbyist users are "bad" and a threat to the larger project of the public order drone; it has also been expanded to encompass visions of drones as potentially detrimental to public order and even national security.

Future critical analysis of public order drones and drone proliferation in civil airspace must take account of this expanding narrative, and explore what happens to the idea of the responsible drone when the narrative of the public order drone incorporates the assignment of blame, efforts to educate, the allocation of liability, and a greater focus on responsible innovation. It will also be important to track resistance to the public order drone, in two senses: first, with regard to the question of whose order, exactly, public order drones uphold; second, with regard to the ways in which drones can "turn back the gaze" and enable activists to monitor public order policing.

Notes

1 The chapter builds on the author's engagement with the drone industry, academia, civil society, and the public; media reports and scholarly literature; and, more generally, on criminological discussions of paramilitary policing and public order.
2 As used here, "drone industry" refers mainly to US-based military manufacturers, but also to (1) established Israeli and European military manufacturers and (2) start-up manufacturers in the United States and elsewhere.
3 In fact, a public order drone can also be a MALE (medium-altitude, long-endurance) drone, like the Predator, or a nanodrone, like the Black Hornet, which can fit into the palm of a hand.
4 See, for example, El-Hasan (2013); for a critique of wildly inflated claims on economic benefits, see Doward (2015).
5 The military's interest in drone terminology comes from a desire to ensure that drones are seen as ethical weapons and logistics platforms. And military contractors are naturally interested in expanding sales to nonmilitary customers.

6 See, for example, Kraska (2007); Balko (2013); Salter (2014); Harwood (2014); Holmqvist (2014); and Li (2014); also see Neocleous critique of the paramilitarization scholarship (2014).
7 As understood here, the notion of "endless possibility" is distinct from the concerns about "function creep" often expressed by surveillance scholars.
8 For a more detailed discussion of the weaponization of police drones, see Sandvik (2015).
9 Examples of such systems include geofencing and built-in restrictions on where drones can fly.
10 Steve Roest, personal communication, November 6, 2014.

References

Aamot, Doug (2014) "Recently in Controversy: Drone Can Tase People with 80,000 Volts," March 10. Available at: http://time.com/19076/recently-in-controversy-drone-can-tase-people-with-80000-volts/ (Accessed April 10, 2016).
AeroVironment (2011) YouTube, November 3. Available at: www.youtube.com/watch?v=ZzHx7AxHmOA (Accessed April 10, 2016).
Bachmann, Jan (2014) Policing Africa: The US military and visions of crafting "good order." *Security Dialogue*, 45 (2): 119–136.
Balko, Radley (2013) Rise of the warrior cop: The militarization of America's police forces. *Public Affairs*.
BBC (2011) "Police Drone Crashes Into River Mersey," October 31. Available at: www.bbc.com/news/uk-england-merseyside-15520279 (Accessed April 10, 2016).
BBC (2014) Available at: www.bbc.com/news/uk-england-london-30446136 (Accessed April 10, 2016).
Birmingham Policy Commission (2014) "The Security Impact of Drones: Challenges and Opportunities for the UK." Available at: www.birmingham.ac.uk/Documents/research/policycommission/remote-warfare/final-report-october-2014.pdf (Accessed April 10, 2016).
Bohman, Dave (2014) "Drone, Helicopter In Near Midair Collision," December 5. Available at: http://wnep.com/2014/12/05/drone-helicopter-in-near-midair-collision/ (Accessed April 10, 2016).
Borges, Andre (2014) "Drones to Patrol Delhi After Alleged Uber Rape," December 11. Available at: www.buzzfeed.com/andreborges/drones-to-patrol-delhi-after-alleged-uber-assault (Accessed April 10, 2016).
Boucher, Phillip (2014) Domesticating the drone: The demilitarisation of unmanned aircraft for civil markets. *Science and Engineering Ethics*, 1–20.
Bowman, John (2014) "Ontario Police Defend Use of Drone Cameras Over Protests," *CBC News*. March 5. Available at: www.cbc.ca/newsblogs/yourcommunity/2014/03/ontario-police-defend-use-of-drone-cameras-over-protests.html (Accessed April 10, 2016).
Brustein, Joshua (2013) "Dear FBI: Keep Guns Off Your Drones, Please. Yours, Congress," July 2, 2013, *Business Week*. Available at: www.businessweek.com/articles/2013-07-02/dear-fbi-keep-guns-off-yourdrones-yours-congress#r=rss (Accessed April 10, 2016).
CBS (2012) "Is The NYPD Experimenting With Drones Over The City? Evidence Points To Yes," January 23. Available at: http://newyork.cbslocal.com/2012/01/23/is-the-nypd-experimenting-with-drones-over-the-city-evidence-points-to-yes/ (Accessed April 10, 2016).

CBS (2013) "Drones: Eyes in the Sky," May 16. Available at: www.cbsnews.com/news/drones-eyes-in-the-sky/ (Accessed April 10, 2016).

Ceballos, Ana (2014) "Santa Bring a Drone? Here's a Few Tips," December 26. Available at: www.montereyherald.com/technology/20141226/santa-bring-a-drone-heres-a-few-tips (Accessed April 10, 2016).

Cenciotti, David (2014) "Italian Police and Military Police Can Use Italian Air Force Predator Drones for a Wide Variety of Missions," November 30. Available at: http://theaviationist.com/2014/11/30/italian-air-force-predators-police-support/ (Accessed April 10, 2016).

Cho, Yeonmin (2014) Lost in debate: The safety of domestic unmanned aircraft systems. *Journal of Strategic Security*, 7.

Chrisafis, Angelique (2015) "French Police Investigate Mystery Drone Flights Over Central Paris," February 26. Available at: www.theguardian.com/world/2015/feb/26/french-police-investigate-drone-flights-central-paris (Accessed April 10, 2016).

Conditt, Scott (2014) "Eye in the Sky: Modern UAVs For Reconnaissance," December 31. Available at: www.tactical-life.com/gear/eye-sky-moden-uavs-reconnaissance-2/#uav-gwle-dec-2014-draganfly-x-6 (Accessed April 10, 2016).

Crang, Mike and Stephen Graham (2007) Sentient cities: Ambient intelligence and the politics of urban space. *Information. Communication and Society*, 10 (6): 789–817.

Culver, Kathleen B. (2014) From battlefield to newsroom: Ethical implications of drone technology in journalism. *Journal of Mass Media Ethics*, 29 (1): 52–64.

De Lint, Willem (2005) Public order policing: A tough act to follow? *International Journal of the Sociology of Law*, 33 (4): 179–199.

Della Porta, Donnatella and Herbert Reiter (2006) The Policing of Global Protest. The G8 at Genoa and its Aftermath, in Donnatella Della Porta, Abby Peterson, and Herbert Reiter (eds.), *The Policing of Transnational Protest*, Aldershot: Ashgate, 2006, pp. 13–41.

Doward, Jamie (2015) "Delivering Pizza, Making Films … Now Safety Fears Grow Over Use of Drones," February 15. Available at: www.theguardian.com/world/2015/feb/15/drones-safety-fears-grow-privacy-pizza-films (Accessed April 10, 2016).

Drone Wars UK (2014) "Back From the Battlefield: Domestic Drones in the UK." Available at: https://dronewarsuk.files.wordpress.com/2014/05/domestic-drones-in-the-uk-final.pdf (Accessed April 10, 2016).

Edwards, Te (2014) "Students Build 3D Printed Search and Rescue Device for L.A. County Fire Department," December 26. https://3dprint.com/32642/student-search-and-rescue/ (Accessed 10 April 2016).

El-Hasan, Muhammed (2013) "Businesses See Opportunity in Civilian Drones, But Regulations Stand in the Way," Los Angeles News Group, June 23. Available at: www.dailyfreeman.com/general-news/20130623/businesses-see-opportunity-in-civilian-drones-but-regulations-stand-in-the-way (Accessed April 10, 2016).

Epema, Kitso (2014) "Drones for Good: Save the Rhino," Program, Unmanned Systems Expo 2015, December 21. Available at: http://tusexpo.com/conference/conference-programme/ (Accessed April 10, 2016).

Finn, Rachel L. and David Wright (2012) Unmanned aircraft systems: Surveillance, ethics and privacy in civil applications. *Computer Law & Security Review*, 28 (2): 184–194.

Finn, Rachel L., David Wright, Anna Donovan, Laura Jacques, and Paul De Hert (2014) "Study on privacy, data protection and ethical risks in civil Remotely Piloted Aircraft Systems operations," Final Report "D3.3: Final report for the European Commission."

Fisher, David (2013) "Police Use Drones to Catch Criminals," March 2. Available at: www.nzherald.co.nz/nz/news/article.cfm?c_id=1&objectid=10868674 (Accessed April 10, 2016).

Fox News (2014) "Predator Drone Helps Convict North Dakota Farmer in First Case of its Kind," January 28. Available at: www.foxnews.com/us/2014/01/28/first-american-gets-prison-with-assistance-predator-drone/ (Accessed April 10, 2016).

Franceschi-Bicchierai, Lorenzo (2012) "Russia is Stockpiling Drones to Spy on Street Protests," July 25. Available at: www.wired.com/2012/07/russia-2/ (Accessed April 10, 2016).

French National Research Agency (2014) "Call for Proposals Flash Drone: 'Protection of Sensitive Sites from Aerial Drones.'" Available at: www.agence-nationale-recherche.fr/en/funding-opportunities/current-calls/aap-en/call-for-proposals-flash-drone-protection-of-sensitive-sites-from-aerial-drones-2015/nc/ (Accessed April 10, 2016).

Friedenzohn, Daniel and Alexander Mirot (2014) The fear of drones: Privacy and unmanned aircraft. *The Journal of Law Enforcement*, 3 (5).

Graham, Steve (2010a) "From Helmand to Merseyside: Unmanned Drones and the Militarisation of UK Policing," September 27. Available at: www.opendemocracy.net/ourkingdom/steve-graham/from-helmand-to-merseyside-military-style-drones-enter-uk-domestic-policing (Accessed April 10, 2016).

(2010b) *Cities Under Siege: The New Military Urbanism*, London: Verso Books.

Greene, Andrew (2014) "AFP Using Drones to Investigate Major Crime as Questions Raised Over Privacy", March 1. Available at: www.abc.net.au/news/2014-03-01/afp-using-drones-tosolve-crime/5292096 (Accessed April 10, 2016).

Hall, Abigail R. and Christopher J. Coyne (2013) The militarization of US domestic policing. *Independent Review*, 17 (4): 485–504.

Hall, Abigail R. and Christopher J. Coyne (2014) The political economy of drones. *Defence and Peace Economics*, 25 (5): 445–460.

Harwood, Matthew (2014) "One Nation Under SWAT," August 14. Available at: www.tomdispatch.com/post/175881/tomgram%3A_matthew_harwood%2C_one_nation_under_swat/ (Accessed April 10, 2016).

Hayes, Ben, Chris Jones, and Eric Töpfer (2014) *"Eurodrones Inc."* London: Transnational Institute and Statewatch.

Hern, Alex (2014) "Got a Personal Drone for Christmas? Use with Caution," December 25, www.theguardian.com/technology/2014/dec/25/personal-drone-christmas-privacy-rules-hazards.

Holmqvist, Caroline (2014) *Policing Wars: On Military Intervention in the Twenty-first Century*. Houndsmill, Basingstoke: Palgrave Macmillan.

IHP (Increasing Human Potential) (n.d.) "Enhancing Public Safety." Available at: http://increasinghumanpotential.org/benefits-of-technology/enhancing-public-safety/ (Accessed April 10, 2016).

KESQ (2013) "Drone Technology Could Be Coming To A Police Department Near You," February 13. Available at: www.kesq.com/kesq/Drone-technology-could-be-coming-to-a-Police-Department-near-you/19098288 (Accessed April 10, 2016).

Kington, Tom (2014) "Italian Reaper Drones To Be Used For Crowd Monitoring," December 17. Available at: www.defensenews.com/story/defense/international/europe/2014/12/17/italian-reaper-drones-to-be-used-for-crowd-monitoring/20528495/ (Accessed April 10, 2016).

Know Before You Fly (2014) Available at: http://knowbeforeyoufly.org/2014/12/auvsi-ama-small-uav-coalition-and-faa-launch-know-before-you-fly-campaign/ (Accessed April 10, 2016).

Kraska, Peter B. (2007) Militarization and policing: Its relevance to 21st century police. *Policing*, 1 (4): 501–513.

Kumparak, Greg (2014) "The Drone That Could Save You From Drowning," December 26. Available at: http://techcrunch.com/2014/12/26/the-drone-that-could-save-you-from-drowning/ (Accessed April 10, 2016).

Kindynis, Theo (2012) "Contours of Control, Eyes in the Sky: The Rise of the Police Drones. Ceasefire," October 14. Available at: http://ceasefiremagazine.co.uk/eye-sky-primer-police-drones/ (Accessed April 10, 2016).

Lemanski, Charlotte (2004) A new apartheid? The spatial implications of fear of crime in Cape Town, South Africa. *Environment and Urbanization*, 16 (2): 101–112.

Li, Shirley (2014). "The Evolution of Police Militarization in Ferguson and Beyond," August 15. Available at: www.thewire.com/national/2014/08/the-evolution-of-police-militarization-in-fergusonand-beyond/376107/ (Accessed April 10, 2016).

Malcolm, Bob (2013) "Police Surveillance Drones Coming to a Sky Near You," April 18. Available at: www.belfasttelegraph.co.uk/community-telegraph/east-belfast/police-surveillance-drones-coming-to-a-sky-near-you-29204839.html (Accessed April 10, 2016).

Matishak, Martin (2014) "FAA Chief: Threat of Drone, Airplane Collisions a 'Serious Concern,'" November 30. Available at: http://thehill.com/policy/transportation/225528-faa-chief-threat-of-drone-airplane-collisions-a-serious-concern (Accessed April 10, 2016).

McLeod, Paul (2014) "Nova Scotia RCMP To Get Drones," January 2. Available at: http://thechronicleherald.ca/novascotia/1177077-nova-scotia-rcmp-to-get-drones (Accessed April 10, 2016).

McNeal, Gregory (2013) "Just Call it a Drone," March 2. Available at: www.forbes.com/sites/gregorymcneal/2013/03/02/just-call-it-a-drone/ (Accessed April 10, 2016).

McNeal, Gregory (2014a) "Senator Feinstein Now Using Safety Concerns To Target The Drone Industry," December 3. Available at: www.forbes.com/sites/gregorymcneal/2014/12/03/senator-feinstein-now-using-safety-concerns-to-target-the-drone-industry/ (Accessed April 10, 2016).

McNeal, Gregory (2014b) "Alleged 'Near-Collision' Between Drone And Helicopter Caught On Video, But Questions Linger," July 17. Available at: www.forbes.com/sites/gregorymcneal/2014/07/17/alleged-near-collision-between-drone-and-helicopter-caught-on-video-but-questions-linger/ (Accessed April 10, 2016).

Monahan, Torin and Jennifer T. Mokos (2013) Crowdsourcing urban surveillance: The development of homeland security markets for environmental sensor networks. *Geoforum*, 49: 279–288.

Murphy, Douglas W. and James Cycon (1999) "Applications for Mini VTOL UAV For Law Enforcement," *Enabling Technologies for Law Enforcement and Security*. International Society for Optics and Photonics. Available at: www.dtic.mil/dtic/tr/fulltext/u2/a422459.pdf (Accessed April 10, 2016).

Neocleous, Mark (2014). *War Power*, Edinburgh: Edinburgh University Press.

Palmer, Darren and Ian Warren (2014) The pursuit of exclusion through zonal banning. *Australian & New Zealand Journal of Criminology*, 47: 429–446.

Pilkington, Ed (2014a) "What's Keeping America's Private Drone Industry Grounded?" September 30. Available at: www.theguardian.com/world/2014/sep/29/drone-testers-faa-aviation-frustration-grows (Accessed April 10, 2016).

Pilkington, Ed (2014b) "'We See Ourselves as the Vanguard': The Police Force Using Drones to Fight Crime," October 1. Available at: www.theguardian.com/world/2014/oct/01/drones-police-force-crime-uavs-north-dakota (Accessed April 10, 2016).

Presutti, Carolyn (2014) "Drones at Work Worldwide, but US Still Lacks Laws," February 25. Available at: www.voanews.com/content/drones-at-work-worldwide-but-us-still-lacks-laws/1859180.html (Accessed April 10, 2016).

Randerson, James (2007) "Eye in the Sky: Police Use Drone to Spy on V Festival," August 21. Available at: www.theguardian.com/uk/2007/aug/21/ukcrime.musicnews (Accessed April 10, 2016).

Reilly, Claire (2014a) "Man Fined For Crashing Drone Over Police Operation in Melbourne," December 19. Available at: www.cnet.com/au/news/man-fined-by-casa-crashing-drone-police-operation-melbourne/ (Accessed April 10, 2016).

Reilly, Claire (2014b) "Rural Fire Service Calls to Ban Drones From Bushfire Areas," November 11. Available at: www.cnet.com/au/news/calls-to-ban-drones-from-bushfire-areas-over-safety-concerns/ (Accessed April 10, 2016).

Rieland, Randy (2012) "Drawing the Line on Drones," October 15. Available at: www.smithsonianmag.com/innovation/drawing-the-line-on-drones-72749356/?no-ist= (Accessed April 10, 2016).

Robbins, Seth (2013) "Colombia Develops UAV Technology to Fight Drugs, Rebels, Illegal Mining," January 8. Available at: http://dialogo-americas.com/en_GB/articles/rmisa/features/regional_news/2013/08/01/colombia-drones (Accessed April 10, 2016).

Salter, Michael (2014) Toys for the boys? Drones, pleasure and popular culture in the militarisation of policing. *Critical Criminology*, 22 (2): 167–177.

Sandvik, Kristin B. (2015) "The Political and Moral Economies of Dual Technology Transfers: Arming Police Drones," in Ales Završnik (ed.), *Drones and Unmanned Aerial Systems: Legal and Social Implications for Security and Surveillance*," New York: Springer.

Sandvik, Kristin B. and Kjersti Lohne (2014) The rise of the humanitarian drone: Giving content to an emerging concept. *Millennium: Journal of International Studies*, 43 (1): 145–164.

Segar, Mike (2014) "'Reckless or Malicious' Civilian Drone Use 'Harassing' Public – Police," November 18. Available at: http://rt.com/uk/206547-drones-public-use-nuisance/ (Accessed April 10, 2016).

Smith, D. (20 June 2014). "Pepper-Spray Drone Offered to South African Mines for Strike Control," *The Guardian*. Available at: www.theguardian.com/world/2014/jun/20/pepper-spray-drone-offeredsouth-african-mines-strike-control (Accessed September 30, 2014).

Thalen, Mikael (2013) "Drone Lobbyist Makes Shocking Comment About 'Indiscriminate Killing' policy," February 22, Examiner.com.

The Hague Security Delta (2014) "Winners SBIR Call for Innovative Security Solutions Against Mobile Unmanned Systems Announced," November 14. Available at: www.thehaguesecuritydelta.com/news/newsitem/257 (Accessed April 10, 2016).

The Press Project (2014) "Is Greece to Lead the Way for Europe in the Use of Drones for Domestic Policing and Surveillance?" June 23. Available at: www.thepressproject. net/article/64356/Is-Greece-to-lead-the-way-for-Europe-in-the-use-of-drones-for-domestic-policing-and-surveillance (Accessed April 10, 2016).

UAVS (2014) Available at: www.uavs.org/aboutuavs, "with an active interest in UAVs [unmanned aerial vehicles] and the development of opportunities to use these systems on a routine basis for the overall benefit of mankind." (Accessed April 10, 2016).

UAVS (2015) Available at: www.uavs.org/aboutuavs (Accessed April 10, 2016).

Vijayan, Jaikumar (2012) "Drone Industry's Code of Conduct Disappoints," July 12. Available at: www.computerworld.com/article/2472278/data-privacy/drone-industry-s-code-of-conduct-disappoints.html (Accessed April 10, 2016).

Viydo, Taylor and KREM Staff (2014) "ISP Using Drone to Take Crime Scene Pics," December 5. Available at: www.ktvb.com/story/news/crime/2014/12/05/isp-using-drone-to-take-crime-scene-pics/19955727/ (Accessed April 10, 2016).

Waddington, Peter A.J. (2000) Public order policing: Citizenship and moral ambiguity. *Core Issues in Policing*, 2: 156–175.

Waddington, Peter A.J. (2007) Policing of public order. *Policing*, 1 (4): 375–377.

Wall, Tyler and Torin Monahan (2011) Surveillance and violence from afar: The politics of drones and liminal security-scapes. *Theoretical Criminology*, 15 (3): 239–254.

Waterfield, Bruno (2014) "EU 'Spent £320 Million on Surveillance Drone Development,'" February 12. Available at: www.telegraph.co.uk/news/worldnews/europe/eu/10632262/EU-spent-320-million-on-surveillance-drone-development. html (Accessed April 10, 2016).

WDTN (2014) "Drone Delays Medical Helicopter Landing at OH Hospital," August 27. Available at: www.12newsnow.com/story/26385252/drone-delays-medical-helicopter-landing-at-oh-hospital (Accessed April 10, 2016).

Whitlock, Craig (2014a) "When Drones Fall From The Sky," June 20. Available at: www.washingtonpost.com/sf/investigative/2014/06/20/when-drones-fall-from-the-sky/ (Accessed April 10, 2016).

Whitlock, Craig (2014b) "Near Mid-Air Collisions With Drones, Airliners Surge, According to New FFA Report," November 26. Available at: www.washingtonpost. com/world/national-security/near-collisions-between-drones-airliners-surge-new-faa-reports-show/2014/11/26/9a8c1716-758c-11e4-bd1b-03009bd3e984_story.html (Accessed April 10, 2016).

Whittle, Richard (2014) "Drone Defender Drops D-word Denial," December 23. Available at: http://breakingdefense.com/2014/12/drone-defender-drops-d-word-denial/ (Accessed April 10, 2016).

Wilcox, Lauren B. (2015) *Bodies of Violence: Theorizing Embodied Subjects in International Relations*, Oxford: Oxford University Press.

Wolverton, Joe (2012) "Drone Group Drafts Code of Conduct Citing Public Relations Problem. New American," July 3. Available at: www.thenewamerican.com/usnews/item/11948-drone-group-drafts-code-of-conduct-citing-public-relations-problem (Accessed April 10, 2016).

Wolverton, Joe (2013) "Why Is Homeland Security Taking Control of Local Police?" *New American*, December 7. Available at: www.thenewamerican.com/usnews/item/17110-why-is-homeland-security-taking-control-of-local-police (Accessed April 10, 2016).

6 A revolution in agricultural affairs
Dronoculture, precision, capital

Brad Bolman

Introduction

There were more than two hundred news articles published between October and November of 2014 about the potential of agricultural drones.[1] The rhetorical economy of these pieces is well developed: each discusses enthusiastically the appearance of "cutting-edge and exciting" (Faria 2014) devices imported from another sphere – for instance, "Once strictly a military machine" (Associated Press 2014) – onto farms across the United States where they promise to be the "next big thing" (Yamanouchi 2014) in agricultural innovation. Even a cursory search confirms the remarkable consistency of these tropes. Jumping back five years, we find an almost identical constellation of think pieces on agricultural drones: a 2009 *Wired* article claimed, for instance, "Future Farming Is (Finally) Now" (Madrigal 2009). The future, in all of these pieces, is droned. Yet before 2007, beyond a scattered few studies of UAVs in precision farming, there was no public discussion of this particular "future farming." The future was not yet in sight. Though we have apparently not yet reached *Wired's now*, something seems to have changed quite dramatically in the relationship between this military import and the forecasted transformations of American agriculture.

The term "drone," a recently popularized nickname for unmanned aerial vehicles (UAVs), suffers a great degree of definitional elasticity: a drone can be a tiny hover vehicle purchased on Amazon.com or a billion dollar military aircraft fitted out with cutting edge weapons systems. Yet in the prevailing public imaginary, drones remain tied to their military usage, unmanning the front lines of America's "Overseas Contingency Operations." Recently, in a spate of academic articles on the growing "Predator Empire" (see Shaw 2013) and the numerous projects to count the causalities of America's "Drone War,"[2] drones, which once promised to remove American casualties from warfare, have become *bad*, horrifying but necessary tools of a shy imperial power. In turn, critics have lined up to proffer analyses of the changing face of "future warfare." In every context, drones announce the future, perhaps also the delayed success of Donald Rumsfeld's failed "Revolution in Military Affairs." And yet alongside this noisy chorus, another discourse on drones has appeared, one in which the drone becomes *good* again, a kind of fantasy object, the solution to problems as varied as firefighting, filmmaking, and agriculture. "There are good uses for drones, I'm not saying there's not, but we need to get a handle on it," noted Gilbert Landolt, president of the Des Moines Veterans for Peace chapter and an anti-drone organizer (Doering 2014). "The good drone," an object of curiosity and confusion, sits awkwardly along an imagined continuum between "military" and "peaceful" technology, "war" and "economy," swords and plowshares. Faced with the importation of "drones" from battlefields to cornfields, we want, intuitively – how could we not? – to applaud the arrival of the good drone, the *best* drone, even, one of the least objectionable in the sky: the agricultural drone, promising a domestication of violent Wasps, Gnats, Predators, and Global Hawks – the transspecies bestiary that comprises the United States drone force. Many yearn for a rehabilitated reaper. Particularly in America, unmanned agricultural flying machines have been endowed with great expectations and equally great reservations. The agricultural drone promises to save, even revolutionize, small farming – and all farming, if the drone "industry" has its way.

The aim of the present chapter is to analyze the paradoxical status of the agricultural drone: its possibilities and faults, promises and disavowals. While discourses surrounding its emergence promise a revolution for farms and farmers, the agricultural drone also raises alarming new possibilities of unequal capital accumulation and land dispossession. My use of the singular – *the* agricultural drone, not *some* agricultural drones – aims to draw the reader's attention to the two registers in which drones operate: in the skies and in the mind. As a historian and anthropologist, here I will combine a return to the archives, a search for drone origins, with speculation about what the long-prophesized drone future may be. Because agricultural drones remain (despite the profusion of media attention) under-studied and misunderstood, this chapter seeks to outline the question concerning agro-drone technology and offer avenues for further research.

I begin with the basics: What *are* agricultural drones? How is the market structured and what models currently exist? I will then briefly analyze the paucity of literature on agricultural drones. These devices, made to conduct "dull, dangerous and dirty jobs" have been, in the agricultural context, so dull and dirty that the attention given to the sexier topic of drones on the battlefield has *not* been paralleled for farming drones. Contrary to many present perspectives, agricultural drones were not always an inevitable development in the Hegelian march to farming perfection. Instead, drones were progressively normalized, eventually understood to be devices that are *useful* and *necessary* for farming. In the second section, I will focus on the predictions of an early "drone expert" in order to demonstrate the existence of *civilian* drones as a critical counterpart to their military siblings. In the third section, I will explore the intersections between precision *agriculture* and precision *targeting*, between the new normal of ag-drones and the old implausibility of flying data gatherers. The transformations that have made drones not simply palatable but deeply *desirable* mirror, in significant ways, the reasons that drones have found such a welcome niche in the arsenals of global militaries. Crucial in all of this is the role of capital: agricultural drones emerged from global trade, military development, and technological transformations in farming. With this in mind, I will offer a few precise – for precision is always *the* question or *in* question – implications of globalized drone farming for historical processes of land acquisition and enclosure. Finally, I will put forth suggestions for further scholarship on global drone farming.

The new drones

Viviane Faria, an analyst at Agri-Trend, a farm consulting firm that claims to "help farmers allocate scarce resources to produce a safe, reliable and profitable food supply in an environmentally sustainable manner," (Agri-Trend 2014) notes that drones are "One of the hottest new areas in precision agriculture" and "not just for [their] 'boys and their toys' appeal" (Faria 2014). "Growers," she writes, "are already using information coming from drones for drought management, disease detection, irrigation and pesticide application." It is worth noting that, despite frequently inflated rhetoric about their myriad possibilities, agricultural drones are predominantly *information* gathering and producing machines. A flood of data is driving the drone boom and a deficit of precision measurements is made out to be the reason for the failures of farming. Despite, or perhaps because of this, picking the right drone and getting the best deal remains difficult: "Solid, unbiased reviews remain scant," and prospective buyers need to understand complex technical issues like "sensor spectrum range, spatial resolution, noise correction during the flight time," as well as having a predetermined "methodology for [their] analysis" (ibid.). Faria lays out the three kinds of information that farm UAVs can provide:

1. Aerial imagery, which reveals patterns in the field caused by anything from irrigation problems to soil variation to nutrient deficiencies. It can even spot pest infestations that aren't always obvious at field level.
2. Multispectral images taken by onboard cameras capture data from the infrared as well as the visual spectrum, highlighting differences between healthy and distressed plants in a way that can't be seen with the naked eye.
3. Time lapsed images, in which a drone can survey a crop every week, every day or even every hour. These combined images create an animation that can reveal changes in the crop, highlighting trouble spots or opportunities for better crop management (ibid.).

The drone advantage comes from a new *gaze*,[3] which in the agricultural context can be broken down in three ways: first and foremost, a new view *from above* that can reveal otherwise invisible deficiencies in one's agricultural planning; second, a capacity to see a farm thermographically or in spectra otherwise unavailable to the human eye; and third, by extending the temporal viewing capacity of the human eye. What is worth stressing is that seeing fields "from above" is not, in itself, a novel experience in agriculture: UAVs are not only a replacement for human perception but are considered more manageable and customizable than the satellite imaging or manned vehicles farmers have employed for decades.

The drones being discussed in agricultural contexts are really an assemblage of two components that are frequently blurred: a *sensor* (or camera) and a *platform* (or frame). The camera, Faria stresses, will determine what one can get out of their drone. She recommends multispectrum cameras – for one, the Tetracam Mini MCA (Tetracam Inc. 2014) – or hyper-spectrum cameras, which divide the three light bands visible to the human eye (Red, Green, Blue) into many more bands (Shippert 2003), like the Rikola Hyperspectral Camera (Rikola Ltd. 2014), combined with LiDAR scanning technology.[4] Faria and others draw a distinction between intermediate-level buyers (in essence, tech-interested novices) and those trying to produce "more advanced studies" who might benefit from the most complex forms of airborne imaging. After the camera comes the question of which platform is best for a specific imaging task, and this in turn opens onto two subcategories: rotary wing and fixed wing UAVs. Even though the hulking image of the flying drone plane prevails in the broader cultural imagination, the platform or frame of the drone is, in large part, determined by the camera or sensor one purchases and whether the platform can carry that payload. The lowest possible tier of drones includes those readily available on consumer shopping websites like Amazon, ranging in the hundreds of dollars. The second tier, Faria writes, "include eBee – SenseFly, X4ES – DraganFly, AgDrone – HoneyComb and PaceSetter – Precision Drone." The PrecisionHawk Lancaster platform can carry a 2.2 pound payload. "Priced at US$10,000 to US$30,000, these models represent options for those who want to buy a drone without making a significant investment" (Faria 2014). At the highest level, for those who *do* want to make a significant investment – from $50 to $72,000 dollars – are the "Aibotix X6, Accuas Fixed Wing, ING Robotic Responder and AutoCopter G15" (ibid.). The final step before you are "ready to fly" is acquiring image-processing software, which Faria places between $2,800 and $6,000.

But how many of these devices are currently in the air? Media reports on the rapid take-up of drones emphasize the extent to which farmers are already flying drones on farms all across America. How accurate is this picture? Firm statistics are difficult to come by in part because of one major stumbling block to large-scale drone farming: currently, the FAA bans commercial use of drones in United States airspace and a November 2014 decision by the National Transportation Safety Board confirmed their regulatory powers (Isidore 2014). Federal Aviation Administration restrictions on drone licenses are covered in nearly every article published over the last few years about agricultural drones. One sign of how contentious the debates over drone restrictions have become, or perhaps of how much money and influence is being placed on legalizing drone flight, is a page on the FAA website titled, "Busting Myths About the FAA and Unmanned Aircraft." There, in response to "Myth #6: The FAA is lagging behind other countries in approving commercial drones," we read the following:

> Developing all the rules and standards we need is a very complex task, and we want to make sure we get it right the first time. We want to strike the right balance of requirements for UAS to help foster growth in an emerging industry with a wide range of potential uses, but also keep all airspace users and people on the ground safe.
>
> (Federal Aviation Administration 2014)

The FAA must carefully dance between the economic agents pushing for looser regulations and a post-9/11 atmosphere of American security that mandates serious and enforceable control of civilian airspace. One way of interpreting this mythbusting act is to say that the FAA is simply trying to reassure a public, greedy for unmanned aircraft, that change is on the way. As John Goglia, a technology journalist for *Forbes*, writes, "sometimes the genie" – which here is drones, of course – "just can't be put back in the bottle" (Goglia 2014). The FAA's original estimate from 2011 was for 10,000 drones in the air in the next five years with 30,000 by 2030 (Schoffstall 2013). Those estimates have since been revised, and the newest estimate is 7,500 small UAV devices littering the skies by 2018. A significant chunk of those drones are predicted to be performing agricultural tasks. This drone arithmetic is a sign of both the operational difficulties under the current regulatory environment and the frequently exaggerated drone proliferation on the part of many supporters. The original deadline for the FAA's legal guidelines was September 2015, but lawmakers have already been warned that progress has been slower than expected (Dillow 2014).

Despite all the restrictions, farmers *are* flying drones, a fact attested to by multiple near-collisions between UAVs and small passenger aircraft (Henn 2014). According to Kevin Price, a former Kansas State professor who now works for drone retailer RoboFlight, "In the next 10 years almost every farm will be using" drone technologies in one way or another (Doering 2014). And yet, despite this, very few authors have attempted to analyze the movement of drones "from the battlefield to the farmer's field" (ibid.). Unmanned aerial vehicles in agriculture have obviously not gone uncommented upon, but the vast majority of publications fall into one of two camps: the aforementioned media pieces on the future of farming with drones which verge, all too often, into the zone of outright propaganda and, on the other hand, a set of articles in technical and scientific journals detailing new imaging techniques and the success of UAV pilot projects.[5] While many of these scholars have weighed in on the possibilities of unmanned agriculture, the conclusions presented are significantly more tempered than those of their media counterparts: no forecasts of revolutions, transformations or paradigm shifts in farming. In their place are statements like this one from a recent literature review by Chunhua Zhang and John M. Kovacs, two academic geographers in Canada: "[T]here are still many significant shortcomings related to UAS [Unmanned Aircraft Systems] remote sensing including high initial costs, platform reliability, sensor capability, and lack of standardized procedure to process large volumes of data … if UAS aviation regulations could be relaxed and research scientists be more engaged with the farming community a greater adoption of UAS in [Precision Agriculture] may occur" (Zhang and Kovacs 2012: 706). Research interest in drones spans engineering journals, agricultural publications, and numerous international conferences over the last decade, but social scientists and historians have let farming drones slip almost entirely from view. And yet from Australia to Finland, Brazil to the United States, there is intense interest in converting the emerging field of drone agriculture into an area of national expertise. Though there are nationally specific economic analyses, one element of these publications remains relatively unchanged. When authors sketch out a history of agricultural drones, they invariably look to the same nation: Japan. Before explaining why, I want to follow drones backward a little, to a time when they were not only *not* inevitable in agriculture, but not even particularly interesting. How did this inevitability become normalized? We have to turn to a relatively unknown NATO-sponsored conference to understand.

From the battlefield to the cornfield: drone normalization

In an unclassified paper, "UAVs – Current Situation and Considerations for the Way Forward," presented in Belgium at the 1999 NATO Research and Technology Organization conference on "Development and Operation of UAVs for Military and Civil Applications," Peter van Blyenburgh, long-time president of Unmanned Vehicles Systems International and an early "drone expert," addressed "the current situation pertaining to unmanned aerial vehicles (UAV) systems" in order "to give some indications on what the future may have in store for us" (van Blyenburgh 1999: 2). Van Blyenburgh's presentation was an impressionistic account of the global drone industry, seeking to cover everything from the sizes of drones, their changing costs, utility in a wide variety of fields, and more. "At the onset," he noted, "it is considered worthwhile to try to define what is meant by the term UAV, therewith hopefully avoiding any misunderstandings" (ibid.). That members of the "Applied Vehicle Technologies" panel still needed terminological clarification about UAVs in 1999 demonstrates that less than two decades ago, there was serious uncertainty about the ontology of unmanned vehicles, about what these new objects *were*. Van Blyenburgh's definition was wide-ranging:

UAVs are to be understood as uninhabited and reuseable motorized aerial vehicles, which are remotely controlled, semi-autonomous, autonomous, or have a combination of these capabilities, and that can carry various types of payloads, making them capable of performing specific tasks within the earth's atmosphere, or beyond, for a duration, which is related to their missions.

(Ibid.)

Beyond their aerial and unmanned nature, very little connects the uses and functions of the devices under his umbrella – everything from lethal aerial vehicles to aerial decoys to agricultural machines. The definitional elasticity created a further problem because "the separation line with cruise missiles is not really clear." This distinction, however, was crucial to distinguishing a more lethal and decidedly militaristic technology from the "UAV," which promised to be something different. Despite this promise, "funding for the development of UAVs" at the time of van Blyenburgh's report had been largely "put up by the military," and he expected this "to remain so for the foreseeable future," even though their complementarity with other weapons systems had been generally disputed or ignored by those in the "military hierarchy and the political establishment" (ibid.).

By the time of this report, UAVs had already proven themselves in combat situations: they appeared during the Gulf War both as tactical UAVs (produced by Exdrona, Pointer, Pioneer – all American companies – and Mart of France) and tactical decoys (Chukar and TALD, both American)[6] (van Blyenburgh 1999: 2); they provided reconnaissance during the conflict in Bosnia and Kosovo; and were beginning to take shape as the future of military affairs for many defense contractors and planners. Whereas original UAVs were envisioned as multi-task operating systems, the tendency in the late 1990s and early 2000s was "to develop UAVs directed at fulfilling specific missions" (van Blyenburgh 1999: 3): "modular" UAVs, in other words, that could do anything from airborne mine detection, urban warfare, surveillance, to helicopter flight path reconnaissance. And while the military side of the equation was growing, van Blyenburgh was sure to note that "UAVs are [also] being used for an ever-growing number of civilian applications." The civilian market was critical, he wrote, because large-scale production and purchasing in multiple industries could produce economies of scale and further capital to invest in innovation. Of the present civilian applications, the first and foremost was the "extremely active" Japanese use of UAVs for "crop spraying, fertilizing and seading [sic] purposes," and a parallel market for such devices in South Korea. In the early 1990s, then, there was a split in the trajectory for the UAV: for America and its allies, it would become sword and surveillance; in Japan and South Korea, it would assist in the fields. If the majority of UAV development had come from war, whence this agricultural drone?

In 1989, Noboru Kawamura and Kiyoshi Namikawa, Agricultural Engineering faculty at Kyoto University, authored an article titled "Robots in agriculture" that sought to outline the vast benefits of autonomous farm machinery for Japanese farming. "Considering the principal food crops," they note, "the ratio of labour costs and agricultural machine costs to the total production costs is high," and even a tremendously expensive machine could create substantial cost savings. Their solution was "robots" or "unmanned farm machinery" (Kawamura and Namikawa 1988: 311) that could utilize new visualization and mechanization technologies, potentially resolving the manpower problem and decreasing overall costs in one fell stroke. Their paper, which focused primarily on machines that could automate the picking of fruit – a relatively trivial task because oranges contrast well with the surrounding foliage and thus provide little real engineering challenge – emerged out of a conference, the "First International Conference on Robotics and Intelligent Machines in Agriculture," in Tampa, Florida, in 1983. The party line of this conference was a relatively predictable one: robots are here, more are coming, and we – agricultural engineers – have to adapt agricultural labor to this new world. As Gerald Isaacs put it in his "Wrap-Up" talk: "Future world market conditions will require agriculture to be competitive, thus the principal issues may be how we help labor adapt to new mechanization, not how we halt the trend toward more mechanization" (Isaacs 1984: 156).

Many presentations at the conference dealt with technical questions: the quality of microprocessors, vision software, remote controls, etc. But a broader, if somewhat implicit, issue was the comparative difference between "intelligent machines" in the agriculture of *Japan* and those in *America*. In his presentation, "Japan's Technology Farm," Noboru Kawamura argued that Japan's unique agricultural situation – intensive yet small-scale farming – has required significantly more innovation in its technological practices than the "large scale farming" techniques used in America and Europe (Kawamura 1984: 52). To stay competitive on the open market, Kawamura argues, Japan would have to embrace "driverless" farm vehicles. Japan's agricultural machinery would have to unman.

At the conference, the focus of Japanese attendees was automating – now we might say "dronifying" – conventional agricultural vehicles. Nobutaka Ito noted that initial experiments had succeeded in removing the driver from the combine harvester, allowing "radio control" of rice combines (Ito 1984: 69). He cautioned, however, that it looked "impossible" for the majority of farmers to adopt this technology, due to Japanese agriculture's small scale and the size of their farms: increasingly complex remote control technologies would outstrip both the needs and capacities of the Japanese farmer. Ito's presentation ended on a cautionary note: improvements in quality were coming, but commercialization of driverless combines had been slow due to tremendous costs and insufficient specialization of the machines. A perceptive reader will note that a very similar tone of caution about the difficult integration of high-tech machinery into agricultural production appears in contemporary accounts of agricultural drones.

Americans at the conference responded to the Japanese presentations with a degree of jealousy and even incomprehension. W.F. McClure, a professor of biological and agricultural engineering at North Carolina State University, observed that Japanese farmers produced in quantity and quality "with enviable efficiency" (McClure 1984: 76). McClure pointed to an obvious "lag" in

American agriculture compared to Japan: first, "the economic incentives are not yet in place" to push farmers into adopting new high-tech fixes. For nearly 30 years, "American industries, including agriculture, have been rather short sighted. Long range planning has not been one of our strong points" (ibid.). Unlike the Japanese farming sector, Americans had not needed to "utilize every morsel produced. Our overproduction is wrought not by efficiency but by brute force – big acreage, big machines, powerful chemicals, etc. – and in the process we waste more than any other nation" (ibid.). The challenge was a large one, and he argues that American farming should "not become involved in high technology simply for the prestige of being in the technological fore-front. The challenge is to be involved because it will help us take full advantage of our food potential, provide us with a higher quality fresh product, and will speed the flow of food to the consumer" (ibid.: 80).

All of these presentations, despite their agricultural focus, carried the implicit undertones of a global technology race. In his presentation, "Robotics: Economic, Technical, and Policy Issues," Delbert Tesar made the geopolitical picture clear. In his narrative, georobotics was a race between national science regimes: Japan and France were in the lead, America was somewhere behind them, and Russia and the Soviet Bloc nations were even further back (Tesar 1984: 2). Tesar claimed, in passing, that agricultural robotics had significant military roots, "derived from the urgent needs associated with handling nuclear materials" (ibid.: 3). In Tesar's view of the future of robotics, prosthetic technologies in various industries would maintain and cement American technological and industrial leadership – it is, in retrospect, hardly surprising that one of the most yearned-for robots in his paper is a deep-sea oil-driller and that agricultural technologies are given short shrift. What Tesar's predictions made clear is the divergence in the "national" perception of technological utility, part of why Japan and South Korea would beat America to agricultural UAV devices by more than two decades. A "proof-of-concept" mission by NASA's solar-powered Pathfinder Plus UAV, as late as 2003, to demonstrate whether a coffee field could be usefully monitored and surveyed is thus symptomatic (Herwitz et al. 2004). Researchers note that "Agriculture is becoming an increasingly knowledge-based industry" and point to "rapidly" evolving UAV platforms that will offer "new alternatives for agricultural and other users needing high spatial resolution imagery delivered in near-real time" (ibid.: 51). American engineers, scientists, and farming industry members are busy rediscovering a device that has been utilized elsewhere for quite a while.

This history demonstrates the paradoxes and non-linearities of technology uptake. It was not enough for drone farming to be *feasible* or even "proven" in one context for it to become widely used. Without a broader social arrangement in which utilization *made sense*, epistemically and economically, agricultural drones would we be largely forgotten in the American context.[7] At that moment, very few decision-makers had any interest in the massive investments required to "take the farmer out of the combine." The vast quantities of new "data" about fields, vegetation, and disease, the idea that one might tap into this unseen world of agri-information through special optical pros-thetics – all of this was nowhere in sight. We can read the prophecies of "inevitability" and "revolution" surrounding agricultural drones today as the symptoms of smaller agricultural changes, ones in subterranean preparation for many years. They are discursive tactics, intentional or not, to prime a social order for the uptake of technologies that are not, in and of themselves, *actually* inevitable. But for these discursive strategies to be successful, two prior elements needed to be in place: first, the claim that *technology* was key to the future of *agriculture* needed to be spread widely and made convinc-ing; second, both the possibility and the utility of the drone's gaze had to be proven. We will explore the former – the discourse of "precision farming" – in the next section, but we will finish the current discussion by fleshing out the transition so commonly discussed with regard to agricultural drones: the shift from the battlefield to the cornfield.

In van Blyenburgh's 27-page report on the future of the "UAV industry," 20 pages were spent on the most detailed military and police considerations: the benefits of vertical takeoff UAVs for "urban reconnaissance surveillance, EW and psy ops roles during conditions of civilian unrest, strife and war, littoral warfare, land and sea mine detection"; the "feasibility of equipping UAVs with laser designators" or "fitting... larger UAVS with existing missiles" (van Blyenburgh 1999: 13). Civilian applications were always a secondary element in the broader military–industrial push. Van Blyenburgh rattled off a list of possible civilian uses that would look familiar to any contemporary reader of Gizmodo: the motion picture industry, TV broadcasting of sports events, rock concerts, meteorology, telecommunications (ibid.). But commercial use, he cautioned, was "still in its infant shoes" (ibid.: 5). Of the entire global industry, the only companies producing agricultural UAVs at the turn of the twenty-first century were in Asia: Fuji Heavy Industries, Kawada, Kubota, Yamaha Motor, and Yanmar Agricultural Equipment in Japan; Daewoo in South Korea. Van Blyenburgh hoped that between 2005 and 2010 there would be a generalized "acceptance of UAVs by users and the general public" along-side "ever increasing use of commercial UAVs" (ibid.: 25). The key, he noted, would be "A substantial effort ... by industry to make the possible future commercial users more aware of the potential offered by UAVs" through:

> responsible coverage in the specialized and general public press, as well as on television, organized educational briefings, inviting possible future users to UAV exhibitions and demonstrations, and bringing the issue of UAVs to the attention of technical universities, engineering schools, research institutes, as well as military academics.
>
> (Ibid.)

This technical report was, by its end, much closer to a manifesto for the drone future – with an outline of all necessary tools to get there – than simply a "consideration" of the "current situation." These strategies were normalization techniques, attempts to stress and confirm both the viability and necessity of drones in the consumer and public sphere. We are living inside the reality that van Blyenburgh advocated. The dramatic profusion of publications about the good drone, and the agricultural drone specifically, are merely one strong indication.

Farming precision

But to understand the significance of agricultural drones in the American context, one also needs to take into account a broader trend in farming over the last two decades: "precision agriculture." "Precision agriculture" (or "precision farming") designates the movement toward increasingly technology- and information-centric farming practices – everything from "grid sampling," "variable rate fertilizer application," "yield monitors," and "yield mapping" (Daberkow and McBride 2001). As this list makes clear, precision agriculture is about the application of information technologies from other domains in order to achieve higher levels of efficiency and cost-savings in agriculture. In the most basic sense, it means deploying GPS technology, mapping software, and statistical tracking in soybean fields and peach orchards. The term made perhaps its first academic appearance in a report by four University of Minnesota agriculture researchers. In "Agricultural Competitiveness, Farm Fertilizer and Chemical Use, and Environmental Quality: A Descriptive Analysis," Runge et al. offered a historical explanation for why American agriculture thoroughly leapfrogged its international competition: "The revolution in the application of scientific knowledge to increasing crop yields through the addition of fertilizers and chemicals shows the importance of these inputs to the substantial productivity gains of the post-war period" (Runge et al. 1990: iv). Runge and his colleagues ended up agreeing with the claims that McClure made in the early 1980s – America has traditionally focused on big yields across big acreage – but they suggest that America remains ahead in agricultural science insofar as advancement after World War II has been traditionally a question of *chemical* science. Peter Sloterdijk notes as well that the shift to an "environmental" perspective in both warfare and science was significantly influenced by the massive advances in chemical science throughout the two World Wars (2009). The use of chemical weapons on a vast scale, Sloterdijk claims, triggered an increased awareness of the growing role of the *atmosphere* – rather than simply the body – as a zone of defense, strategy, and threat. "Precision" emerges thus as a response to the over-utilization of fertilizers and chemicals in American agriculture, which create "environmentally catastrophic" conditions (Runge et al. 1990: 1). The solution, according to the Minnesota researchers, was "precision farming techniques": everything from "new biotechnologies, biocontrols, plant genetics, crop management, and fertilizer and pesticide sources" to "improved timing, placement, and targeting of nitrogen and pesticide applications" (ibid.: 70). Chemical clouds gave way to the need for precision accuracy.

The ideal of "precision agriculture" has always *responded to* contemporary technological conditions and mutated when those conditions changed. The historicity of the term is telling:

> Over the years the emphasis has changed from simply "farming by soil" ... through variable-rate technologies, to vehicle guidance systems and will evolve to product quality and environmental management. At various places throughout the world the degree of development, and consequently the focus, varies.
>
> (McBratney et al. 2005: 7)

"Precision" and "Precision agriculture" have no stable referent at all. They are, rather, empty signifiers referring back only to the broader technological context within which agricultural practices occur, within the space of the technological milieu (see Lundberg 2012: 73–4). While discourses about the potential for precision agriculture to completely revolutionize the industry were popular in the 1990s, today most advocates and analysts admit that adoption of the heralded techniques and devices has been very slow, with large farms dramatically outpacing smaller farmers in percentages of uptake. "Precision agriculture" has had ambiguous success so far.

Part of the difficulty is awareness. In 1998, 70 percent of farmers were largely or almost entirely unfamiliar with precision farming technologies, despite years of general availability (Daberkow and McBride 2003: 163). Another problem, however, is cost. If you own a small herd of cattle or manage a few fields of wheat, investing in costly technological trinkets may not be particularly appealing. Stan Daberkow and William McBride, analysts for the Economic Research Service of the US Department of Agriculture, argue, "Since technological change is typically associated with enhanced opportunities for greater productivity and income, understanding the processes by which entrepreneurs become aware of and adopt new technologies is of interest to the private sector, researchers and policymakers" (ibid.: 164). Technological change receives a decisively positive gloss, and there is a relatively linear relationship between technological change and both productivity and income: more technology equals more crops, more technology equals more money. The farming industry or broader "agricultural sector" is reconstituted as a cohort of "entrepreneurs" whose interest and role is understanding and adopting new technologies. Knowledge about this process, about how farmer-entrepreneurs chose to adopt or not adopt technological tools for their practice, becomes a domain of state knowledge with clear and important implications for both the "private sector" and "policymakers." Big business and the government want to understand why farmers are not using all of the devices that are being produced – and how to accelerate the uptake process.

The classification of farmers as rational tech-entrepreneurs should come as no surprise in a world where so many increasingly want or try to package themselves as one form of tech-entrepreneur or other via social media, do-it-yourself tech projects, etc. But Daberkow and McBride, two government researchers working to determine how the Department of Agriculture can encourage a particular conduct of farming, do more than fall in with this trend. Their definition closely fits Foucault's articulation of neoliberal man (*homo economicus*) as "the subject who is an 'entrepreneur of him/herself' ... meant to fit into the frame of society remade as an 'enterprise society'"(Lazzarato 2009: 110). Farmers are repackaged as purely economic actors, who "actively gather information when they expect it to provide an economic return" and decide the form of their farming based on complex profit–loss calculations (Daberkow and McBride 2003: 164). Agriculture is a project of free enterprise articulated along relatively narrow neoliberal lines. After outlining the form and results of their empirical study on technology diffusion, Daberkow and McBride conclude with another sort of thought experiment: "In a world of perfect access to information, producers would be aware of and adopt new technologies that raise profits or well-being more generally ... Awareness and adoption therefore would only depend on factors associated with profitability" (ibid.: 174). In short, if farmers were hyper-rational decision-makers with access to all information – if they were not, in short, farmers, or even really human beings – they would operate their farms along pure profit lines and would adopt each new technology if it promised efficiency and cost-savings.

And yet Daberkow and McBride's study ends up only applying to, or targeting, a specific sub-set of farmers. For a large number of those who run smaller farms, or particular sorts of farms, precision agriculture technologies are both unprofitable and unattractive. The ideal farmers, the ones that government programs and private businesses should target, then, are "well-educated, computer-literate operators of large, row-crop farms in the Heartland" (ibid.: 175). Built into their analysis is the continued shift away from small farming toward monocultures. Daberkow and McBride's conclusions end up being relatively banal and tautological: only the farmers who can afford to buy new-fangled gadgets and GPS devices are going to be interested in buying them. Their research, however, is a contribution to the broader discourse about what type of *subjects* farmers are. Foucault calls this the "conduct of conduct," the notion that individual behaviors and individual subjects can be shaped through non-coercive discursive measures. The ideal farmer, they make clear, the one who will survive in these new and challenging times, has the money and the willingness to make somewhat risky financial decisions to opt into new technological devices. Today's farmer must be a digital speculator.[8] The drone industry has taken notice.

Brandon Basso, the lead researcher for 3D Robotics, a smaller drone startup that provides tailored "solutions" for different industries, explains, "We want them to use drones the same way that they use their other farming equipment" (Sharma 2013). Basso and 3D Robotics want farmers to feel comfortable with drones and the encroachment of new technological ways of acting and seeing. Yet his statement is misleading, because 3D Robotics and others are attempting to market drones by stressing how much they fundamentally *change* traditional modes of farming. Rather than "spray pesticides uniformly over their crop to protect them from fungal infections … farmers can choose to not spray pesticides based on an aerial survey of their crop using drones. Alternatively, they can selectively spray pesticides only on plants that need attention" (Henn 2014). Drones bring targeting, quite literal forms of "precision," to "precision agriculture."

What is critical in these dronified narratives is the extent to which drones alter not only farming but also the farmer, transforming the relationship between farmers and their crops. "Modern farming," *NPR* explains, "is a data-driven business." The ideal farmer, one well suited to the era of "big data" (Morozov 2014), would be "Like a software programmer or Web developer," and he would run "an endless series of tests on his land, altering things like crop density, fertilizer and planting width" (Henn 2014). Avital Ronell's claim that "We exist under [technology's] sway, so much so that one could assert that [it] has now transformed the world into so many test sites" is verified (Ronell 2007: 160). Farms, literal plots of land, soil, and crops, become information, data. Tilling a field is, after all, just like assembling a Wordpress site. "Modern" farmers become experimentally minded tech-entrepreneurs who utilize optical and mapping capabilities to extract crops from their fields as efficiently as possible. The drone provides the missing link in a series of farming possibilities because of its prosthetic and visual capabilities, its ability to bring scanning and action "from the air," in Sloterdijk's terms. The broader re-articulation of farmers as data laborers helps cement what Mikko Joronen calls "neoliberal monopolitics," the increasing re-interpretation of the world through the lens of profit and loss, information and rational decision (Joronen 2013: 8–9).

It should come as little surprise, then, that the drone "industry" is putting its eggs into the agricultural basket. As in Japan, advertising and targeting, in precisely the mode outlined by van Blyenburgh, are normalizing drones as agricultural devices. The changes that drones bring to agriculture *are* somewhat more dramatic than those they bring to military strategy: cruise missiles and fighter jets were able to strike pinpoint enemy locations for decades before drones, but the kinds of precision now available for corn fields or soya crops are quite unique. What is fascinating about the discourse on drones in "precision" farming is the way that it mirrors much of the proselytizing about drones in military and surveillance contexts. What began as a rather different kind of "precision" starts to take on, via cultural osmosis, the characteristics and significance of "precision" in the military context. "Precision" agriculture ceases to be about "precise" measurements and starts to focus much more heavily on *targeting, precise strikes*. The very same revolution in aerial imaging and mapping that the drone provided for US military operations in Pakistan and

Afghanistan comes home to North Dakota and Iowa, where a bird's eye view of thousands of acres allows for mapping entire fields in heretofore unknown ways: the very same logic of pinpointing an individual – whether an aphid on a soybean or a terrorist suspect carrying an assault weapon – "targeting" and acting prosthetically to resolve a pest. The extreme cross-applicability of discourse about drone possibilities in civilian and military spheres is one of the paradoxes of those who are anxious about drones in one area – say, policing Pakistan's mountains – but who support them so vigorously elsewhere – say, monitoring rural areas. Precision *agriculture* is not simply an offshoot of precision *weapons*, but a co-emergent technological and cultural force, drawing on capacities and networks of knowledge with heavily military origins. The expansion of targeting logic across cultural domains led Rey Chow to call our time the "age of the world target," a riff on Martin Heidegger's suggestion that the metaphysical shift in modern times was toward the "age of the world picture," the world conceived as one grand frameable image. For Chow, "To conceive of the world as a target is to conceive of it as an object to be destroyed" (2006: 30).

We have perceived signs that point to the emergence of a new sort of farmer – and not simply a new sort of *farmer*, but a new sort of *person* as well, novel subjectivities that emerge from the combined growth of the economic-distance imperative and prosthetic-drone possibilities. This subjectivity, *homo dronomicus* (drone-man), is not an evolved state or absolute threshold, but nonetheless *is* the harbinger of a certain future, or a certain version of the future. In this future, sold for varying prices and at different speeds depending on who you are, the possibility for profit from an emerging and increasingly intense dronification of the world is nearly infinite. So is the possibility of loss. We should be aware of these dangers not only because killing with a drone is more than pushing a button (Asaro 2013: 200), but because the drone shift promises to multiply and reinforce other socioeconomic shifts. And the farmers, the companies, the armies, and the civilians who do not find ways to understand, adapt themselves to, and control the "dronified" world will fall irretrievably behind.

Unmanned land grabs

As mapping technology and prosthetic action transition from the mountains of Afghanistan to the fields of North Dakota, as the new evangelists of agricultural drones rediscover agriculture Japanese-style, this dronified "Revolution in Military Affairs" is becoming a "Revolution in Agricultural Affairs." Not only will agricultural drones provide the necessary economies of scale and a degree of social diffusion and normalization for military drones, but the near-euphoria over drone farming in the Global North runs the risk of whitewashing the "other danger" of agricultural drones: contributing to and magnifying many of the negative tendencies of contemporary large-scale farming. Here we are entering uncharted analytic territory: global drone farming is only in its "infant shoes," to reuse a phrase from Peter van Blyenburgh, and very little attention – scholarly or otherwise – has been placed on its significance beyond narrow economic calculations. Nonetheless, I want to consider in this final section how agricultural drones may allow for unique forms of global agriculture. Agricultural drones, appearing "in a slew of countries including Canada, Australia, Japan and Brazil," (Doering 2014) offer new possibilities for global land acquisition by major multinational corporations – unmanned, long-distance displacement, and a novel modality of David Harvey's "accumulation by dispossession" (Harvey 2004: 64).

Harvey, following Marx, points to a general trend under capitalist social organization toward the "commodification and privatization of land and the forceful expulsion of peasant populations" (2004: 74). This "accumulation by dispossession" allows a system that has traditionally relied on expansion into untouched landscapes and enclosure of global commons to maintain processes of accumulation in the face of geographical "limits to capital" (Harvey 2006). Though the quasi-dialectical movement between commons and enclosures in relation to the management and ownership of land represents a long-term dynamic of the system, many analysts have noted a recent increase in land grabs. Why? Ben White and colleagues note in their introduction to a special collection on land enclosures that agricultural "land grabbing" is, by all available estimates and despite secrecy surrounding many of the deals, rapidly increasing (White et al. 2012). Two broader trends are worth highlighting. First, incentives to develop agrofuel feedstocks like jatropha, palm oil, and sugar have caused billions of dollars to flow into land purchases (Hildyard et al. 2012: 33–5). Particularly concerning in these new "energy grabs" or "energy enclosures" is that, beyond "interfering with local people's access to land, water, forests, fishing grounds and other means of livelihood, they also generally deny or limit local people's access to energy" (ibid.). Extractive economies thus established preserve unsustainable global energy flows and deprive smaller economies of energy resources they desperately require. "The resource curse," the tendency for poverty and war to dominate in areas "amidst bountiful natural resource endowment," becomes even more disastrous (Omeje 2008: 1). Costis Hadjimichalis points to a second major factor driving global land dispossession: the use of speculative capital to seize land in areas hit by poverty. In his analysis of land politics in Greece, Hadjimichalis notes that the Greek debt crisis provided an opportunity for government and business elites to sell off public lands "as a price that is necessary to pay in order for Greece to exit the crisis": "What had been won through generations – materially, institutionally but symbolically also – is now lost over a small amount of time through the dispossession of land, of public property and of small ownership" (Hadjimichalis 2014).

We can look at the growing role of drones in South and Central America as one indicator of the potential significance of drones for questions of land control and global justice. In Colombia, where land dispossession by multinational corporations has caused massive controversy (Otis 2013b), UAVs have been heavily utilized by the government since at least 2006 to provide surveillance for the war against FARC (Revolutionary Armed Forces of Columbia People's Army). In 2014, Colombia unveiled its first domestically produced drone, initially meant to provide intelligence for the war against FARC but also useful, according to Air Force engineer Alejandro Vargas, for monitoring "meteorological and volcanic activity, as well as oil pipelines and the drugs trade" (Willis 2014). The ostensibly "civilian" tasks, monitoring oil pipelines or taking environmental readings, remain within a military realm as well, since FARC "often carry out attacks on oil pipelines and energy stations throughout the country" (Fox 2012). In Colombia, then, we are already seeing a repetition of the process whereby military drones are partially sanitized of their violent capacities through the litany of benign tasks they can perform. Significantly, Colombia and its neighbors represent sites of competition between the burgeoning American drone industry, restricted in what models can be sold outside the United States, and that of Israel, which provides the majority of the devices in use by Latin American governments (Koebler 2013). The growing market for UAV technology in both civilian and security matters has caused American military producers to aggressively court these governments as potential clients. Yet also getting involved in the drone market in South and Latin America are companies like UTC Aerospace Systems, whose small, hand-launched "Vireo" drones claim to provide "actionable data to law enforcement, government agencies, agriculture producers and first responders" (UTC Aerospace Systems 2013). The appearance of these small drone platforms at an aerospace expo in Colombia appears to be a sign that the agricultural future will not *only* hit American farmers. Brazil is the largest market for drone technology in South America. There, devices are used by the government to monitor the rainforest and border regions and by farmers as well, also interested in "precision farming" practices (Otis 2013a). A similar process is also occurring in Argentina (Cupolo 2013). By all accounts, the rest of the Western Hemisphere is also trying to get in on the action, although from Mexico to Panama to Ecuador, the vast majority of purchases have been surveillance drones to battle drug trafficking (ibid.). Commentators have alternated between overt concern about the seeming inextricability of *military* and *agricultural* drone use in these markets – the complementary relationship that reappears conspicuously – and a more laissez-faire approach to the technology that writes off this connection to the inevitable desirability of high-tech farming practices.

It remains difficult now to make entirely confident predictions about the role of agricultural drones in these markets and those across the globe, and the questions raised here remain, by necessity, incomplete. Further scholarship will need to pay attention to the increasing interconnection between drone technologies and international agriculture projects. We can, however, utilize the preceding analysis to posit two theses about the agricultural drone future.

First: Increasing capabilities of commercially available drones (along the lines of their visual-cartographic capacities as well as the ability to remain airborne for longer periods of time) will both accelerate and allow for new modes of international speculation and surveillance of lands beyond the strict confines of national borders. The benefits that drones have for military surveillance and intelligence gathering apply in numerous, quite obvious ways to agricultural land acquisition, although they also raise issues of international airspace violations. There are two levels here: on the one hand, large multinational corporations can utilize advanced imaging techniques and geological analyses in order to gain more detailed information about potential acquisitions, offering a data supplement to decisions about advantageous purchases; on the other hand, drones can be deployed in newly acquired lands as both prosthetic labor *and* a form of security/surveillance. Much of the land acquisition occurring over the last ten years has been motivated by concerns about national food insecurity (Borras Jr. and Franco 2012: 40), and a security-driven pseudo-militaristic framing has predominated in both the media and national discourse. Andrew McMurry calls this latter assemblage of actors and discourses the "food security complex," which tends to focus on "logic-driven appeals to the latest techno-agricultural and market mechanisms for meeting world demands and defeating hunger" (McMurry 2012). Drones fit easily and effectively within this discourse because they occupy a strange in-between place of traditional farming tech fixes and the more overtly militaristic technologies of security. Thinking within the broader discourse of food insecurity and its tendency to reduce complex questions of international resource distribution to simplistic concerns about national security, we can confidently posit that drones are set to play a significant role in the future politics of food control. To what extent remains to be seen. That they will be used is a certainty.

Second: Drone agriculture will exacerbate global resource inequality. We can admit one possibility: the narrative told by American drone manufacturers about the tremendous possibility of drones for small farmers is true, that small farmers around the world will gain access to newfound information and data about their fields which will allow for yield improvements and increased efficiency. Further, drones will allow them to spend less time on tedious, labor-intensive processes and increase the automation of farming practices. This seems, at the moment, a Panglossian prediction. A look at the history of technology in the "Green Revolution" provides little reason for optimism (Buckland 2004). Ben White and colleagues wonder why it is that "much-touted win–win solutions" in global agricultural development have been "so difficult to realize." Their conclusion is that "powers of exclusion" – the interacting processes of regulation, force, the market, and legitimation – tend to produce deals with unequal compensation, poor benefits, and exposure to unacceptable risks. The predominant trend in the military application of drones – powerful nations have been able to use drone violence and disproportionate force throughout the global South – seems highly likely in the context of the new precision agriculture because the political and ideological barriers to the equal deployment of technology remain relatively insurmountable. A resolution to the problem of global land grabs and resource inequality more broadly will require more than new eyes in the sky.

Conclusion: drone on the range

The present contribution has attempted to resituate the media fascination with agricultural drones within a history of military research and development as well as changes in the conception of the agriculture-technology nexus inside American farming paradigms. Agricultural drones emerged, I have argued, from many of the same processes that produced hunter-killer drones and they were perceived at the time as supplements to military drones that might both expand UAV markets and increase public acceptance of the technology. There was no one-way trip from the battlefield to the cornfield, however, and I have pointed to Japan's early leadership in unmanned agricultural devices to show the potential for alternative trajectories in the development of this technology. I have linked the increased acceptance of drones to increased interest in "precision agriculture" among farmers across the globe, which is connected to but also importantly distinct from the passion for "precision targeting" in military strategy. Finally, by analyzing the market for drones in areas where global land dispossession issues remain particularly salient, I have set out my own tentative position on the potential for drones to reconfigure global agricultural practices.

There remain, however, quite a few unanswered questions that I hope other researchers can assist in examining further. First, deeper analysis of specific regions will be crucial to understanding how the global dynamics of the drone market are being implemented in different contexts (how drone purchases in the Middle East are differing from those in South and Central America). Second, research on agricultural drones will be strengthened by statistical analyses and further information about the developing American market for agricultural drones as the US legal regulations transform. Third, though certainly not finally, discussions with farmers and corporations in unique regions alongside a global approach to the diffusion and transformation of "precision agriculture" will help us to treat this trend in all of the detail it requires. If agricultural drones *are* the future of farming, it behooves us to track their socio-historical flight paths and understand the historically unequal social relations that this future may inaugurate. The point is not that every drone is bad, but that every drone is dangerous (Dreyfus, Rabinow, and Foucault 1983), and it is time to focus as closely on drones on the range as we have on drones above the battlefield.

Notes

1 The number is based on analysis of Google News archives for the period. The number would be higher if we included blogs and other independent media.
2 One leading example is The Bureau of Investigative Journalism's (2014) "Covert Drone War" project: www.thebureauinvestigates.com/category/projects/drones/.
3 Without embarking into an explicit analysis of drone vision, I should note that I use this term with an eye toward its conspicuous presence across nearly all academic literature on UAVs (see, for one example among many: Shaw and Akhter 2012).
4 LiDAR uses laser illumination of a target to measure distance. In agriculture, the technology has been deployed to map drainage patterns or crop elevations requiring additional pesticide spray.
5 More than 700 journal articles have been published since 2000 on the topic of unmanned aerial vehicles in precision agriculture.
6 Where tactical UAVs gathered intelligence and returned it to ground forces, tactical decoy drones were used to trick enemy air defense installations. During the Yom Kippur War, for instance, Israel successfully conned the Syrian military into believing a large air attack was imminent by flying Chukar decoys toward the Golan Heights.
7 I lack the space to offer a full theorization of sociotechnical change, but many fascinating texts complement the story offered here (see, for instance, Bijker 1997 or Mackenzie 1993).
8 Which is not to say that farming had, before this moment, escaped speculation: the use of the cotton gin or new pesticides always required a willingness to make risky economic calculations. But what appears new in these writings is the naturalized wedding of "old" farming to "new" cyberculture.

References

Agri-Trend (2014) "About Us." Available at: www.agritrend.com/about-us.aspx (Accessed April 10, 2016).

Asaro, P.M. (2013) The labor of surveillance and bureaucratized killing: New subjectivities of military drone operators. *Social Semiotics*, 23 (2): 196–224. doi:10.1080/10350330.2013.777591.

Associated Press (2014) "Dreams of Drone-Assisted Farming Are Taking Flight," *East Valley Tribune*, November 21. Available at: www.eastvalleytribune.com/life/article_73495394-6f51-11e4-a725-4b662de729c6.html (Accessed April 10, 2016).

Bijker, W. (1997) *Of Bicycles, Bakelites, and Bulbs: Toward a Theory of Sociotechnical Change*. Cambridge: The MIT Press.

Borras Jr, S.M. and Franco, J.C. (2012) Global land grabbing and trajectories of agrarian change: A preliminary analysis. *Journal of Agrarian Change*, 12 (1): 34–59. doi:10.1111/j.1471-0366.2011.00339.x.

Buckland, J. (2004) *Ploughing up the Farm: Neoliberalism, Modern Technology and the State of the World's Farmers*. London: Zed Books.

Chow, R. (2006) *The Age of the World Target: Self-Referentiality in War, Theory, and Comparative Work*. Next Wave Provocations. Durham: Duke University Press.

Cupolo, D. (2013) "Drone Use Soars in Latin America, Remains Widely Unregulated," *Upside Down World*. December 19. Available at: http://upsidedownworld.org/main/international-archives-60/4615-drone-use-soars-in-latin-america-remains-widely-unregulated (Accessed April 10, 2016).

Daberkow, S.G. and McBride, W.D. (2001) "Adoption of Precision Agriculture Technologies by U.S. Farmers," in *Proceeding of the 5th International Conference on Precision Agriculture, Bloomington, Minnesota, USA, July 16–19, 2000*, 1–12. Madison, Wisconsin: American Society of Agronomy.

Daberkow, S.G. and McBride, W.D. (2003) Farm and operator characteristics affecting the awareness and adoption of precision agriculture technologies in the US. *Precision Agriculture*, 4 (2): 163–77. doi:10.1023/A:1024557205871.

Dillow, C. (2014) "Despite FAA Dithering, a Drone Economy Sprouts on the Farm," *Forbes*, September 16. Available at: http://fortune.com/2014/09/16/despite-faa-dithering-a-drone-economy-sprouts-on-the-farm/ (Accessed April 10, 2016).

Doering, C. (2014) "Growing Use of Drones Poised to Transform Agriculture," *USA Today*, March 23. Available at: www.usatoday.com/story/money/business/2014/03/23/drones-agriculture-growth/6665561/ (Accessed April 10, 2016).

Dreyfus, H.L., Rabinow, P., and Foucault, M. (1983) *Michel Foucault: Beyond Structuralism and Hermeneutics* (2nd edn). Chicago: University of Chicago Press.

Faria, V. (2014) "Bird's Eye View," *AgAdvance*, June 1. Available at: www.agadvance.com/issues/jun-2014/birds-eye-view.aspx (Accessed April 10, 2016).

Federal Aviation Administration (2014) "Busting Myths About the FAA and Unmanned Aircraft," December 26. Available at: www.faa.gov/news/updates/?newsId=76240 (Accessed April 10, 2016).

Fox, E. (2012) "Colombia Producing Its Own Drones," *InSightCrime*, October 26. Available at: www.insightcrime.org/news-briefs/colombia-producing-drones (Accessed April 10, 2016).

Goglia, J. (2014) "Listen Up Drone Operators: FAA Has 7 Myths To Bust," *Forbes*, March 3. Available at: www.forbes.com/sites/johngoglia/2014/03/03/listen-up-drone-operators-faa-has-7-myths-to-bust/ (Accessed April 10, 2016).

Hadjimichalis, C. (2014) Crisis and land dispossession in Greece as part of the global "land fever." *City*, 18 (4–5): 502–8. doi:10.1080/13604813.2014.939470.

Harvey, D. (2004) The "new" Imperialism: Accumulation by dispossession. *Socialist Register*, 40.

Harvey, D. (2006) *The Limits to Capital*. Updated Edition. New York: Verso.

Henn, S. (2014) "High-Ho, The Derry-O, The Farmer And The Drone," *All Tech Considered, NPR*. Available at: www.npr.org/blogs/alltechconsidered/2014/05/10/311143655/high-ho-the-derry-o-the-farmer-and-the-drone (Accessed April 10, 2016).

Herwitz, S.R., Johnson, L.F., Dunagan, S.E., Higgins, R.G., Sullivan, D.V., Zheng, J., Lobitz, B.M., Leung, J.G., Gallmeyer, B., Aoyagi, M., Slye, R.E., and Brass, J. (2004) Imaging from an unmanned aerial vehicle: Agricultural surveillance and decision support. *Computers and Electronics in Agriculture*, 44 (1): 49–61. doi:10.1016/j.compag.2004.02.006.

Hildyard, N., Lohmann, L., and Sexton, S. (2012) *Energy Security For Whom? For What?*. The Corner House. Available at: www.thecornerhouse.org.uk/resource/energy-security-whom-what (Accessed April 10, 2016).

Isaacs, G.W. (1984) "Conference Wrap-Up," in *Robotics and Intelligent Machines in Agriculture: Proceedings of the First International Conference on Robotics and Intelligent Machines in Agriculture*. St. Joseph: American Society of Agricultural Engineers.

Isidore, C. (2014) "FAA Can Regulate Drones," *CNN Money*, November 19. Available at: http://money.cnn.com/2014/11/19/technology/faa-drones/index.html (Accessed April 10, 2016).

Ito, N. (1984) "Application of Agricultural Robots in Japan," in *Robotics and Intelligent Machines in Agriculture: Proceedings of the First International Conference on Robotics and Intelligent Machines in Agriculture*. St. Joseph: American Society of Agricultural Engineers.

Joronen, M. (2013) Conceptualising new modes of state governmentality: Power, violence and the ontological mono-politics of neoliberalism. *Geopolitics*, 18 (2): 356–70. doi:10.1080/14650045.2012.723289.

Kawamura, N. (1984) "Japan's Technology Farm," in *Robotics and Intelligent Machines in Agriculture: Proceedings of the First International Conference on Robotics and Intelligent Machines in Agriculture*. St. Joseph: American Society of Agricultural Engineers.

Kawamura, N. and Namikawa, K. (1988) Robots in agriculture. *Advanced Robotics*, 3 (4): 311–20. doi:10.1163/156855389X00253.

Koebler, J. (2013) "American Defense Companies Try to Break Israel's Grasp on Latin American Drone Market – US News," *US News & World Report*, July 15. Available at: www.usnews.com/news/articles/2013/07/15/american-defense-companies-try-to-break-israels-grasp-on-latin-american-drone-market (Accessed April 10, 2016).

Lazzarato, M. (2009) Neoliberalism in action inequality, insecurity and the reconstitution of the social. *Theory, Culture & Society*, 26 (6): 109–33. doi:10.1177/0263276409350283.

Lundberg, C. (2012) *Lacan in Public: Psychoanalysis and the Science of Rhetoric*. Tuscaloosa: The University of Alabama Press.

Mackenzie, D. (1993) *Inventing Accuracy: A Historical Sociology of Nuclear Missile Guidance*. Cambridge: The MIT Press.

Madrigal, A. (2009) "Self-Steered Tractors and UAVs: Future Farming Is (Finally) Now," *Wired*, October 19. Available at: www.wired.com/2009/10/precisionfarming/all/ (Accessed April 10, 2016).

McBratney, A., Whelan, B., Ancev, T., and Bouma, J. (2005) Future directions of precision agriculture. *Precision Agriculture*, 6 (1): 7–23. doi:10.1007/s11119-005-0681-8.

McClure, W.F. (1984) "Agricultural Robotics in Japan: A Challenge for U.S. Agricultural Engineers," in *Robotics and Intelligent Machines in Agriculture: Proceedings of the First International Conference on Robotics and Intelligent Machines in Agriculture*. St. Joseph: American Society of Agricultural Engineers.

McMurry, A. (2012) Framing Emerson's "farming": Climate change, peak oil, and the rhetoric of food security in the twenty-first century. *Interdisciplinary Studies in Literature and Environment*, 19 (3): 548–66. doi:10.1093/isle/iss065.

Morozov, E. (2014) "The Planning Machine," *The New Yorker*, October 13. Available at: www.newyorker.com/magazine/2014/10/13/planning-machine (Accessed April 10, 2016).

Omeje, K. (2008) "Extractive Economies and Conflicts in the Global South: Re-Engaging Rentier Theory and Politics," in *Extractive Economies and Conflicts in the Global South: Multi-Regional Perspectives on Rentier Politics*. Aldershot: Ashgate.

Otis, J. (2013a) "Brazil Leads the Way on Global Commercial Drone Boom – Page 2," *GlobalPost*, January 6. Available at: www.globalpost.com/dispatch/news/regions/americas/brazil/130104/brazil-commercial-drones-uavs-coming-soon (Accessed April 10, 2016).

Otis, J. (2013b) "In Colombia, an Alleged American Land Grab Sets Off a Political Storm," *Time*, July 10. Available at: http://world.time.com/2013/07/10/in-colombia-an-alleged-american-land-grab-sets-off-a-political-storm/ (Accessed April 10, 2016).

Rikola Ltd. (2014) "Hyperspectral Camera," *Rikola Ltd*. Available at: www.rikola.fi/site/?page_id=55 (Accessed April 10, 2016).

Ronell, A. (2007) *The Test Drive*. Urbana: University of Illinois Press.

Runge, C.F., Munson, R.D., Lotterman, E., and Creason, J.R. (1990) *Agricultural Competitiveness, Farm Fertilizer and Chemical Use, and Environmental Quality: A Descriptive Analysis*. St. Paul, Minnesota: Center for International Food and Agricultural Policy. CABDirect2.

Schoffstall, J. (2013) "FAA Predicts 10,000 Drones Could Be In the Skies By 2020," *CNS News*, March 25. Available at: http://cnsnews.com/blog/joe-schoffstall/faa-predicts-10000-drones-could-be-skies-2020 (Accessed April 10, 2016).

Sharma, R. (2013) "Growing the Use of Drones in Agriculture," *Forbes*, December 26. Available at: www.forbes.com/sites/rakeshsharma/2013/11/26/growing-the-use-of-drones-in-agriculture/ (Accessed April 10, 2016).

Shaw, I.G.R. (2013) Predator Empire: The geopolitics of US drone warfare. *Geopolitics*, 18 (3): 536–59. doi:10.1080/14650045.2012.749241.

Shaw, I.G.R. and Akhter, M. (2012) The unbearable humanness of drone warfare in FATA, Pakistan. *Antipode*, 44 (4): 1490–509. doi:10.1111/j.1467-8330.2011.00940.x.

Shippert, P. (2003). Introduction to hyperspectral image analysis. *Online Journal of Space Communication*, 3.

Sloterdijk, P. (2009). *Terror from the Air*. Translated by Amy Patton and Steve Corcoran. *Semiotext(e)/Foreign Agents*. Los Angeles; Cambridge, Mass: Semiotext(e); MIT Press.

Tesar, D. (1984) "Robotics: Economic, Technical, and Policy Issues," in *Robotics and Intelligent Machines in Agriculture: Proceedings of the First International Conference on Robotics and Intelligent Machines in Agriculture*. St. Joseph: American Society of Agricultural Engineers.

Tetracam Inc. (2014) "Mini-MCA," November. Available at: www.tetracam.com/Products-Mini_MCA.htm (Accessed April 10, 2016).

The Bureau of Investigative Journalism (2014) "Covert Drone War," The Bureau of Investigative Journalism. Available at: www.thebureauinvestigates.com/category/projects/drones/ (Accessed April 10, 2016).

UTC Aerospace Systems (2013) "VireoTM Unmanned Aerial System," Rosemount Aerospace Inc. Available at: http://stg.utcaerospacesystems.com/cap/systems/sisdocuments/Unmanned%20Aerial%20Systems%20(UAS)/Vireo%E2%84%A2_Unmanned_Aerial_System.pdf (Accessed April 10, 2016).

van Blyenburgh, P. (1999) "UAVs – Current Situation and Considerations for the Way Forward," in *Development and Operation of UAVs for Military and Civil Applications*. Rhode-Saint-Genèse, Belgium: Research and Technology Organization.

White, B., Borras Jr., S.M., Hall, R., Scoones, I., and Wolford, W. (2012) The new enclosures: Critical perspectives on corporate land deals. *Journal of Peasant Studies*, 39 (3–4): 619–47. doi:10.1080/03066150.2012.691879.

Willis, A. (2014) "First Made-in-Colombia Drone to Track Drug Smugglers," *Bloomberg*, October 31. Available at: www.bloomberg.com/news/2014-10-31/first-made-in-colombia-drone-to-track-drug-smugglers.html (Accessed April 10, 2016).

Yamanouchi, K. (2014) "Farmers See Opportunity in Drones," *Atlanta Journal-Constitution*, October 26, sec. Business. Available at: www.ajc.com/news/business/farmers-see-opportunity-in-drones/nhrNm/ (Accessed April 10, 2016).

Zhang, C. and Kovacs, J.M. (2012) The application of small unmanned aerial systems for precision agriculture: A review. *Precision Agriculture*, 13 (6): 693–712. doi:10.1007/s11119-012-9274-5.

7 Wings for wildlife

The use of conservation drones: challenges and opportunities

Serge Wich,[1,2] Lorna Scott[1] and Lian Pin Koh[3]

[1] *School of Natural Sciences and Psychology, Liverpool John Moores University, James Parsons Building, Byrom Street, L33AF, Liverpool, UK.*

[2] *Institute for Biodiversity and Ecosystem Dynamics, University of Amsterdam, Science Park 904, 1098 XH Amsterdam, The Netherlands*

[3] *School of Earth and Environmental Sciences, The University of Adelaide, Adelaide, SA 5005, Australia*

Introduction

Over the past few decades global biodiversity has dramatically changed. The rapid growth of the human population and the per capita increase in consumption of goods has put increasing pressure on biodiversity. As a result of this, plant and animal species in many types of habitat are becoming more threatened. Habitat loss and fragmentation is one of the main threats to global biodiversity as societies continue to grow and develop vast expanses of natural land and the habitats within them are destroyed. Other major threats include over-exploitation such as fishing and hunting (poaching), and climate change (Butchart et al. 2010). Societies all over the world have a responsibility to protect the environment for aesthetic, ethical and economical reasons.

Biodiversity monitoring is a key component of most conservation projects, and gathering accurate data on things such as species distribution, density, threats and habitat is a crucial part of this. Such data often form the basis of conservation management plans in which limited resources can be invested wisely (Stem et al. 2005; Yoccoz et al. 2001). Many of the traditional methods used to monitor wildlife and their habitats have constraints in time and cost, and can be very labour intensive. An alternative method which has emerged to address some of these issues is the use of an unmanned aerial vehicle (UAV) for conservation activities, more broadly known as a conservation drone (Koh and Wich 2012). These drones have already been implemented into an array of studies and have led to many positive results. However, with drone proliferation in conservation comes a set of ethical issues that must be addressed before they can fully develop into a force for good.

This chapter aims to provide an overview of how the good drone is becoming a new tool in the world of conservation science. First, we provide an account of how the conservation drone was developed and how it is assembled and operated. We then highlight some of the main issues encountered with existing conservation methods, and describe how drones can help to alleviate some of these problems. This is followed by a section detailing how drones have already been used in three principal areas of biodiversity conservation: wildlife monitoring, habitat monitoring and anti-poaching. In the final part we address some of the problematic issues that may arise as drone use increases in the scientific community, pertaining to privacy and data protection.

The conservation drone explained

The idea of using low-cost do-it-yourself drones for conservation came in 2011 after two of us (Lian Pin Koh and Serge Wich) discussed the generally high financial and time investments that were made to monitor biodiversity in South East Asia. Particularly when surveying species such as orangutans (*Pongo* spp), it is costly and time-consuming to cover the entire distribution due to the relatively large geographic extent to which they occur and the fairly inhospitable terrain. Population data therefore rely on estimates, which are obtained by counting the number of nests within a small area and extrapolating these results to estimate the wider population (Ancrenaz et al. 2004; Wich et al. 2008). This means that the extent of data is limited and the frequency at which data are collected limited as well. Because orangutans make a new night nest on every night and these had been observed from manned helicopters and planes (Ancrenaz et al. 2004; Wich, pers. obs) we thought that perhaps drones could be used to obtain images of the forest canopy in which the nests could be detected. Because nobody had tried to take pictures of the canopy from drones to detect orangutan nests before, we were eager to test our idea and started to look for opportunities to obtain a drone that was affordable and could be repaired in the field. We quickly realised that it was best to build our own system based on resources available on the internet and components we could easily order via the internet (details below).

Building a conservation drone: methodology and challenges

Conservation drones are made up of four basic components: i) a model aircraft, ii) an autopilot system, iii) a payload, such as a camera or other type of sensing equipment, and iv) mission planning software. Because of the relative simplicity of these systems they can be built by non-engineers with information available online (www.diydrones.com) or purchased from various companies that use similar components. They can be operated by non-specialist users, although some training is needed and automated missions can be planned with open-source software (such as: www.planner.ardupilot.com). To operate, the drone is launched into the air by the user and flies along the pre-programmed mission autonomously before landing (semi) automated. A variety of sensors can be used on these drones such as still cameras, video cameras, thermal imaging cameras, and multi-spectral cameras, which collect data throughout the flight. Flight duration and range varies depending on the model of aircraft used.

In 2012 the first prototype conservation drone was flown over the island of Sumatra, Indonesia (Koh and Wich 2012). From 32 test missions it was established that these drones could have a number of potential applications for conservation scientists. First, the high-resolution images acquired by the drones enabled easy identification of large mammals such as Sumatran orangutans (*Pongo abelii*) and Sumatran elephants (*Elephas maximus*) *sumatranus*. Drones could therefore potentially become an essential tool for surveying and monitoring various species of wildlife. It was also clear from the images obtained that drones could be used to monitor and map habitats, enabling scientists to rapidly detect changes in land cover and differentiate between different types of land cover. Finally, the images obtained from the test missions were of sufficient detail to detect human activities in and around forests, such as logging, forest trails and fires. Therefore, drones could also be used as a tool in the fight against illegal activities such as wildlife poaching and illegal logging, enabling rapid detection of such activities and action to be taken (Koh and Wich 2012). In the following sections we discuss studies that have used the small conservation drone system but also some larger systems.

The drone as a solution to the limitations of existing conservation techniques

Although wildlife conservationists have developed a large array of techniques to monitor biodiversity, the huge task of conducting such monitoring on a global scale asks for continuous integration of novel technologies into the wildlife conservationist's toolkit. In addition, financial constraints are a frequent problem for conservation workers as many organisations are non-governmental and poorly funded (James et al. 1999). Ground or aerial surveys for biodiversity monitoring can be very labour intensive, time-consuming and expensive (Gardner et al. 2008). Because of the rapidly changing situation on the ground it is essential that surveys be conducted on a regular basis, which is difficult for those requiring a large financial input (Meijaard et al. 2012). Conservation drones have been designed to suit those on a low budget and are potentially a highly cost-effective option. A drone used to conduct an aerial survey collects data much faster than an equivalent ground survey, and this can be repeated at a much higher frequency (e.g. multiple flights in one day).

A widespread technique is the use of satellite imagery to create maps and monitor gross changes in land cover and habitat (e.g. Hansen et al. 2013). While sensors such as Landsat (www.landsat.org) offer freely available images, they are often of low spatial resolution and so have limited practical applications for those working on the ground. Higher resolution images can be obtained but often at a much greater cost. Depending on the type of sensor, images are only taken at specified points in time and so cannot be used for regular monitoring. Furthermore, images taken from space are frequently obscured by clouds, which is a particular problem in tropical areas. Drones do not encounter the same obstructions as they fly at a much lower altitude beneath the clouds. The images obtained by a drone are also of a much higher resolution than satellite images, meaning they can be used to study much finer details on the ground, but this comes at the cost of a smaller footprint of the image.

Environmental factors can greatly influence the success of certain monitoring techniques. For example, ground surveys can be very challenging in remote areas or over difficult terrain, in which case aerial surveys using manned aircraft may be preferable (Ancrenaz et al. 2004; Woll et al. 2011). Marine environments pose further challenges to scientists and aquatic surveys are normally conducted using aircraft and/or boats, both of which require skilled personnel to operate and pose a risk to the people on board (Koski et al. 2010). Drones can be operated over challenging terrain or bodies of water which are difficult to survey on foot, provided the environmental conditions are not too extreme (such as strong winds or heavy precipitation which may prevent flight). Being an unmanned flying vehicle, a drone is not as dangerous to operate as a manned aircraft, and the potential impact of a drone crash would be much less damaging to objects and people on the ground. Drones can be operated after a small amount of training, meaning highly skilled or specialist personnel are not always needed.

Both ground, aerial and boat surveys cause some degree of disturbance to the environment which may influence the results of the study. This is especially true if a human observer is within sensing distance of an animal (Jewell 2013; Witmer 2005). Drones offer a much less invasive surveying method as their presence is not as conspicuous as a human observer or a noisy aircraft.

A lot of the work conducted by conservationists requires hours of dedicated labour to obtain relatively limited amounts of data. Modern technology can sometimes help speed up some of this work, but using tools such as radio tags and camera traps is still quite labour intensive. Animals are fitted with radio tags for the purpose of monitoring and tracking and are normally located on foot using a directional antenna, which detects radio frequencies emitted by the tag. Such a process requires many hours of searching in the field, and incurs high costs. Attempts are now under way to use drones to locate these transmitters, in the form of miniature tracking antennae (Körner et al. 2010; Leonardo et al. 2013).

Camera traps are small cameras equipped with infrared motion sensors that can be hidden within the environment. When movement is detected in the vicinity of the trap, the camera is triggered and an image is captured. This method is often used to monitor elusive animals such as snow leopards (*Panthera uncia*) (Jackson et al. 2006). Similarly, remote microphones are used to remotely record the vocalisations and other sounds produced by animals. The main disadvantage of such methods however is that camera traps and microphones must be re-visited in order to retrieve data from their memory cards. This is costly if they have been sparsely distributed across large and usually remote landscapes. With the progression of drone technology it is hoped that drones will be able to fly over a camera or microphone trap and retrieve such data, saving a great deal of time and effort.

How conservation drones have already been used

Wildlife monitoring

Drones (both fixed-wings and multi-rotors) are rapidly becoming an important fieldwork tool in wildlife research. One of their most beneficial features is that they cause minimal disturbance to the environment in which they are being used, making them appropriate for surveying and monitoring a variety of animal taxa. This is especially true for those that are easily disturbed, such as flocks of birds. Drones have been used for data collection in a number of bird studies, including monitoring temporal changes in breeding populations of Black-headed gulls (*Chroicocephalus ridibundus*) (Sarda-Palomera et al. 2012) and estimating population densities of Canada geese (*Branta canadensis*) and Snow geese (*Chen caerulescens*) (Chabot and Bird 2012). Additionally, drones have been used to conduct line transect surveys to estimate Elephant density (*Loxodonta africana*) (Vermeulen et al. 2013).

The bird's eye view of a drone provides a novel opportunity to gather information from a different perspective. Species which inhabit the forest canopy, such as arboreal primates or nesting birds, may be difficult to observe from the ground. Weissensteiner et al. (2015) used a drone to overcome this problem: obtaining data on nest occupancy, number of offspring and breeding success of hooded crows (*Corvus cornix*) which nest in the canopy. These data are normally acquired by climbing trees using specialist equipment, which is dangerous for the researcher and causes high levels of disturbance. Not only were drones less intrusive, but there was much less risk involved for the researcher and data was acquired seven times faster than previous surveys (Weissensteiner et al. 2015). The Sumatran orangutan (*Pongo abelii*) was the driving force behind the development of conservation drones. Orangutan distribution and density are determined by counting the nests that they build (van Schaik et al. 1995), which is a very time-consuming and costly process when applied to large areas or has to be repeated often. Data on orangutan distribution and relative abundance can now also be acquired with a drone collecting aerial imagery of the canopy (Wich et al. 2016). The same methods have also been applied to African apes, where drones have been used to determine the presence of chimpanzees (*Pan troglodytes*) and their associated fruiting trees in Gabon (Van Andel et al. 2015).

Flexibility is an important feature of any tool used by a conservation scientist, often working in unpredictable conditions and facing ever-changing challenges. There are a variety of sensors available to use in conjunction with drones, which make them a highly flexible data-acquisition platform. Most commonly used are RGB photo and video cameras, but recent developments have seen a rise in the use of other sensors. For instance Mulero-Pázmány et al. (2014) mounted a thermal imaging camera to a drone to detect rhinoceros (black rhinoceros: *Diceros bicornis* and the white rhinoceros: *Ceratotherium simum*) in Africa.

As well as helping to improve upon traditional monitoring techniques, drones are being used to help solve human–wildlife conflicts. Such conflicts are common, and as human settlements continue to encroach into natural land, an increase in such conflict seems inevitable and therefore strategies to mitigate such problems become more pertinent. In Kenya, drones have been deployed as a tactic to drive elephants from inhabited areas where they come into contact with local villagers and cause severe damage to their crops (Schiffman 2014). Human infrastructure poses further risks for wildlife, and many raptor and bird species are electrocuted on power lines. In an attempt to combat this problem Mulero-Pázmány et al. (2013) conducted an environmental impact assessment by using drones to collect images of power lines. The geo-referenced data were then used to assess the relative hazards posed to soaring birds, which in turn helped to inform conservation measures to prevent further mortalities.

Though used most extensively in terrestrial surveys, the use of drones in marine environments is increasing. Their small frame and lightweight design means they do not encounter the same limitations as manned surveys using aircraft or boats, such as sea turbidity and disturbance of wildlife (Hodgson et al. 2013), but may face other challenges such as wind and large areas that need to be covered which might make the smaller drone systems less suitable. Marine mammals are a particularly challenging group to survey as they may not spend much time at the surface of the water and can have very large ranges. To test the suitability of drones for marine mammal surveying, Koski et al. (2009) obtained drone imagery from a section of open water where simulated whale targets had been dispersed. From these images, overall detection rates were similar to those obtained by manned aircraft. Similarly, drones have been used in Australia to conduct marine mammal surveys, where drone images identified dugongs, whales, dolphins, turtles and other fauna (Hodgson et al. 2013). While the ability of drones to conduct such surveys has been clearly demonstrated, a problem that remains is that the detection of marine mammals from aerial images is rather difficult and normally requires specialist personnel. It is expected though that future research will further the development of automatic object recognition algorithms, such as those tested by Maire et al. (2013) for detecting dugongs. For terrestrial surveys, automatic object recognition is also becoming more common for animals or their signs (Chen et al. 2014; Van Gemert et al. 2014).

Habitat monitoring

An important aspect of biodiversity conservation is mapping and monitoring the extent and changes of various land-cover classes. As with wildlife studies, drones are being deployed in both terrestrial and marine environments.

In coastal environments drones have been used to monitor variables that indicate the health of a marine habitat such as algal blooms, ice distribution, temperature and contaminants such as oil spills (Lomax et al. 2005). Drones are rapidly becoming an important tool for conservationists working to protect the world's oceans and monitor marine protected areas (Soarocean 2015). For example, the National Oceanic and Atmospheric Administration (NOAA) have been using drones for a variety of tasks (NOAA 2015), including surveying sea ice habitat in the North Pacific in order to study Alaskan ice seals (*Phoca hispida*) (NOAA 2009).

The ability of drones to capture sequential images with overlap and side-lap during a survey allows for the creation of orthorectified geo-referenced mosaics. Researchers have used these mosaics to identify and classify different types of land cover. For example, Chabot et al. (2014) used a drone to conduct an aerial survey over an area of wetland inhabited by Least Bitterns (*Lxobrychus exilis*). The images obtained were used to classify areas, such as freshwater, floating vegetation, and reed beds, which directly informed species and habitat management. Compared to ground surveys, drones improved the precision and efficiency of field data collection and caused less environmental disturbance. Land-cover classifications are usually created using satellite images, such as Landsat, which are of medium spatial resolution. By flying at a much lower altitude, drones provide images of higher resolution, and can be used to improve the accuracy of maps created using satellite generated imagery. For example, Szantoi et al. (in review) used Landsat images to classify various land-cover types in an area of Sumatra where orangutans occur. A drone was then used to collect "drone-truth" data of the same area and these data were subsequently applied as training datasets to improve the accuracy of the Landsat-based classifications and distinguish more land-cover types. Similarly, drones were used as part of a study investigating peat fires in Southeast Asia, where drone imagery was used to evaluate the accuracy of Landsat-based maps and refine vegetation classifications (Gaveau et al. 2014).

The low operation and maintenance costs of drones allow for surveys to be repeated frequently, enabling scientists to closely monitor the condition of forests. In the United States, the USDA Forest Service have been using drones to monitor and map forests, for road maintenance and for surveillance of timber theft and trespassers (Horcher and Visser 2004). Additionally, Getzin et al. (2012) have used drone images of canopy gaps to assess floristic biodiversity in the forest understory. To improve forest conservation there is a large scope for drones to become part of community-based forest monitoring (CBFM) programmes. Such programmes play an important role in involving local people in the conservation of their forests. Drones may be a useful addition to CBFM programmes, as they can provide detailed and accurate data without the need for processing satellite images that are often unavailable for such communities or do not provide the required resolution (Paneque-Gálvez et al. 2014).

Anti-poaching

Wildlife crime is a growing international problem; the illegal trade in ivory and rhinoceros horn has dramatically increased in recent years (Wilson-Wilde 2010). It is a lucrative, multi-billion dollar industry, fuelled by organised crime, and the growing sophistication with which poachers operate must be met with new anti-poaching technologies. Poachers often target vulnerable populations of wildlife occurring over vast land expanses and unforgiving terrain, making it difficult for rangers to patrol adequately (Bergenas et al. 2013). Conservation drones present a new form of aerial surveillance to be used in the fight against wildlife crime.

In 2011, the UK-based marine conservation charity Sea Shepherd used a drone to successfully intercept a Japanese whaling ship in the southern ocean (Sea Shepherd 2011). In 2012, The World Wildlife Fund (WWF) deployed drones in the Chitwan and Bardia National Parks (Nepal), as part of a strategy against rhinoceros (*Rhinoceros unicornis*) and tiger (*Panthera tigris tigris*) poaching (Goodyer 2013). Anti-poaching drones are sometimes equipped with cameras that transmit real-time data to a control station on the ground, enabling conservation workers to rapidly detect illegal activities and the location of wildlife or poachers. This information can then be used to deploy rangers on the ground and intercept the poachers (Goodyer 2013).

The use of drones for anti-poaching has also been demonstrated in South Africa, where poaching is the main threat to rhino conservation. Mulero-Pázmány et al. (2014) compared the capabilities of different on board sensors for detecting rhino poaching activity. Still photographs were found to be of the highest image quality and offered accurate location data, but required lengthy processing after the flight had returned. Video footage transmitted back to the control station offered the best option for real-time monitoring, and would be of great use during a pursuit of poachers. Infrared thermal imaging cameras enabled night-time surveillance, and obtained accurate imagery provided there was sufficient thermal contrast between the targets and the surrounding environment (Mulero-Pázmány et al. 2014). The usage of drones in combination with smart predictive algorithms to predict the location of rhinoceros in Africa is particularly promising as drones can then be deployed to areas that have a high probability of having rhinoceros and poachers (Snitch 2015). As well as poaching, drone imagery has also been used to detect illegal logging activity in Sumatra (Koh 2014).

Problematic issues

Privacy concerns

An important concern with the use of drones for conservation (as well as for other purposes) is that still images or video acquired with a drone might contain people and that this may violate their personal privacy. Although it is beyond the scope of this chapter to fully explore this aspect we will highlight some questions relating to this in the conservation context. The chances of accidentally obtaining images that contain a person are low in the use of conservation drones because they are used primarily in remote locations to monitor wildlife and their habitats. But instances in which people are in images and could be recognised might occur and it is thus important to determine what are the potential privacy right implications of this. Privacy laws generally state that surveillance in a public place does not violate personal privacy rights, as is the norm in many of today's societies, which are under constant CCTV surveillance (Finn and Wright, 2012). Protected areas can be both public areas and private areas for which it is likely that varying privacy laws apply. Access to many protected areas needs a permit from the relevant government authorities or other owners, but despite this, trespassing is common. It is important to determine whether privacy aspects relating to drone imagery change if images are obtained from someone that trespasses a protected area compared to someone who obtained permission to access the area. There is a need to clarify these issues and determine what needs to be done. It is important to not only evaluate such concerns for the usage of drones, but also for other data gathering methods that conservation workers use such as satellite images, camera traps and remote microphones.

Local participation

The participation of local communities is an important component for the success of many conservation efforts. People living in communities adjacent to protected areas are most prone to having a drone fly over their area on the way to a protected area. This means that consideration of privacy issues as it relates to local communities is important as well as other concerns they might have. This raises some questions such as whether local communities should be forewarned about drone use in their area, and whether this is a feasible task for conservationists. Contacting all nearby villages may be very difficult due to logistical constraints and communication barriers, but there are fears that without prior warning local people may think they are under surveillance and begin to distrust drones (Humle et al. 2014). This could lead to conflicts between members of the local communities and conservation workers, which should be avoided in order for conservation efforts to be successful (Paneque-Gálvez et al. 2014). One suggestion may be to create a type of privacy impact assessment before flying the drone mission.

Data and control hacking

There are several potential concerns linked to hacking. The first concern relates to the possibility of someone hacking into the control system of the drone and subsequently taking over the controls to do something that was not intended by the original operators. The conservation drone systems that we and many others used are not using encrypted control systems and therefore could be taken over and/or jammed without having to break into an encrypted system. This could potentially lead to people intercepting a drone that would contain data on the location of wildlife. The second concern is that data that are transmitted back to the ground control station could be hacked into. This could potentially allow people to access data on the location of wildlife. So far we have never had such an issue nor have we heard of others in the conservation context having these issues, but in the near future this is certainly something that could arise and therefore it is very sensible to start thinking about such possibilities and develop systems that are less susceptible to these risks.

Using drone data on illegal activities

Illegal activities such as logging and poaching are a persistent problem within protected areas. What if a drone records an individual participating in illegal activity? If a drone gathers incriminating evidence that a person is conducting illegal activities, can this be passed on to the local authorities if the individual was unaware that they were under surveillance? For example, in the UK the Data Protection Act 1998 stipulates that individuals must be told if a surveillance system is in operation (Finn and Wright, 2012). Is it therefore necessary to put warning signs in and around protected areas to warn people that they may be under surveillance? In the USA, if drones are used for surveillance and footage is consequently used as evidence in criminal or court proceedings, then law enforcement should firstly have obtained an area warrant prior to their use (Schlag, 2012). There are often signs to indicate that logging and hunting are not permitted, so the addition of surveillance warning signs would perhaps not be an impossible task.

Drones are relatively difficult to detect by poachers, and it is hoped that their presence will increase surveillance capacity and may begin to deter poachers from committing wildlife crimes (Bergenas et al. 2013). However, the utilisation of the good drone in anti-poaching operations carries its own risks; poachers may too adapt this technology to assist in locating animals or gathering information about the whereabouts of local authorities. In addition, when local authorities use drones to intercept poachers there are dangerous consequences for those involved on the ground. Poachers are often heavily armed and the ensuing violence may lead to loss of human life, as was the case in South Africa in 2014 where two poachers were killed by a ranger acting upon information gathered by a drone (ShadowView 2014). It remains an open question at this moment whether such instances will impact the general notion of good use of drones in the conservation context, but it is important to note here that poachers often shoot rangers as well. So deaths occur on both sides. An important question in the debate on the use of technology to find and arrest poachers that can have lethal consequences is whether it is the use of drones that is seen as a concern or whether the concern is the use of technology in general. Binoculars (for day and night), radios and other technologies have been used for many years to find and arrest poachers. It could be that using drones as a tool for anti-poaching efforts is being treated differently than other technologies because of the annotation that drones have for military purposes (Humle et al. 2014). A discussion on the use of technology in general for anti-poaching efforts would be beneficial because it could elucidate whether it is the use of drones that is the main concern or the use of technology in general. It is important to realise that for anti-poaching efforts the drone is a visual aid for the rangers to obtain an aerial viewpoint, much like manned-surveillance (microlight) aircrafts that are used in various areas. In addition to this, rangers might soon be using camera traps sending up images via satellite links that will also provide information on the location and activities of poachers. So there is a variety of technological aids that rangers use for their work. Remote microphones are also being used to detect gunshots. And of course rangers have been using other visual aids such as (night) binoculars for many decades. Thus even though drones are the newest tool in the toolbox it is relevant to determine how they differ from other technologies and whether the concern about the use of drones is not purely because of the military annotations of drones, whereas the use of drones is merely another tool in the rangers' technology toolbox.

Conclusion

The introduction of drones into the world of conservation is an important example of using drones for a good cause because many people consider conservation to be a good cause. The usage of drones in the conservation context has often been highlighted in the media and is becoming increasingly popular among conservation workers. Conservation workers frequently use drones as tools to collect data on wildlife distribution and density as well as their habitats, and these reasons are commonly seen as good ones, but in the conservation context, drones are also increasingly being used as a tool to obtain information on poachers with the aim of intercepting their purpose, which sometimes has lethal consequences. It has been argued that this might backfire on the promotion of "good" drones for non-poaching related conservation efforts such as wildlife surveys and habitat monitoring. It is therefore important that concerns are researched and discussed so that the debate can be based on solid data.

References

Ancrenaz, M., Gimenez, O., Ambu, L., Ancrenaz, K., Andau, P., Goossens, B., Payne, J., Sawang, A., Tuuga, A. and Lackman-Ancrenaz, I. (2004) Aerial surveys give new estimates for orangutans in Sabah, Malaysia. *PLOS ONE*, 3 (1): e3.

Bergenas, J., Stohl, R. and Georgieff, A. (2013) The other side of drones: Saving wildlife in Africa and managing global crime. *Conflict Trends*, 3: 3–9.

Butchart, S.H.M., Walpole, M., Collen, B., van Strien, A., Scharlemann, J.P.W., Almond, R.E.A., Baillie, J.E.M., Bomhard, B., Brown, C., Bruno, J., Carpenter, K.E., Carr, G.M., Chanson, J., Chenery, A.M., Csirke, J., Davidson, N.C., Dentener, F., Foster, M., Galli, A., Galloway, J.N., Genovesi, P., Gregory, R.D., Hockings, M., Kapos, V., Lamarque, J.-F., Leverington, F., Loh, J., McGeoch, M.A., McRae, L., Minasyan, A., Hernandez Morcillo, M., Oldfield, T.E.E., Pauly, D., Quader, S., Revenga, C., Sauer, J.R., Skolnik, B., Spear, D., Stanwell-Smith, D., Stuart, S.N., Symes, A., Tierney, M., Tyrell, T.D., Vie, J.-C. and Watson, R. (2010) Global biodiversity: Indicators of recent declines. *Science*, 328 (5982): 1164–1168.

Chabot, D. and Bird, D.M. (2012) Evaluation of an off-the-shelf unmanned aircraft system for surveying flocks of geese. *Waterbirds*, 35 (1): 170–174.

Chabot, D., Carignan, V. and Bird, D.M. (2014) Measuring habitat quality for least bitterns in a created wetland with use of a small unmanned aircraft. *Wetlands*, 34: 527–533.

Chen, Y., Shioi, H., Montesinos, C.F., Koh, L.P., Wich, S. and Krause, A. (2014) Active detection via adaptive submodularity, *Proceedings of The 31st International Conference on Machine Learning*.

Conservation Drones (2015) "What are Conservation Drones?" Available at: http://conservationdrones.org/what-are-conservation-drones (Accessed 10 April 2016).

Finn, R.L. and Wright, D. (2012) Unmanned aircraft systems: Surveillance, ethics and privacy in civil applications. *Computer Law & Security Review*, 28 (2): 184–194.

Gardner, T.A., Barlow, J., Araujo, I.S., Avila-Pires, T.C., Bonaldo, A.B., Costa, J.E., Esposito, M.C., Ferreira, L.V., Hawes, J., Hernandez, M.I.M., Hoogmoed, M.S., Leite, R.N., Lo-Man-Hung, N.F., Malcolm, J.R., Martins, M.B., Mestre, L.A.M., Miranda-Santos, R., Overal, W.L., Parry, L., Peters, S.L., Ribeiro-Junior, M.A., da Silva, M.N.F., da Silva Motta, C. and Peres, C.A. (2008) The cost-effectiveness of biodiversity surveys in tropical forests. *Ecology Letters*, 11: 139–150.

Gaveau, D. L., Salim, M.A., Hergoualc'h, K., Locatelli, B., Sloan, S., Wooster, M., Marlier, M.E., Molidena, E., Yaen, H., DeFries, R., Verchat, L., Murdiyarso, D., Nasi, R., Holmgren, E. and Sheil, D. (2014) Major atmospheric emissions from peat fires in Southeast Asia during non-drought years: Evidence from the 2013 Sumatran fires. *Scientific Reports*, 4 (6112): 1–7.

Getzin, S., Wieg, K. and Schöning, I. (2012) Assessing biodiversity in forests using very high-resolution images and unmanned aerial vehicles. *Methods in Ecology and Evolution*, 3: 397–404.

Goodyer, J. (2013) "Drone Rangers," *Engineering and Technology*, 8 (5): 60–61.

Hansen, M.C., Potapov, P.V., Moore, R., Hancher, M., Turubanova, S.A., Tyukavina, A., Thau, D., Stehman, S.V., Goetz, S.J., Loveland, T.R., Kommareddy, A., Egorov, A., Chini, L., Justice, C.O. and Townsend, J.R.G. (2013) High-resolution global maps of 21st-century forest cover change. *Science*, 342 (6160): 850–853.

Hodgson, A., Kelly, N. and Peel, D. (2013) Unmanned aerial vehicles (UAVs) for surveying marine fauna: a dugong case study. *PLOS ONE*, 8: e79556.

Horcher, A. and Visser, R.J.M. (2004) "Unmanned aerial vehicles: Applications for natural resource management and monitoring," *Proceedings of the Council of Forest Engineering*.

Humle, T., Duffy, R., Roberts, D.L., Sandbrook, C., St John, F.A.V. and Smith, R.J. (2014) Biology's drones: Undermined by fear. *Science*, 344 (6190): 1352.

Jackson, R.M., Roe, J.D., Wangchuk, R. and Hunter, D.O. (2006) Estimating snow leopard population abundance using photography and capture-recapture techniques. *Wildlife Society Bulletin*, 34 (3): 772–781.

James, A., Gaston, K. and Balmford, A. (1999) Balancing the Earth's accounts. *Nature*, 40 (23): 323–324.

Jewell, Z. (2013) Effect of monitoring technique on quality of conservation science. *Conservation Biology*, 27 (3): 501–508.

Koh, L.P. (2014) "Evidence of Illegal Logging Activity Detected by Conservation Drones in Gunung Leuser National Park." Available at: http://conservationdrones. org/2014/09/30/illegal-logging/ (Accessed 10 April 2016).

Koh, L.P. and Wich, S.A. (2012) Dawn of drone ecology: Low-cost autonomous aerial vehicles for conservation. *Tropical Conservation Science*, 5: 121–132.

Körner, F., Speck, R., Göktoğan, A.H. and Sukkarieh, S. (2010) "Autonomous airborne wildlife tracking using radio signal strength," *The 2010 IEEE/RSJ International Conference on Intelligent Robots and Systems*, 18–22 October, Taipei, Taiwan.

Koski, W.R., Abgrall, P. and Yazvenko, S.B. (2010) An inventory and evaluation of unmanned aerial systems for offshore surveys of marine mammals. *Journal of Cetacean Research and Management*, 11 (3): 239–247.

Koski, W.R., Allen, T., Ireland, D., Buck, G., Smith, P.R., Macrander, A.M., Halick, M.A., Rushing, C., Sliwa, D.J. and McDonald, T.L. (2009) Evaluation of an unmanned airborne system for monitoring marine mammals. *Aquatic Mammals*, 35 (3): 347.

Leonardo, M., Chen, Y., Jensen, A.M., Coopmans, C. and Mckee, M. (2013) "A miniature wildlife tracking UAV payload system using acoustic biotelemetry," *Proceedings of ASME 2013 International Design Engineering Technical Conferences & Computers and Information in Engineering Conference IDETC/CIE*. Portland, Oregon, USA.

Lomax, A.S., Corso, W. and Etro, J.F. (2005) "Employing unmanned aerial vehicles (UAVs) as an element of the Integrated Ocean Observing System," *Oceans 2005*. Proceedings of MTS/IEEE (184–190). IEEE.

Maire, F., Mejias, L., Hodgson, A. and Gwenael, D. (2013) "Detection of dugongs from unmanned aerial vehicles," in *Proceedings of IEEE/RSJ International Conference on Intelligent Robots and Systems*. Tokyo: Tokyo Big Sight.

Meijaard, E., Wich, S., Ancrenaz, M. and Marshall, A.J. (2012) Not by science alone: Why orangutan conservationists must think outside the box. *Annals of the New York Academy of Sciences*, 1249 (1): 29–44.

Mulero-Pázmány, M., Negro, J.J. and Ferrer, M. (2013) A low cost way for assessing bird risk hazards in power lines: Fixed-wing small unmanned aircraft systems. *Journal of Unmanned Vehicle Systems*, 2: 5–15.

Mulero-Pázmány, M., Stolper, R., Van Essen, L.D., Negro, J.J. and Sassen, T. (2014) Remotely piloted aircraft systems as a rhinoceros anti-poaching tool in Africa. *PLOS ONE*, 9 (1): e83873.

NOAA (2009) Unmanned aircraft helping scientists learn about Alaskan ice seals. *Marine Pollution Bulletin*, 58: 1100.

NOAA (2015) "NOAA UAS in the news." Available at: http://uas.noaa.gov/news/ (Accessed 10 April 2016).

Paneque-Gálvez, J., McCall, M.K., Napoletano, B.M., Wich, S.A. and Koh, L.P. (2014) Small drones for community-based forest monitoring: An assessment of their feasibility and potential in tropical areas. *Forests*, 5 (6): 1481–1507.

Sardá-Palomera, F., Bota, G., Vinolo, C., Pallares, O., Sazatornil, V., Brotons, L., Gomáriz, S. and Sarda, F. (2012) Fine-scale bird monitoring from light unmanned aircraft systems. *Ibis*, 154 (1): 177–183.

Schiffman, R. (2014) Drones flying high as new tool for field biologists. *Science*, 344 (6183): 459.

Schlag, C. (2012) The new privacy battle: How the expanding use of drones continues to erode our concept of privacy and privacy rights. *The University of Pittsburgh Journal of Technology Law & Policy*, 13: 1–23.

Sea Shepherd (2011) "Sea Shepherd Intercepts the Japanese Whaling Fleet with Drones." Available at: www.seashepherd.org/news-and-media/2011/12/24/sea-shepherd-intercepts-the-japanese-whaling-fleet-with-drones-1299 (Accessed 10 April 2016).

ShadowView (2014) "Poachers Caught by ShadowView Drones." Available at: www.shadowview.org/news/poachers-caught-shadowview-drones/ (Accessed 10 April 2016).

Snitch, T. (2015) "Satellites, Mathematics and Drones Take Down Poachers in Africa." Available at: http://theconversation.com/satellites-mathematics-and-drones-take-down-poachers-in-africa-36638 (Accessed 10 April 2016).

Soarocean (2015) "Low Cost Drones for Ocean Conservation." Available at: http://soarocean.org/ (Accessed 10 April 2016).

Stem, C., Margoluis, R., Salafsky, N. and Brown, M. (2005) Monitoring and evaluation in conservation: A review of trends and approaches. *Conservation Biology*, 19 (2): 295–309.

Szantoi, Z., Koh, L.P. and Wich, S.A. "Mapping of land cover relevant for orangutans using landsat imagery augmented with unmanned autonomous vehicle photography." (in review). *PLOS ONE*.

Van Andel, A.C., Wich, S.A., Boesch, C., Koh, L.P., Robbins, M.M., Kelly, J. and Kühl, H. (2015) Locating chimpanzee nests and identifying important fruiting trees with an unmanned aerial vehicle. *American Journal of Primatology*, 77: 1122–1134.

van Gemert, J.C., Verschoor, C.R., Mettes, P., Epema, K., Koh, L.P. and Wich, S. (2014) "Nature conservation drones for automatic localization and counting of animals," in European Conference on Computer Vision workshop on Computer Vision in Vehicle Technology.

van Schaik, C.P. and Azwar, P.D. (1995) "Population estimates and habitat preferences of orangutans based on line transects of nests," in Nadler, R.D., Galdikas, B.M.F., Sheeran, L.K. and Rosen, N. (eds.), *The Neglected Ape*. Plenum Press, NY, pp 129–147.

Vermeulen, C., Lejeune, P., Lisein, J., Sawadogo, P. and Bouché, P. (2013) Unmanned aerial survey of elephants. *PLOS ONE* 8: e54700.

Weissensteiner, M.H, Poelstra, J.W. and Wolf, J.B.W. (2015). Low-budget ready-to-fly unmanned aerial vehicles: An effective tool for evaluating the nesting status of canopy-breeding bird species. *Journal of Avian Biology*, 46: 1–6.

Wich, S.A., Dellatore, D., Houghton, M., Ardi, R. and Koh, L.P. (2016) A preliminary assessment of using conservation drones for Sumatran orangutan (Pongo abelii) distribution and density. *Journal of Unmanned Vehicle Systems*, 4 (1): 45–52.

Wich, S.A., Meijaard, E., Marshall, A.J., Husson, S., Ancrenaz, M., Lacy, R.C., van Schaik, C.P., Sugardjito, J., Simorangkir, T., Traylor-Holzer, K., Doughty, M., Supriatna, J., Denon Geonis, R., Gumal, M., Knott, C.D. and Singleton, I. (2008) Distribution and conservation status of the orang-utan (*Pongo* spp.) on Borneo and Sumatra: How many remain? *Oryx*, 42: 329–339.

Wilson-Wilde, L. (2010) Wildlife crime: A global problem. *Forensic Science, Medicine and Pathology*, 6: 221–222.

Witmer, G.W. (2005) "Wildlife Population Monitoring: Some Practical Considerations," USDA National Wildlife Research Center – Staff Publications. Paper 70. Available at: http://digitalcommons.unl.edu/icwdm_usdanwrc/70 (Accessed 10 April 2016).

Woll, C., Prakash, A. and Sutton, T. (2011) A case-study of in-stream juvenile salmon habitat classification using decision-based fusion of multispectral aerial images. *Applied Remote Sensing Journal*, 2 (1): 37–46.

Yoccoz, N.G., Nichols, J.D. and Boulinier, T. (2001) Monitoring of biological diversity in space and time. *TRENDS in Ecology & Evolution*, 16 (8): 446–453.

Websites:

http://diydrones.com/.
http://landsatlook.usgs.gov/ (Accessed 10 April 2016).
http://ardupilot.org/ardupilot/index.html (Accessed 10 April 2016).

8 Drone/body

The drone's power to sense and construct emergencies

Mareile Kaufmann

Introduction

At present, we are witnessing an increasing acceptance of drone deployment, especially in emergencies where the drone has demonstrated its power: it can find victims, screen dangerous territory, direct aid, guide people out of chaotic emergency situations, and provide data for early warning systems. At the same time, drones are increasingly promoted as a tool that eventually outperforms human physical capacities: it is better suited than the human body to oversee emergency situations. Different authors of this volume investigate the drone's capability to identify bodies (Wich, Scott and Koh), to do surveillance (Karlsrud and Rosén; Jumbert), to provide for reconnaissance, documentation and sorting (Sandvik and Lidén) – and to do so with new levels of precision (Krasmann). These functionalities, however, are largely discussed as intimately linked to the visual. While a critical appraisal of the "drone stare" is shared by most chapters, this contribution explores how the drone moves beyond the stare as it is increasingly designed to combine its seeing capabilities with different sensing technologies. The drone offers more than new lines of sight: it hears sounds that may point to danger, it feels radiation, smells chemicals and interprets data. In exploring this trend, this chapter firstly presents an inventory of such additional sensors. The combination of different sensing technologies within one vehicle is especially studied as a novel phenomenon that is likely to proliferate rapidly. In line with the other chapters this contribution explores these "better-than-body" functions with respect to their potential to further enhance emergency management capacities and foster an argument about benevolent drone deployment. It describes how the drone pushes "doors open to new fields of use" (Jumbert and Sandvik), how it continues to blur boundaries between military and humanitarian use and how it acquires the status of the "good drone." While the sensing drone promises the acceleration and an increase in efficiency of emergency response – effects that are easily invoked to legitimise its use – this chapter does not stop with an assessment about what the sensing drone can do for emergency management. Rather, it addresses an overarching question in asking how the dynamic development of this sensing technology actually changes emergency management altogether. It does so by reflecting the benevolent argument vis-à-vis the drone's ability to function as a "quasi-body," a link between the body and the drone that is currently underexplored. Building on theories that acknowledge the formative power of technology, this chapter fleshes out to what extent the drone's sensing capabilities influence the construction of emergency situations and the human body. It describes how the drone combines electronic sensing capabilities with heightened mobility and the political economy of data collection and computation, through which it eventually contributes to the construction of what an emergency actually is.

The aim of this chapter is thus to explore how the emergency drone's sensing abilities imitate human bodies and what kind of power that implies. It develops the argument that through its sensing capabilities the drone does not only do something *for* emergency management, but also *to* emergency management (cf. Sandvik et al. 2014). By emulating and technically perfecting human senses, the good drone contributes to the construction of many different aspects of emergency governance. This includes the construction of the emergency situation per se, regulatory discourses and reasoning around emergencies, as well as the human body that is part of it. In all of these respects the drone has the capacity to sense and un-sense phenomena. It is thus not only important to explore how these abilities enhance and change emergency management practices, but also to highlight the power that the emergency drone exercises by assuming these functions.

In order to point out how the sensing drone constructs emergency governance, this chapter builds upon insights from political philosophy and critical security studies. More specifically, it draws on the literature which discusses the mutually constitutive relationship between technology, society and governance (cf. Woolgar 1991; Grusin 2010; Adey et al. 2011; Gregory 2011; Boyd and Crawford 2012; Amoore 2013; Duffield 2013), between technology and legal discourses (cf. Krasmann 2012; Leander 2013; Sandvik and Lohne 2014) as well as the relationship between technology and the body (cf. Bijker, Hughes and Pinch 1987; Woolgar 2012; Berkowitz 2014; Black 2014). Technology's role within society, the bulk of this literature suggests, is not one of a mere tool that is shaped by a specific culture, but in interaction with human beings it redefines relationships, practices and epistemologies of emergency governance. Technology, then, has the ability to construct rationalities and perform actions. This ability, so the chapter argues, also applies to the way in which the drone emulates human senses and constructs emergencies.

This chapter follows a broad understanding of emergencies as unforeseen and disruptive situations that emerge "against a background of ostensible normalcy, causing suffering or danger, and demanding urgent response" (Calhoun 2010: 30), since these situations pose a risk to life, health, property or environment (Drager et al. 2012: 19; Oxford Dictionary, Merriam Webster Dictionary). This may include emergencies of a smaller scale, for example missing persons, but also large-scale emergencies such as natural disasters, pandemics or terror attacks. This chapter references examples from emergency contexts in the global north and south. It excludes, however, cases of benevolent drone deployment in so-called "complex" (Wisner and Adams 2003) or "permanent emergencies" (Duffield 1994, cf. Hannigan 2012), such as conflicts, large-scale movements of people, famines or failing economies (Wisner and Adams 2003), as they refer to differing politics and practices of intervention. Broadly speaking, this chapter traces the narrative of the benevolent emergency drone in opposition to the killing drone. While drones are best known from the context of targeted killings in the global south and police operations targeting individuals in the north (Swaine 2013), actually functioning rescue drones have very recently emerged as its possible counterpart. The drone is now re-framed in terms of its potential to save the lives of individuals and groups during emergencies in the global north and south, spreading its wings from war zones to emergency areas (Seri 2014).

Generic emergency drones are increasingly tested by first responders. Some of them are already being deployed in the field. The use of the search and rescue drone in the aftermath of typhoon Haiyan, for example, entailed a leap forward in the acceptance of the emergency drone (Santos 2013). As of today, the secretariat of the pacific community (SPC 2014) uses drones to the Solomon Islands Country Office to obtain precise imagery of flooded areas, while the Austrian Red Cross also tests the use of drones for search and rescue operations (ORF.at 2014), just to name a few. While most of these emergency drones are handheld micro-drones, long-haul UAV Global Hawk has also been deployed for damage assessment after the 2010 Haiti Earthquake (Snyderman 2010). Most of the emergency drones currently in use are equipped with visual sensors for overview and location purposes, either to collect data for situational analysis, or to identify endangered individuals, groups or entombed bodies (cf. Franzen 2013). Other emergency drones feel and hear avalanches (Coghlan 2014) or smell the leak of dangerous gas (Bermúdez i Badia et al. 2007), all of which can be used to contain emergencies or avoid cascading effects.

Since the emergency drone of the near future is likely to combine various sensors, the first part will describe the different sensing capabilities that are being developed and tested in research projects or presented as narratives of opportunity by non-governmental organizations, technology enthusiasts and policymakers. This review presents what the various sensing capabilities are doing *for* emergency management. Since some of these narratives argue that the drone may be better suited than human bodies to perform specific emergency management tasks, this part furthermore discusses how these technological sensing capabilities relate to the human body.

The subsequent part will more thoroughly explore the role that sensors play for processes of construction – as opposed to processes of destruction – and point to the power that is inherent in the ability to construct something. By focusing on what the sensing drone does *to* emergency management the chapter will discuss the drone's potential to construct and transform four central elements of emergencies: the perception of the emergency situation, the regulatory discourse about drone deployment, reasoning about urgency and the human body as such. How these processes of construction and transformation may challenge the "good" in the good drone is reflected upon in the conclusions.

The "sensing drone" in emergency management

The following review presents the various sensing capabilities embodied in the "emergency drone" and what this drone does *for* emergency management.

An inventory of the "five sensors"

> *So if in the future you are unfortunate enough to find yourself caught up in a terrorist attack or natural disaster and see a robot hovering above your head, take heart – help may be closer than you think.*
>
> (Shaw 2012: 2)

The image of an infrared sensor, a 3 mm diode, generally evokes little association with the human body. However, performing the very meaning of the word, a sensor perceives and feels; it detects a stimulus and translates it into impulses – a process that is not too different from the human body's capacity to sense. It is not only the process of sensing itself that creates a link between the sensor and the human body, but generally new sensor technology serves as a means for the human body to expand its sensory reach and to act upon the received information, for example emergencies, as discussed here.

At times, this relationship complicates a clear distinction between the human body and the technological artifact: where does the body end and where do artifacts begin? Black (2014) argues that the boundary between the body and the artifact is fluid, since humans create artifacts for a specific purpose, but these artifacts also re-influence human bodies and the relation to their environments. The equipment of UAVs with sensors for the detection of lost persons, dangerous gas, or damaged areas can thus be understood as an attempt to extend the human capacity to sense for the purpose of emergency management. It is then expectable that the use of this sensing drone also re-influences the human body. However, in the case of the sensing drone, this mutual influence is much determined by the sophistication of the artifact. As opposed to a mere tool, a prosthetic device that adds to the mechanical abilities of the human body (Woolgar 2012), the sensing drone actually mimics, emulates and technically perfects human senses, to the extent that it seems to outreach the human body's capacities. Through that, the artifact itself, the sensing drone has already begun to re-influence the human body within the context of emergency management.

The following overview of the "five sensors" illustrates how sensing drones are being used for emergency response and how they – vis-à-vis the limits of

the human body – create opportunities for improving emergency management. The section furthermore leads us to understand how the drone's senses
contribute to the construction of emergency management.

Sight – Drones have always had an intimate relationship to visual
technologies. However, distance-measuring sensors (Spendlove 2014), wide-
area surveillance cameras, full motion video and hyperspectral imaging,
that is, sensors picking up on light across the electromagnetic spectrum
(Weinberger 2014), have radically redefined the drone's ability to see. Not
only does a sensing drone see more than the human eye due to its increased
mobility, but the combination of several cameras allow for a view at different
angles at the same time. Such overview functions do by no means entail that
a drone sees less detail. The opposite is the case: as opposed to humans,
night vision cameras see in low light conditions, sensors for spectral imaging
perceive more wavelengths than the human eye, other optical sensors can
measure exact distances to an object, determine pigmentation or identify at
which angle an object moves. Such visual functions can be used for scanning
complex terrains, identifying damage zones and casualties, which allows
for the monitoring of at-risk sites. Visual sensors mounted on drones are
currently used for situational analysis during floods (Falcon 2013; FEMA
2014), bushfires (Palmer 2013) and other emergencies. Since drones can
discriminate specific bodies they are currently being deployed to identify
endangered individuals and groups at sea or on land (cf. Franzen 2013).
Drones are furthermore deployed to gather information for analyzing the
dynamics of large groups and motion prediction (Wang et al. 2013) to control
crowds during emergencies. The remote measurement of pigmentation can
be useful to detect the spreading of dangerous bacteria (McGlashen 2013),
which may soon be used to monitor pandemics. All of these visual sensing
capacities exceed the human eye and carry the potential to improve emergency
management.

Touch – Another technology often associated with drones are thermal
infrared sensors, which allow for the detection and measurement of
precise temperature. Meteorological sensors expand these capacities as
they can measure humidity, wind direction, pressure and solar radiation
(cf. IRDAM's website). These sensors do not only sense heat, but they
outreach the human body's capacity to touch by their ability to measure
and determine precise values of diverse physical conditions. Others can
detect minimal seismic signals. In the context of emergency management
this ability allows drones to find bodies that are lost or that cannot be
seen by the human eye, because these bodies are buried under avalanches
or rubble (Molina et al. 2012). These drones can discriminate whether
bodies are dead or alive, but they can also warn about extreme weather or
earthquakes, which has lately also been presented as a new opportunity
to save lives (cf. National Oceanic and Atmospheric Administration;
Politecnico di Milano's "Prometeo Project").

Hearing – Acoustic sensors allow drones to detect, localize, filter and classify sounds (cf. SARA). While the estimation of the geographic location of an acoustic source can also be performed by humans, the removal of distracting noises in sound adverse environments and the classification of sounds is something that fewest humans can accomplish. Different research projects, some of them in cooperation with the Federal Emergency Management Agency (FEMA), investigate acoustic approaches to detect mudslides and avalanches (Coghlan 2014) or to locate people under rubble (cf. "Prometeo Project" at Politecnico di Milano). In combination with drones (Klein et al. 2013), these functions can be utilized to find missing persons or to detect ongoing incidents, which may cause further damage.

Smell and Taste – Chemical sensors, such as the "sniffer star" weigh less than most bird feathers (Schachtman, 2003; cf. Sandia National Laboratories) and can easily be mounted on a UAV. Not only do they pick up smells, but they can determine the composition of the chemical (Bermúdez i Badia et al. 2007). As such, they sniff better than humans or even trained detection dogs. Smell and taste sensors detect gases that humans are incapable of smelling. The ability to identify the composition of chemicals and their potential to react with other substances exceeds the capacities of the human nose. Such functions can be deployed in emergency situations to track chemical plumes or to monitor busy areas in order to discover the leakage or spreading of dangerous substances, such as toxic or flammable gas. This would also give emergency managers insights on evacuation plans or offer possibilities to deter cascading effects during emergencies (cf. Case study "Sensing Danger" at Georgia Tech Research Institute).

The sensibilities of sensing

These examples illustrate the considerable potential the sensing drone has to transform the management of complex emergency situations. However, as of today, many of the suggested solutions, tasks and tools can be situated somewhere between "technological fantasies," meaning narratives of technologies that offer effective answers to insecurities (Crang and Graham 2007) and emerging research topics. With the exception of combining conventional high-resolution and infrared cameras, single vehicles including various sensors have rarely been operational. To date, emergency drones are mainly deployed by the police (cf. Franzen 2013), professional emergency responders (ORF.at 2014; SPC 2014; Meier 2014b), private enthusiasts and the DIY movement or the providing companies (cf. Falcon 2013; De Oliveria 2013) to collect visual data for emergency monitoring and situational analysis or to locate missing individuals.

Visual capacities are increasingly combined with the transport of medication into inaccessible areas. In order to ensure that urgently needed medicine or defibrillators reach remote locations in time, Germany, for example, tests the so-called defikopter (Geuss 2014; Definetz 2013). Similar pilot projects have been conducted by the start-up company Matternet in Haiti and the Dominican Republic (De Oliveria 2013). In the same manner drones could also carry dangerous items, such as bombs, away from crowds (Coxworth 2011; Grose 2014). Even though the multi-sensorial emergency drone is currently only emerging and only partly operational, ongoing research projects merge and advance sensing and drone technology: the latest promise are drone swarms that allow for various sensor combinations (cf. Penders et al. 2007; Bürkle et al. 2011; Choi and Lee 2011; Penn State University – Department of Geography). But where does the project of the multi-sensorial drone lead us? The following paragraphs discuss this tentative project of the multi-sensorial drone vis-à-vis different theoretical approaches to technology and the body.

Drones with various sensing capabilities would constitute a powerful quasi-body with access opportunities that exceed those of human bodies. The emergency drone would not only defy physical barriers and dangerous situations, as weight and mobility provide the agility to enter "at-risk sites." More importantly, the drone has a different sensorial access to the emergency situation, since it seems to see, hear, taste, smell and feel more than the human body. If linked to databases, it provides for powerful computational emergency analytics. The drone's quasi-body thus holds the power to outperform the human body in emergency response. A competition between the two, however, is not yet obvious. One reason for that could be that its robotic features are not anthropomorphic. If at all, its bird- or insect-morphology rather creates acceptability problems due to its linkage to the military and killing context.

In the recent emergency management discourse, however, the drone is considered a long-awaited solution for the chaotic emergency situations that human responders face. In the spirit of performing the dull, dirty and especially the dangerous work, the drone and its technological counterparts have long inspired arguments about the partial replacement of human on-site commitments in favor of remote management. The deployment of emergency drones provides more opportunities for accessing emergency situations (Almon 2013), is safer for human responders (ibid.; Moe 2013; Mekki and Kamoun 2014) and improves decision-making: "the key to successful disaster response – amidst all the chaos – is the intelligent allocation of tasks and resources, and humans on the ground are not always best placed to make those life and death decisions" (Shaw 2012: 1).

The assistance that sensing drones can provide to emergency management teams and volunteers thus constitutes the basis for an argument about the deployment of the good drone for emergency management (cf. EU project ICARUS on UAVs for search and rescue). Using drones not only saves responders from dangerous work, in fact, it also provides additional management capacities that cannot be performed by the human body.

More critical technology observers and theorists would argue, however, that the capacity to emulate and outreach the human body's functions is what distinguishes the emergency drone from a mere management tool. While a tool has a direct sensory connection to the body and can be used in an unreflective manner, as if it was a part of our body schema, an emergency drone would constitute what Marx describes as a machine, which has a certain degree of autonomy (Marx 1980; cf. Leroi-Gourhan 1993).

Precisely because the emergency drone emulates sensory functions, it creates an analogy to the body rather integrating itself into the human body schema. As opposed to the optimist view that such autonomous functions assist the human emergency responder, a Marxist argument would focus on the resulting passivity of the human responder, who loses the sensory relationship with the artifact. Instead of acting *with* the machine, the emergency responder would have to act *on* the machine (Marx 1980). Following this argument, the drone would take agency and self-sufficiency away from the emergency responder to the extent that it replaces the human body in particular situations.

While the loss of agency to the machine readily lends itself as an argument to those who are critical of the good drone, Black (2014) argues that the question of agency and capacity is dependent on the modification of our sensory relationship with the environment. He acknowledges that artifacts may have different degrees of sensory connections to the human body, but a low degree of sensory connection to the artifact does not necessarily reduce the agency of the human body. The agency of the human body, he argues, arises from the interaction of the body with the artifact and its environment; the key to identifying agency is then to explore the way in which the interaction between the human body and the artifact modifies the body's sensory relationship with the environment.

Altogether, Black suggests that all sensory relationship arises from interaction and that artifacts simply alter the nature of the interplay between senses and environment. They are facilitators for new forms of agency (Black 2014). Even though the incorporation of new artifacts into everyday practices can at times be smooth and at times be a struggle, the general capacity of the human body to incorporate artifacts in new ways is not to underestimate: "When this capacity is combined with devices able to sense us and sense our sensing in ever more sophisticated ways, the possibilities for new kinds of experience are dramatically expanded" (ibid.: 52). He continues that the ability to incorporate new artifacts into body schemata "extends not only the reach of our capacity to act, but also our sensory reach, through the tool and out into the world" (ibid.: 55).

This argument is not to be mistaken as one that supports technology optimism. Rather, it draws attention away from the idea of a loss of agency and a necessary direct sensory connection to the artifact, and towards the study of how, for example, sensing drones change the human body's sensory relationship to its environment. Or, to take this argument further, it invites the study of how the sensing drone changes the human's relationship to the environment in general, to the emergency situation in particular and to those populations, which are sought to be reached by emergency management activities.

In sum, the impact that the sensing drone has on the human body is two-fold. On the one hand, it influences the responders' capacities to experience and sensitively act on the emergency situation. As such, the drone changes the responders' agency and the sensory relationship to the emergency environment. On the other hand, information collected by the drone's sensors also influences the responders' knowledge about the emergency situation and the emergency population. Through this knowledge the drone contributes to the construction of central elements within emergencies, which are discussed below.

The power of the sensing drone: from destruction to construction

So far, the critical discussion on the relationships between drones and the human body focused on the destruction and elimination of bodies in the context of targeted killings with combat drones (cf. O'Connell 2010). This discourse included different themes, for example the techniques, processes and visual cultures of the aerial gaze in general and air targeting in particular (Adey et al. 2011). It also discussed the role of remoteness and proximity in precision strikes (cf. Gregory's 2011 critique of Grossmann 1995) that are at times not very precise, killing and injuring civilians (Stanford Law School and NYU School of Law 2012). Different critical voices have focused on the constitutive powers of the drone, arguing that the drone contributes to a targeted killing dispositive (Krasmann 2012) and renders democracies more war-prone altogether (Sauer and Schörnig 2012). Others have argued that the drone not necessarily normalizes targeted killings, but also continues controversies about it (Leander 2013).

These literature contributions indicate that causing the destruction of a human is not the only way in which the drone assumes power: What precedes the destruction of a human body is the technology that enables the construction of a targeted human as a particular individual. Without this process of construction the logic of a precision strike is impossible and redundant. Construction then refers to the act of determining the identity of a person and the decision as to whether this person is hostile or harmless. Following this understanding of construction, the drone's sensory setup contributes to the establishment of a particular kind of human body as a threat, which constitutes a powerful act. Through its novel abilities to sense, gather and analyze data, the drone contributes to constructions and categorizations not only during warfare, but also during emergency situations, where the identification of human bodies and their categorization is equally central. In latter context, however, they are vulnerable bodies, in need of being rescued.

Sensing and un-sensing: the role of the sensor for processes of construction

The sensing drone mobilizes the production and circulation of information. It mediates interactions between people with the aim of generating data that can be used to effectively govern emergency populations (cf. Grusin 2010). Sensing is thus an essential constituent of the drone's power, because it plays a key role in collecting and analyzing information, through which it constructs the phenomena and contexts it is deployed for (cf. Woolgar 1991; Bijker, Hughes and Pinch 1987). The drone operator, for example, experiences, perceives and (re-)constructs the emergency situation by means of the drone's sensing capabilities, and by means of its increasingly sophisticated sensors, the drone can (re-)construct emergency situations in an ever more detailed manner, creating new modi of acting within such situations.

However, despite the drone's ability to emulate human senses, the operator's experience is never a direct one. It is delivered and enabled by an intermediary. The sensing drone transmits a copy of the situation and the responder deals with an incomplete image of reality. This incompleteness can be attributed to the sensor itself. Sensors are specialized to recognize particular shapes, substances, sounds or appearances over others. For example, despite the existence of so-called sensor arrays that recognize several smells (Albert et al. 2000), many sensors are designed to identify a particular substance of interest (Nanto et al. 1998). The sensor recognizes that particular substance, but it does not sense any other phenomena, which may, as a result, not be prioritized for emergency help. This problematique of sensing and un-sensing becomes particularly illustrative, for example, in the context of search and rescue operations, where un-sensing or selective sensing may have deadly consequences for the sought-after individual.

While technology optimists would argue that it is just a matter of developing better sensor technology to identify different appearances, the drone's reconstruction of a phenomenon is furthermore limited by the way in which the sensor transforms impulses into data and the way in which this data is then processed. In other words: the drone may sense particular phenomena, but it still needs to make sense of that information. In the same way in which humans need to analyze, interpret and categorize sensory impulses, information sensed by the drone also needs to be processed. Such analyses are conducted by human professionals, but information can also be organized, multiplied, searched and analyzed by algorithms.

Algorithmic analysis, however, imposes its own constitutive effects. Data does not exist objectively, out there, ready to be measured (Amoore 2013). Before analyzed, decisions are taken about which variables will be counted and which will be ignored. The process of imagining data is always bound to a specific context (Boyd and Crawford 2012). It is thus the process of imagining data and the programming of the algorithm that give data form. Algorithms that analyze data collected by specific sensors make visible whatever they can detect. What lies outside of this setup is not being identified (Gregory 2011) or reconstructed. It is un-sensed and unperceived. As such, algorithms have the power "to act, to affect, and to be affected" (Amoore 2013: 133).

Combined in the emergency drone, sensor and algorithm construct visibilities and invisibilities. Dependent on the reach of their sensors and the configuration of the algorithm, emergency drones discover, identify and (re-) construct specific phenomena during emergency situations, but they neglect, "un-sense" (cf. Sandvik and Lohne 2014) and render others invisible. This structural shortcoming of the sensor is complemented by other instances of un-sensing, such as human inobservance, technical miscalculations and malfunctions, as well as politically framed decisions to focus on some phenomena over others. The sensing drone thus not only emulates or potentially outreaches human senses, influencing human capacities to experience and act upon their environment, it also enables its own modi of reconstructing emergency situations by gathering information, creating knowledge and making sense of emergency management environments through purpose-built sensors and computation. These (re-)constructions are only ever as encompassing as the drone's architecture allows.

Thus, through its combination of sensorial, analytic and mobile capacities, the drone forms a powerful quasi-body that – within the limits of its configuration – affects and constructs various aspects of emergency governance, which this chapter will turn to now.

Constructing emergencies

To begin with, the drone not only (re-)constructs emergency situations for responders, but also for the recipients of emergency help. Within the context of military drone operations, it is well studied that the presence of a drone transforms the public and private space of those who reside in areas in which drones are being deployed: "The fear of strikes undermines people's sense of safety to such an extent that it has at times affected their willingness to engage in a wide variety of activities, including social gatherings, educational and economic opportunities, funerals" (Stanford Law School and NYU School of Law 2012: 55).

The drone's presence within an emergency management setting is less likely to evoke such dramatic effects. It does, however, influence the environment and the perception of emergencies by recipients and bystanders. A discussion on the deployment of drones for emergency management with representatives of the Norwegian Red Cross, technology experts, legal and ethical advisers and sociologists[1] highlighted that the mere presence of a drone, as opposed to the presence of human volunteers only, may influence the way in which individuals relate to emergencies. In particular, it was pointed out that the drone's association with military use,[2] and the known effects it creates in such contexts, may create discomfort on the one hand. Once more broadly accepted, it may create the exact opposite effect on the other, namely a false sense of security in the face of acute danger. Another factor influencing the construction and perception of emergency situations is the widespread connotation of the drone as an instrument of surveillance. Even though deployed for emergency management, a drone equipped with multiple sophisticated sensors may face difficulties in being socially accepted. As opposed to meeting a human volunteer, the encounter with drones is likely to evoke negative emotions (ibid.). In the context of search and rescue operations, for example, bystanders may perceive the presence of a drone as a violation of privacy, whereas the encounter with a volunteer may be positively connoted or at least accepted as a necessity, given the search and rescue operation.

While the drone has the power to shape the recipients' experience of emergency situations on the one hand, its increased deployment also transforms emergency management on the other. The current emergency management discourse predominantly emphasizes the drone's capacities to positively impact the course of the emergency situation (cf. Choi and Lee 2011; Meier 2013). Some of them claim quite literally that the "drone can transform emergency response" (Pennic 2014). Through its various abilities to sense, collect and process information, the drone not only accelerates situational analysis and helps in determining strategic response, but in some cases it also implements emergency measures, for example by providing specific medical supplies (ibid.; Geuss 2014; Definetz 2013).

The key here is that both data collection and response are dependent on the particular configuration of the drone's senses: it hears, smells and sees some stimuli, but not others. Following this understanding, the sensing drone actively contributes to the construction and definition of a situation as being urgent. It transmits information about what its algorithms determine to be dangerous and safe, whether that is gas (Bermúdez i Badia et al. 2007), bacteria (McGlashen 2013), sounds (Coghlan 2014) or actions. In terms of the latter, ideas have been forwarded that the drone could detect unusually high amounts of activities in, for example, hospitals, which can be used as an indicator for a spreading pandemic (Tucker 2014; cf. Sandvik 2014 for a critical take). By gathering and analyzing information about emergencies – within the boundaries of its technological configuration, the drone influences the conception of what an emergency is and what it is not. Sensing specific indicators and un-sensing others, it feeds this data directly into a situational analysis. As such, it affects both the scientific practice of emergency management and the definition and the governance of emergencies.

The drone's capacity to influence perceptions and constructions of emergency situations has thus the potential to influence the very rationales of emergency governance. A different kind of political implication has already become visible in the way in which the drone's deployment in emergency situations influences legal discourses.

Constructing regulatory discourses

The use of drones has long been addressed in regulatory discourses. The fact that the drone elicits regulatory lacunae further illustrates its formative capacities. Arguing already in 2008 that unmanned vehicles have a persistent and profound influence over the daily lives of citizens, Gogarty and Hagger question whether existing laws "adequately protect the principles they are designed to uphold in the face of the robotic revolution" (2008: 144). Ever since, the legal debate over the use of unmanned aerial vehicles (UAVs)[3] has kept growing and, over the past years, the drone has created continued controversy over legal boundaries (Leander 2013). This has also become apparent in the context of the good drone. Firstly, the emergency drone generates complications due to differing regulations for deploying drones during emergencies. More importantly, it creates discourses about the tensions between the drone's very sensing capabilities and regulations about (body) privacy and data protection. Both are briefly discussed below.

While seemingly less controversial and met with more optimism than the armed drone (cf. Almon 2013; Davis 2013; Baron 2014, UAViators. org),[4] the regulations for actually deploying drones for emergencies is still ambiguous. The certification of drone pilots, flight regulations and liability issues vary internationally, which creates problems for accountabilities in terms of unintended physical damage or illegal data collection. Most legal guidance is still being developed and "many countries in the global South (...) may have very little regulation at all" (OCHA 2014: 9). In many cases drone operations have to be cleared on an ad hoc basis (ibid.), as was the case after Typhoon Yolanda in the Philippines, on Hawaii after Hurricane Sandy and in Ludian County, China after an earthquake, where emergency drones were used for damage assessments. All of these cases were framed as a value-added to rescue efforts (Meier 2014a and b). That does not mean, however, that the use of emergency drones is free of legal controversy. Falcon's emergency drone, which was deployed to support response during the 2013 Colorado floodings, was, for example, grounded by FEMA (Falcon 2013). Similarly, the online dissemination of aerial images of the tornado-struck Mayflower caused an investigation by the US Federal Aviation Administration (Rutkin 2014).

The use of civil drones in the US remains a regulative issue, despite the launch of Section 333 by the Federal Aviation Administration (FAA 2014), which is an attempt to define special rules for UAVs. Canada's Aviation Regulations, in contrast, allow for the use of UAVs in accordance with a certificate that discloses details about the purpose and date of the operation, the vehicle itself and the detailed operation route (Transport Canada 2010) – all of which may complicate ad hoc operations for emergency response. The European Commission issued Regulation 216/2008/EC (Official Journal of the European Union 2008), which foresees the licensing of drones over 150kg by the European Air Safety Agency. UAVs below 150kg are regulated by the National Aviation Authorities of the member states. Germany, for example, adopted laws that allow such drones to fly up to 100 meters above the ground (Deutsches Luftverkehrsgesetz 2012), but only after permission has been granted. Similar regulations exist in most EU member states (Finn et al. 2014). Both the US and the European Union plan the integration of civil and commercial UAVs into national airspace by 2016. This would also solve one of the current key problems for operating emergency drones, since they are presently not allowed to interfere with traditional air traffic, but often have to operate around logistics hubs, a fact that currently complicates their spontaneous application (OCHA 2014: 9).

One of the most striking ambiguities in the regulation of drone use, however, refers to the drone's very ability to sense and to collect information through which it acquires panoptic power. This power is expansive, because it constrains individuals' opportunities to act on and assume fundamental rights. The application of the European Charter of Fundamental Rights (Official Journal of the European Communities 2000) to drone use for emergency management is not as straightforward as it seems. Article 7, the respect for private and family life, as well as Article 8, the protection of personal data, complicate the usage of drones equipped with sensors. Since the drone introduces "new points of access to historically protected spaces" (Calo 2012) regulation concerning the relationship between privacy, data protection and the emergency drone is still in the making. Both aspects are often sidelined in environments in which the protection of bare human life seems to gain primacy over private life and personal data.

The fact that data protection laws vary across the globe further complicates the situation. According to German regulation, for example, a drone is not allowed to fly into private zones and it has to respect data protection and safety regulations (BMVI 2014). However, flying into private zones, especially during search and rescue operations and for damage assessments, seems at times unavoidable and damage assessments easily produce visual data about private zones. A report for the European Commission more concretely discusses the concept of body privacy, "the right to keep body functions and body characteristics (...) private" (Finn et al. 2013: 15). Indistinct thermal pictures produced by emergency drones, for example, would then not intrude upon body privacy (Finn et al. 2014). Throughout the report's analysis it becomes clear, however, that the risk of intruding on body privacy and the potential objectification of the body is linked to the question of intentionality (ibid.: 220).

Accordingly, within the emergency management context, the argument about saving bare human life will once more overshadow the concern for body privacy, even though the various intentionalities that convene during emergency management procedures cannot always be clearly distinguished from another and personal data may not always be stored and used for its original purposes. If linked to intentionality, the guarantee of body privacy stays unresolved. A widespread response to such concerns is the call for improved technology development. Whether "Privacy by Design" (cf. Cavoukian et al. 2010), the integration of privacy into systems engineering, or "Secure by Design," which refers to secure software coding (CERT 2011), the next level of data protection looks for solutions that are built into the technology itself – not into the regulation of the data collection in the first place.

The question as to whether and how the mere presence of the emergency drone changes and infringes upon people's behavior, movements, everyday activities, as well as contents and modalities of expression is not addressed by such design concepts – even though they are equally anchored in the Charter of Fundamental Rights (Art. 11 Freedom of Expression and Information and Art. 45 Freedom of Movement and of Residence, OJEC 2000). A suggestion forwarded by the OCHA is to better contextualize emergency drone use and make data collection as transparent as possible, for example by implementing more rigorous informed consent measures (OCHA 2014: 10). Whether and how an informed consent procedure can be implemented during emergency situations is, however, still underexplored. Furthermore, even if specifically designed for the emergency management context, the drone's information gathering and ever-more sophisticated sensing capabilities may acquire more power over time than originally foreseen. As will be discussed next, sensing drones contribute to the overarching trend of a calculative politics as computerized sensorial equipment construct new modi of reasoning about emergencies.

Constructing reasoning

Despite the regulatory lacunae it creates, the drone's emergency management capacities remain promising. It takes on dirty, dull and dangerous missions and holds "the capacity to perform specific tasks with efficiency, reliability and mechanical rationality" (Berkowitz 2014: 160; De Shaw Rae 2014). It is this mechanical rationality that requires more exploration. Due to its ability to sense, gather and mechanically process information, the drone begins to emulate reasoning. Engineering efforts are increasingly directed at creating drones that can prepare and take decisions via algorithmic programming (Panella 2008). Some of these projects, in fact, seek "to emulate human pilot thought processes" (Eng et al. 2009: 329). Such processes require systems that take decisions based on a specific set of rules and on the information provided by sensors in order to meet overall mission requirements (Cummings et al. 2007: 4). Decision-making is already a standard feature in most computerized aerial vehicles, including traditionally piloted aircrafts. Most sensing and calculating technologies have the capacity to prepare a decision and replace human reasoning for particular tasks, which has lately become subject to criticism (Black 2014; Berkowitz 2014). However, since tools and machines have always assumed functions that either assisted or extended human action, it is useful to venture beyond this replacement rhetoric. It is more insightful to describe and problematize how the machine's decision-making functions inform and transform human reasoning.

Since the drone is given a set of parameters it abides by, decision-making is primarily considered a matter of programming, of "finding the rights sensors and algorithms" (Majumdar 2014: 10). Following a specific set of rules, the drone's calculative power breaks complex problems into a set of manageable decisions. This is a skill that humans rarely exhibit – especially not under stress – and it is thus easy to be "infatuated by [its] perfection" (Berkowitz

2014: 162). This perfection of "mechanical rationality" (ibid.: 160) constitutes the major difference between a drone's and human reasoning.

How so? In his dystopian novel *The Glass Bees*, Ernst Jünger summarizes as early as 1957 that "Technical perfection strives towards the calculable, human perfection towards the incalculable" (Jünger 1957: 155). This statement becomes particularly significant in the context of decision-making by sensing drones (cf. Berkowitz 2014). Even if a drone learns from data rather than following programmed instructions, drones are always designed to argue within the realm of the calculable. For that reason, some critics argue that machines "lack morality and mortality" (Christof Heyns[5] cited in Berkowitz 2014: 167) to decide over human lives and deaths – also in emergency situations. However, there may still be situations in which a drone's "purely logical decisions could be more ethical than human decisions, as they are not emotionally value-laden" (Tucker-Lowe 2012: 17). Drones may thus even exceed human decision-making capacities with calculative sophistication and precision. Their calculative power can neutralize "the advantage of experience" (Garry Kasparov[6] cited in Berkowitz 2014: 164) – at least when it comes to logical decisions.

Experiential and emotional knowledge, however, may be the missing piece in calculative decision-making. Drones cannot be convinced of the opposite. They are not intended to act on instinct or spontaneously. Drones have limited capacities to understand emotionally ambiguous situations. The fact that calculation is the only available means to a drone to take decisions is what distinguishes it fundamentally from humans. As long as it is not demonstrated that the human body, human acting and thinking itself is a result of calculation only, there will always be a difference between the human and the drone's way of reasoning. Berkowitz points out that it is the imperfections and ambiguities, the "perceived human weaknesses of distraction, emotion, exhaustion, quirkiness, risk, and unreliability" (Berkowitz 2014: 163), which mark us as human and that we risk losing if we succumb to our desire for perfect reliability, efficiency and calculative decision-making.

Positively framed, the drone's calculative powers could indicate the neutrality of its decision-making. This calculative neutrality, however, is unable to emulate human reasoning in all its complexity: drones may be designed to take autonomous decisions, but not to have an opinion or to act intentionally. The drone does not have a motivation; it does not invest itself into a specific cause. It reasons without thought (Berkowitz 2014). The sensing drone may fulfill its mission with calculative perfection, but it is humans that ultimately give sense to that mission. As a result, the increased effort to automatize emergency help by means of drones may have the power to change human engagement with emergencies altogether. It can change the humanness of helping and it may impact upon the capacity to take spontaneous decisions, which are crucial in the context of emergencies. As such, the sensing drone contributes to the construction of human bodies per se.

Constructing bodies

The increased distribution of drones affects and remodels the relationship between the responder's body and his or her operational environment. A recent news report on emergency drones states: "Operators can watch, talk and instruct those helping the victim by using an on-board camera" (Prigg 2014). Sensing technologies thus increasingly mediate the physical interaction between operators and recipients. While this development toward remote-sensing technologies may be considered an asset by some, recent criticism refers to the gradual removal of emergency responders bodies from the emergency site toward their operational bases. This process entails a growing disconnect to the field, a virtualization of the emergency situation and the establishment of remote control and physical distance (Stoddard et al. 2010; Duffield 2013). Another curious instance of remote sensing is the gamification of operational emergency management (Holdeman 2011; Crowe 2012), which, for example, suggests the embedding of visual data from emergency sites into online computer games for analysis (IRL 2013).

This discourse shows that the sensing drone may instantiate remoteness on the one hand, but it also creates new forms of closeness to the emergency situation for the operator and for public volunteers on the other (for a similar argument in the context of targeted killing cf. Gregory 2011). The sensing drone enables the seeing, smelling, touching and hearing of phenomena that are impossible for the operator to access without a drone. As such, the drone creates opportunities for sensitively acting upon emergency situations. This form of closeness, however, is something that operators and volunteers would first have to learn to deal with. On that background, it is necessary to inquire how the shift in the operator's physical presence and absence influences the emergency responders' mission, motivations and self-conception.

Sensing drones not only contribute to the construction of the responder's body, but also to that of the recipient. Visual reconstructions of the drone's operational environment and the human bodies located in it, which originally allowed for the opportunity to evade detection through camouflage (Adey et al. 2011), are now complemented by a variety of sensors. While the multi-sensorial setup of drones may change the character of camouflage over time, it currently represents the impossibility to hide. In the context of the recent upsurge of the Ebola virus, for example, speculative suggestions were made to deploy thermal cameras to feel the temperature of bodies as an indicator to identify potential symptoms and categorize individuals as sick (DIYDrones.com; cf. Sandvik 2014). While such scenarios clearly transgress borders of body privacy and may inspire novel phenomena of camouflage, the emergency management context is otherwise marked by the hope and an urgency to be seen, found and identified. The impossibility to hide is here turned into an asset, not only to drone operators, but also to those who are supposed to receive emergency help.

Within the context of emergency management, a drone's ability to sense, detect and follow bodies contributes to the construction of the body in need.

The body in need of help is suffering; it is wounded or contaminated, so it has to be distinguished from those bodies that are not. Establishing particular categorizations for human bodies and deciding upon their survivability, prioritizing more urgent cases over others, is the basis of triage. Current research in the field of engineering suggests building drones that not only assist in conducting triage, but that actually perform such procedures autonomously (White 2013), which also ties in with the discussions on decision-making. This underlines the powerful role that drones play in the construction and categorization of human bodies: not only in the context of targeted killings, but also in the context of emergency management, the drone increasingly decides over life and death by identifying and constructing different categories of bodies in need.

While triage deals with the overwhelming presence of bodies, the emergency drone also contributes to the (re-)construction of absent bodies. Its deployment in search and rescue operations establishes the category of the missing body that needs to be found and whose intactness is sought to be determined (Doherty and Rudol 2007). During such operations drones target mainly singular or specific human bodies. Emergency drones, however, also construct the collective body of the crowd, which, especially in the context of emergencies during mass gatherings, has been framed in terms of panic and its potentially deadly consequences (Heise 2013). In the context of emergency management during big events, the emergency management drone exercises power by actively controlling this crowd, for example by the use of pepper spray in critical situations (Desert Wolf; Smith 2014). Thus, the emergency drone does not only become a powerful quasi-body and a machinic extension of human agency through its various sensing capabilities, but it also contributes to construction and transformation of the human body itself.

Conclusion: the drone and the body – a sensitive relationship

The ambition of this chapter was to map out the way in which the drone's sensing capabilities influence emergency management and to engage in a reflection about the emergency drone as a powerful quasi-body that contributes to the construction of the emergency situation, regulatory discourses and reasoning around emergencies, as well as the human body that is part of it. This discussion of the drone's sensing capabilities not only expands an understanding of the drone's constitutive powers, but it also introduces this critical debate into the emergency management domain, where the benevolent argument of the emergency drone affords a strong legitimating effect vis-à-vis responders, lawmakers and possibly society at large.

The promise that the sensing drone offers to emergency management is indeed powerful. It provides the technological potential to reinvent, speed up and render more precise management activities, such as search and rescue, first response, crowd control, as well as the detection and handling of emerging risks (cf. Doherty and Rudol 2007; Almon 2013; Mekki and Kamoun 2014). This potential, however, also implicates the transformative power of the drone to construct emergencies – at times in inconspicuous ways, which need identification, acknowledgment and critical discussion.

The drone's main capabilities to construct and influence emergencies lie in its emulation and calculative perfection of sensing. However, through its sensors, the drone also mediates experiences. It constructs situations and bodies through information gathering and algorithmic analysis, both of which feed into broader categories, for example bodies in need that begin to structure and define emergency situations. Such constructions, however, are always constrained by the technological limits of the drone's design. Despite its increased capability to detect and view phenomena, the drone senses only particular modes of urgency and specific kinds of bodies and it un-senses others. In doing so, the drone creates new forms of presence and absence of both the emergency manager and of the recipients of emergency management. The drone is furthermore likely to influence the way in which an emergency situation is perceived by drone operators, as well as by recipients and bystanders. By focusing on specific situations and by sensitively mediating them, it contributes to the construction of the emergency situation as such. The drone's sensing capabilities have the power to create regulatory discourses and they generate a technically engineered form of autonomous decision-making, a form of reasoning that takes the humanness out of emergency engagements.

The major unintended effect of the good drone is thus that it affects human–human relationships. It changes the experience of emergencies and emergency help for both managers and recipients. When humanity, a core principle and driver for emergency management organizations, is to an increasing extent technologically mediated, it is important to identify the point at which the drone's way of constructing emergencies can no longer be considered a value-added to emergency management. At this point, it is instructive to confront the enormous potential that the sensing drone offers to emergency management with the ways in which its very sensing capabilities can challenge the "good" of the good drone. This refers to the potential of un-sensing suffering, evoking distrust, creating dependencies and redefining emergencies. When deploying the sensing drone for doing good it is not only essential to consider how it may infringe upon rights and how it challenges accountabilities, but also to consider situations in which its perfectly calculated decision can become too resolute and gain too much power over the emergency situation. More scholarly attention must be given to the way in which the sensing drone influences human reasoning, human presence in the field and the human bodies that emergency management seeks to save. Hence, engineering emergency aid Jünger's insight may function as a guiding principle: What are the incalculable aspects of emergency management that cannot be delivered by the calculative perfection of a drone, even if it emulates and expands the human capacity to sense?

Notes

1 The Peace Research Institute Oslo and the Norwegian Board of Technology hosted a workshop on March 7, 2013, discussing whether drones could and should be used in search and rescue operations in Norway. This workshop, developed in cooperation with the Norwegian Red Cross, involved over 25 experts from fields such as military and defense, law, ethics and fundamental rights, technology and emergency management. It was part of the FP7-funded DESSI project (Decision Support on Security Investment).
2 Gogarty and Hagger write that although UAVs "have begun to transition to the civilian sector they still retain many of their military characteristics." (2008: 144). The same problem is touched upon by the OCHA report, pointing out that humanitarian organizations wish not to be associated with military technology https://docs.unocha.org/sites/dms/Documents/Unmanned%20Aerial%20Vehicles%20in%20Humanitarian%20Response%20OCHA%20July%202014.pdf, p. 9.
3 The naming for drones varies according to legislation. This section uses the terminology forwarded in the respective regulations.
4 The OCHA report "Unmanned Aerial Vehicles in Humanitarian Response" points out that the rising interest in the use of drones for emergency management may also be the result of marketing campaigns (2014: 3).
5 When cited, in 2013, Christof Heyns was Special Rapporteur on Extrajudicial, Summary or Arbitrary Executions.
6 Garry Kasparov is the first World Chess Playing Champion to fall to the chess playing machine "Deep Blue."

References

Adey, P., Whitehead, M. and Williams, A.J. (2011) Introduction. Air-target: Distance, reach and the politics of verticality. *Theory Culture Society*, 28 (7–8): 173–187.
Albert, K.J., Lewis, N.S., Schauer, C.L., Sotzing, G.A., Stitzel, S.E., Vaid, T.P. and Walt, D.R. (2000) Cross-reactive chemical sensor arrays. *Chemical Reviews*, 100 (7): 2595–2626.
Almon, G. (2013) Exploring the use of drones for emergency response. Available at: www.tech4relief.com/2013/10/09/exploring-the-use-of-drones-in-emergency-response/ (Accessed April 10, 2016).
Amoore, L. (2013) *The Politics of Possibility. Risk and Security Beyond Probability*. Durham/London: Duke University Press.
Baron, G. (2014) UAVs and Emergency Management: Progress and Regress. Available at: www.emergencymgmt.com/emergency-blogs/crisis-comm/UAVs-and-Emergency-Managementprogress-and-regress.html (Accessed April 10, 2016).
Berkowitz, R. (2014) Drones and the question of "the human." *Ethics & International Affairs*, 28 (2): 159–169.
Bermúdez i Badia, S., Bernadet, U., Guanella, A., Pyk, P. and Verschure, P. (2007) A biologically based chemo-sensing UAV for humanitarian demining. *International Journal of Advanced Robotic Systems*, 4 (2): 187–198.
Bijker, W., Hughes, T. and Pinch, T. (1987) *The Social Construction of Technological Systems: New Directions in the Sociology and History of Technology*. Cambridge MA/London: MIT Press.
Black, D. (2014) Where bodies end and artefacts begin: Tools, machines and interfaces. *Body & Society*, 20 (1): 31–60.

188 *Mareile Kaufmann*

BMVI (2014) Kurzinformation über die Nutzung von unbemannten Luftfahrtsystemen. Available at: www.bmvi.de/SharedDocs/DE/Publikationen/LF/unbemannte-luftfahrtsysteme.pdf?__blob=publicationFile (Accessed 10 April 2016) (Accessed April 10, 2016).

Boyd, D. and Crawford, K. (2012) Critical questions for big data. Provocations for a cultural, technological, and scholarly phenomenon. *Information, Communication and Society*, 15 (5): 662–679.

Bürkle, A., Segor, F. and Kollmann, M. (2011) Towards autonomous micro UAV swarms. *Journal for Intelligent Robotic Systems*, 61: 339–353.

Calhoun, C. (2010) The idea of emergency: humanitarian action and global (dis)order, in Fassin, D. and Pandolfi, M. (eds.), *Contemporary States of Emergency: The Politics of Military and Humanitarian Interventions*. New York: Zone Books. 29–58.

Calo, R.M. (2012) Robots and Privacy, in Patrick Lin, Keith Abney and George A. Bekey (eds.), *Robot Ethics: The Ethical and Social Implications of Robotics*. Cambridge: MIT Press. 187–202.

Cavoukian, A., Stoddart, J., Dix, A., Nemec, I., Peep, V. and Shroff, M. (2010) Privacy by Design Resolution. 32nd International Conference on Data Protection and Privacy Commissioners. Available at: www.ipc.on.ca/site_documents/pbd-resolution.pdf (Accessed April 10, 2016).

CERT (2011) Top 10 Secure Coding Practices. Software Engineering Institue Carnegie Mellon University. Available at: www.securecoding.cert.org/confluence/display/seccode/Top+10+Secure+Coding+Practices (Accessed April 10, 2016).

Choi, K. and Lee, I. (2011) A UAV based close-range rapid aerial monitoring system for emergency responses. International Archives of the Photogrammetry, Remote Sensing and Spatial Information Sciences, Vol. XXXVIII-1/C22 UAV-g 2011. Available at: www.geometh.ethz.ch/uav_g/proceedings/lee (Accessed April 10, 2016).

Civil Aviation Authority UK (2012) CAP 722 Unmanned Aircraft System Operations in UK Airspace – Guidance. Available at: www.caa.co.uk/application.aspx?catid=33&pagetype=65&appid=11&mode=detail&id=415 (Accessed April 10, 2016).

Coghlan, A. (2014) Mudslides Could Be Predicted With Acoustic Sensors. Available at: www.newscientist.com/article/dn25289-mudslides-could-be-predicted-with-acoustic-sensors.html#.VIbLoDHF98E (Accessed April 10, 2016).

Coxworth, B. (2011) Matternet Would Use UAVs to Deliver Supplies to Remote Villages. Available at: www.gizmag.com/matternet-goods-transporting-uav-network/19663/ (Accessed April 10, 2016).

Crang, M. and Graham, S. (2007) Sentient cities: Ambient intelligence and the politics of urban space. *Information, Communication and Society*, 10 (6): 789–817.

Crowe, A. (2012) *Disasters 2.0. The Application of Social Media Systems for Emergency Management*. Boca Raton: Taylor and Francis CRC Press.

Cummings, M.L., Bruni, S., Mercier, S. and Mitchell, P.J. (2007) Automation architecture for single operator, multiple UAV command and control. *The International C2 Journal*, 1 (2): 1–24.

Davis, R.L. (2013) The Practicality of Using Unmanned Aerial Vehicles for Damage Assessments, Austin Fire Department, Austin, Texas. Available at: http://austintexas.gov/sites/default/files/files/Fire/Wildfire/RescueRobotics/UAVforDamageAssessments_Davis.pdf (Accessed April 10, 2016).

Definetz.de (2013) Defikopter: Drohnen können Leben retten. Available at: www. definetz.de/index.php?option=com_content&view=article&id=769:defikopter-drohnen-koennen-leben-retten&catid=91:defikopter&Itemid=122 (Accessed April 10, 2016).

De Oliveira, R. (2013) Flying Aid Drones Tested in Haiti and Dominican Republic. Available at: www.theguardian.com/global-development/2013/jan/09/flying-aid-drones-haiti-dominican-republic (Accessed April 10, 2016).

De Shaw Rae, J. (2014) *Analyzing the Drone Debates*. New York: Palgrave Macmillan.

Deutsches Luftverkehrsgesetz (2012) § 16 Absatz 1 Nummer 7 LuftVO. Available at: www.gesetze-im-internet.de/luftvg/__16.html (Accessed April 10, 2016).

Doherty, P. and Rudol, P. (2007) A UAV search and rescue scenario with human body detection and geolocalization. AI advances in artificial intelligence. *Lecture Notes in Computer Science*, 4830: 1–13.

Drager, K.H., Nicolae, S., Hagen, J. and Ion, P. (2012) *Training for Rural Communities in Emergency Management and Emergency Situations*. The International Emergency Management Society.

Duffield, M. (1994) Complex emergencies and the crisis of developmentalism. *IDS Bulletin*, 25 (4).

Duffield, M. (2013) Disaster Resilience in the Network Age. Access-Denial and the Rise of Cyber-Humanitarianism. DIIS Working Paper 23.

Eng, P.C., Mejias, L., Liu, X. and Walker, R.A. (2009) Automating human thought processes for a UAV forced landing. *Journal of Intelligent and Robotic Systems*, 57 (1–4): 329–349.

Falcon (2013) Falcon UAV Supports Colorado Flooding Until Grounded by FEMA. Available at: www.falconunmanned.com/falcon-uav-news/2013/9/14/-falcon-uav-supports-colorado-flooding-until-grounded-by-fem.html (Accessed April 10, 2016).

Federal Aviation Administration (2014) Section 333. Available at: www.faa.gov/uas/legislative_programs/section_333/ (Accessed April 10, 2016).

FEMA (2014) Flood Zone Determination Companies. Available at: www.fema.gov/national-flood-insurance-program/flood-zone-determination-companies (Accessed April 10, 2016).

Finn, R.L., Wright, D. and Friedewald, M. (2013) Seven types of Privacy, in Gutwirth, S., Leenes, R., De Hert, P. and Poullet, Y. (eds.), *European Data Protection: Coming of Age*. Dordrecht: Springer. 3–32.

Finn, R.L., Wright, D., Donovan, A., Jacques, L. and De Hert, P. (2014) Privacy, data protection and ethical risks in civil RPAS operations; D3.3: Final report for the European Commission. Available at: http://ec.europa.eu/DocsRoom/documents/8550 (Accessed April 10, 2016).

Franzen, C. (2013) Canadian Mounties Claim First Person's Life Saved by a Police Drone. Available at: www.theverge.com/2013/5/10/4318770/canada-draganflyer-drone-claims-first-life-saved-search-rescue (Accessed April 10, 2016).

Geuss, M. (2014) German Company to Use "parcelcopter" drone to bring medicine to remote island. Available at: http://arstechnica.com/tech-policy/2014/09/german-company-to-use-parcelcopter-drone-to-bring-medicine-to-remote-island/ (Accessed April 10, 2016).

Gogarty, B. and Hagger, M. (2008) The laws of man over vehicles unmanned: The legal response to robotic revolution on sea, land and air. *Journal of Law, Information and Science*, 19 (1): 73–145.

Gregory, D. (2011) From a view to a kill: Drones and late modern war. *Theory Culture Society*, 28 (7–8): 188–215.

Grose, T. (2014) Are Unmanned Drones the Future of Global Transport? www.newsweek.com/next-chapter-flight-cargo-planes-without-pilots-259717.

Grossman, D. (1995) *On Killing: The Psychological Cost of Learning to Kill in War and Society*. New York: Back Bay Books.

Grusin, R. (2010) *Premediation: Affect and Mediality after 9/11*. New York: Palgrave.

Hannigan, J. (2012) *Disasters Without Borders: The International Politics of Natural Disasters*. Cambridge: Polity.

Heise, K. (2013) When Crowds Kill: How Apps, Drones, And Psychology Can Improve Crowd Control. Available at: www.worldcrunch.com/tech-science/when-crowds-kill-how-apps-drones-and-psychology-can-improve-crowd-control/quake-turbulence-shock-wave-duisburg-helbing/c4s10578/#.VJP_XV4AAA (Accessed April 10, 2016).

Holdeman, E. (2011) SF Heroes – Gamification of Emergency Preparedness. Available at: www.emergencymgmt.com/emergency-blogs/disaster-zone/SF-heroes-gamification-of-emergency-preparedness-072111.html (Accessed April 10, 2016).

IRL (2013) Internet Response League. IRL Moving Forward. Available at: http://internet-response-league.com/2013/07/10/irl-moving-forward/ (Accessed April 10, 2016).

Jünger, E. (2000/1957) *The Glass Bees*. New York: The New York Review of Books.

Klein, D.J., Venkateswaran, S., Isaacs, J.T., Pham, T., Burman, J., Hespanha, J.P. and Madhow, U. (2013) Source localization in sparse acoustic sensor network using UAV-based semantic data mules. *AC Transactions on Sensor Networks*, 9 (3).

Krasmann, S. (2012) Targeted killing and its law: On a mutually constitutive relationship. *Leiden Journal of International Law*, 25 (3): 665–682.

Leander, A. (2013) Technological agency in the co-constitution of legal expertise and the US drone program. *Leiden Journal of International Law*, 26 (4): 811–831.

Leroi-Gourhan, A. (1993) *Gesture and Speech*, Berger, A.B. (trans.). Cambridge, Massachussets: MIT.

Majumdar, D. (2014) Essay: The Legal and Moral Problems of Autonomous Strike Aircraft. Available at: http://news.usni.org/2014/08/21/essay-legal-moral-problems-autonomous-strike-aircraft (Accessed April 10, 2016).

Marx, K. (1980) *Marx's Grundrisse* (2nd edn), D. McLellan (ed.). London: Macmillan.

McGlashen, A. (2013) Research Refines Remote Sensing of Cyanobacteria Blooms. Environmental Monitor. Available at: www.fondriest.com/news/research-refines-remote-sensing-of-cyanobacteria-blooms.htm (Accessed April 10, 2016).

Meier, P. (2013) How UAVs Are Making a Difference in Disaster Response. Available at: http://irevolution.net/2013/12/05/uavs-in-disaster-response/ (Accessed April 10, 2016).

Meier, P. (2014a) Humanitarians in the Sky: Using UAVs for Disaster Response. Available at: http://irevolution.net/2014/06/25/humanitarians-in-the-sky/ (Accessed April 10, 2016).

Meier, P. (2014b) Humanitarian UAVs Fly in China After Earthquake (updated). Available at: http://irevolution.net/2014/08/25/humanitarian-uav-china-earthquake/ (Accessed April 10, 2016).

Mekki, S. and Kamoun, M. (2014) ANCHORS, an UAV Assisted Integrated Approach to Crisis Management. Available at: www.agence-nationale-recherche.fr/fileadmin/documents/2014/wisg/actes/ANCHORS.pdf (Accessed April 10, 2016).

Merriam Webster Online Encyclopedia Available at: www.merriam-webster.com/dictionary/emergency (Accessed April 10, 2016).

Moe, Å.R. (2013) Saken forklart: Sivile droner tar av. Available at: https://teknologiradet.no/sikkerhet-og-personvern/saken-forklart-sivile-droner-tar-av/ (Accessed April 10, 2016).

Molina, P., Pares, M.A., Colomina, I., Vitoria, T., Silva, P., Skaloud, J., Kormus, W., Prades, R. and Aguilera, C. (2012) Drones to the rescue! Unmanned aerial search missions based on thermal imaging and reliable navigation. *Inside GNSS*, (July/August 2012), 36–47.

Nanto, H., Morita, T., Habara, H., Kondo, K., Douguchi, Y. and Minami, T. (1998) Doping effect of SnO_2 on gas sensing characteristics of sputtered ZnO thin film chemical sensor. *Sensors and Actuators B: Chemical*, 36 (1–3): 384–387.

National Oceanic and Atmospheric Administration Available at: http://uas.noaa.gov/ (Accessed April 10, 2016).

OCHA (2014) Unmanned Aerial Vehicles in Humanitarian Response. OCHA Policy and Studies Series. June 2014. 010.

O'Connell, M.E. (2010) Unlawful Killing with Combat Drones: A Case Study of Pakistan, 2004–2009. Notre Dame Legal Studies Paper No. 09–43.

Official Journal of the European Communities (2000) Charter of Fundamental Rights of the European Union. 2000/C 364/01. Available at: www.europarl.europa.eu/charter/pdf/text_en.pdf (Accessed April 10, 2016).

Official Journal of the European Union (2008) Regulation (EC) No 216/2008 of The European Parliament and of The Council of February 20. Available at: http://eur-lex.europa.eu/LexUriServ/LexUriServ.do?uri=OJ:L:2008:079:0001:0049:EN:PDF (Accessed April 10, 2016).

ORF.at (2014) Drohnen für Suche nach Vermissten, August 19. Available at: http://noe.orf.at/news/stories/2663835/ (Accessed April 10, 2016).

Oxford Dictionaries. Available at: www.oxforddictionaries.com/definition/english/emergency?searchDictCode=all (Accessed April 10, 2016).

Palmer, C. (2013) Drones to Forecast Future Bushfires. *Itnews*. Available at: www.itnews.com.au/news/drones-to-forecast-future-bushfires-328040 (Accessed 13 April 2016).

Panella, I. (2008) Aritifical intelligence methodologies applicable to support the decision-making capability on board Unmanned Aerial Vehicles. BLISS '08 Proceedings of the 2008 Bio-inspired, Learning and Intelligent Systems for Security. IEEE Computer Society, 111–118.

Penders, J., Cervera, E., Witkofski, U., Marques, L., Gancet, J., Bureau, P., Gazi, V. and Guzman, R. (2007) Guardians: A swarm of autonomous robots for emergencies, in Krishna, K.M. and Indurkhya, B. (eds.), *Workshop on multirobotic systems for societal applications*. Available at: www.robot.uji.es/documents/guardians/workshops/IJCAI07.pdf#page=16 (Accessed April 10, 2016).

Penn State University, Depratment of Geography, Planning GIS for Emergency Management. Available at: www.e-education.psu.edu/geog588/l2_p5.html (Accessed April 10, 2016).

Pennic, F. (2014) Ambulance Drone Could Transform Emergency Response. Available at: http://hitconsultant.net/2014/12/02/ambulance-drone-could-transform-emergency-response/ (Accessed April 10, 2016).

Politecnico di Milano, Prometeo Project. Available at: www.prometeo.polimi.it/GPE/GPEing/GPE_area_2.html (Accessed April 10, 2016).

Prigg, M. (2014) The Ambulance Drone That Could Save Your Life. Flying Defibrillator Can Reach Speeds of 60 mph. Available at: www.dailymail.co.uk/sciencetech/article-2811851/The-ambulance-drone-save-life-Flying-defibrillator-reach-speeds-60mph.html (Accessed April 10, 2016).

Rutkin, A. (2014) Drone Law: Flying Into A Legal Twilight Zone. Available at: www.newscientist.com/article/mg22229694.400-drone-law-flying-into-a-legal-twilight-zone.html#.VACCfDKSx8F (Accessed April 10, 2016).

Sandvik, K.B. (2014) Fighting the War with the Ebola Drone. Available at: https://matsutas.wordpress.com/2014/12/02/fighting-the-war-with-the-ebola-drone-by-kristin-b-sandvik/ (Accessed April 10, 2016).

Sandvik, K.B. and Lohne, K. (2014) The rise of the humanitarian drone: Giving content to an emerging concept. *Millennium: Journal of International Studies*, 42 (3): 1–12.

Sandvik, K.B., Jumbert, M.G., Karlsrud, J. and Kaufmann, M. (2014) Humanitarian technology: A critical research agenda. *International Review of the Red Cross*, 96 (1): 1–24.

Santos, L.A. (2013) In the Philippines, Drones Provide Humanitarian Relief. Available at: www.devex.com/news/in-the-philippines-drones-provide-humanitarian-relief-82512 (Accessed April 10, 2016).

Sauer, F. and Schörnig, N. (2012) Killer drones: The "silver bullet" of democratic warfare. *Security Dialogue*, 43 (4): 363–380.

Schachtman, N. (2003) Drones See, Smell Evil From Above. Wired.com. Available at: http://archive.wired.com/politics/law/news/2003/03/58173 (Accessed April 10, 2016).

Secretariat of the Pacific Community (SPC 2014) Secretariat of the Pacific Community Brings Drone Technology to Solomon Islands. Available at: www.spc.int/en/component/content/article/216-about-spc-news/1627--secretariat-of-the-pacific-community-brings-drone-technology-to-solomon-islands-.html (Accessed April 10, 2016).

Seri, A. (2014) Drones Spread Wings From War Zones to Disaster Areas. Available at: www.scidev.net/global/innovation/news/drones-spread-wings-from-war-zones-to-disaster-areas-1.html (Accessed April 10, 2016).

Shaw, D. (2012) Disaster Drones. How Robot Teams Can Help in a Crisis. Available at: www.bbc.com/news/technology-18581883 (Accessed April 10, 2016).

Sm̲____ Offered to South African Mines for Strike ____ble at: www.theguardian.com/world/2014/jun/____-african-mines-strike-control (Accessed April 10, 2016).

Sr̲____ Photographs Damage to Help Relief Efforts. ____ov/news/newsarticle.aspx?id=57540 (Accessed ____

Sp̲____ Distance Measurement Sensors for Drones ____ble at: www.engineering.com/DesignerEdge/____/020/LIDAR-Lite-Distance-Measurement-____ccessed April 10, 2016).

St̲____ uman Rights and Conflict Resolution Clinic) ____ice Clinic) (2012) Living Under Drones. Death, Injury and Trauma to Civilians from US Drone Practices in Pakistan. Available at: https://law.stanford.edu/publications/living-under-drones-death-injury-and-trauma-to-civilians-from-us-drone-practices-in-pakistan/ (Accessed April 10, 2016).

Stoddard, A., Harmer, A. and Renouf, J.S. (2010) Once Removed: Lessons and Challenges in Remote Management of Humanitarian Operations for Insecure Areas. Humanitarian Outcomes. Available at: www.humanitarianoutcomes.org/sites/default/files/resources/RemoteManagementApr20101.pdf (Accessed April 10, 2016).

Swaine, J. (2013) Barack Obama "has authority to use drone strikes to kill Americans on US soil," *The Telegraph*, March 6. Available at: www.telegraph.co.uk/news/worldnews/barackobama/9913615/Barack-Obama-has-authority-to-use-drone-strikes-to-kill-Americans-on-US-soil.html (Accessed April 10, 2016).

Transport Canada (2010) Unmanned Aerial Vehicle. Available at: www.tc.gc.ca/eng/civilaviation/standards/general-recavi-brochures-uav-2270.htm (Accessed April 10, 2016).

Tucker, P. (2014) Fighting Ebola with Data, Satellites and Drones. Available at: www.defenseone.com/technology/2014/09/fighting-ebola-data-satellites-and-drones/95171/ (Accessed April 10, 2016).

Tucker-Lowe, N. (2012) RPAS and the ethical landscape of contemporary conflict. *Air Power Review*, 15 (3): 12–27.

Wang, Z., Li, M., Khaleghi, A.M., Xu, D., Lobos, A., Vo, C., Lien, J.M., Liu, J. and Son, Y.J. (2013) DDDAMS-based crowd control via UAVs and UGVs. *Procedia Computer Science*, 18: 2028–2035.

Weinberger, S. (2014) 4 Drone Sensors That Changed Warfare and What Happens When They Come Home. Popular Mechanics. Available at: www.popularmechanics.com/technology/military/planes-uavs/4-new-drone-sensors-that-changed-warfare-and-what-could-happen-when-they-come-home-9549377#slide-1 (Accessed April 10, 2016).

White, D. (2013) How Drones Can Provide Eyes in the Sky for EMS. Available at: www.ems1.com/ems-products/cameras-video/articles/1432458-How-drones-can-provide-eyes-in-the-sky-for-EMS/ (Accessed April 10, 2016).

Wisner, B. and Adams, J. (2003) Environmental health in emergencies and disasters: a practical guide. World Health Organization, 2002.

Woolgar, S. (1991) The turn to technology in social studies of science. *Science Technology Human Values*, 16 (1): 20–50.

Woolgar, S. (2012) Reconstructing Man and Machine: A note on Sociological Critiques of Cognitivism, in Bijker, W., Hughes, T.P. and Pinch, T. (eds.), *The Social Construction of Technological Systems. New Directions in the Sociology and History of Technology*. Cambridge, Massachusetts: MIT Press. 303–320.

Websites

Desert Wolf. Be Anywhere, See Everywhere. www.desert-wolf.com/dw/products/unmanned-aerial-systems/skunk-riot-control-copter.html

DIYDrones.com. Could UAVs be used to detect people with Ebola. http://diydrones.com/forum/topics/could-uavs-be-used-to-find-people-with-ebola?page=1&commentId=705844%3AComment%3A1800527&x=1#705844Comment1800527

EASA. www.easa.europa.eu/

Georgia Tech Research Institute. Case Study "Sensing Danger." http://gtri.gatech.edu/casestudy/sensing-danger

IRDAM. Meteorological Instruments. Weather and Operational Management. www.irdam.ch/2010042850/weather-sensors-security/measure-of-directional-wind-temperature-humidity-weather-sensors/mapping-of-smell-spreadings.html

Project ICARUS. Unmanned Search and Rescue. www.fp7-icarus.eu/project-overview

Sandia National Laboratories. Microsensors and Sensor Microsystems. www.sandia.gov/LabNews/LN01-24-03/key01-24-03_stories.html#sniffer; https://share.sandia.gov/news/resources/releases/2003/mat-chem/SnifferSTAR.html (Accessed 10 April 2016).

SARA. Scientific Applications & Research Associates, Incorporated. Acoustic Sensors for Unmanned Aerial Vehicles. www.sara.com/ISR/acoustic_sensing/LOSAS.html

UAViators.org. http://uaviators.org/

Index

accountability 78
"accumulation-of-events" doctrine 39n21
actor-network theory 38n12
Adey, P., Whitehead, M. and Williams, A.J. 29
AEROCEPTOR project 102
Afghanistan 112, 116
AFISMA (African-led International Support Mission in Mali) 53
agriculture, drone use in 19, 129–47; components 132; data collection 131, 138; global resource inequality 146; and normalization of drones 130, 134–8, 139, 142; "precision agriculture" 139–43
agrofuel 144
airspace see civil airspace
All Sources Information Fusion Unit see ASIFU
Alston, Philipp 35
Amoore, L. 177
analytical framework 8, 9–16, 17
Anderson, K. 36
antisocial behavior 110, 116
Arab Spring 90
Aradau, C. 30, 39n16
Argentina 145
ARGUS (autonomous real-time ground ubiquitous surveillance) 10, 11, 97
Arias Fernandez, Gil 101
Arquilla, John and Ronfeldt, David 32, 33
ASIFU (All Sources Information Fusion Unit) 50
Australia 89, 119, 158
AUVSI (Association for Unmanned Vehicle Systems International) 15, 112, 113
awareness campaign 120
Azerbaijan 57

"bad" drones 13, 14
Balkans 65, 80
Bangladesh 54
Basso, Brandon 141, 142
Becker, J. and Shane, S. 35
Berkowitz, R. 182, 183
biodiversity monitoring 153, 155–9, 160
Black, D. 171, 175
Boko Haram 82
"boomerang effect" (Foucault) 114
border surveillance 89–103; and control 97; cost of 8; and EU 18, 19; and sense of control 99–100; social sorting and triage 97–8
Bosnia 69, 135
Bosnia and Herzegovina 81, 82
Boucher, Philip 100, 101
boundary demarcation and public order 7, 110
Brazil 89, 145
Breakey, Hugh 66, 79, 80
Brennan, John 27, 32
Buckland, J. 146
Bukavu, DRC 52

C-34 committee 48
Calhoun, C. 169
Calo, R.M. 181
Cammaert, Patrick 53
Canada 117, 180
CAR (Central African Republic) 46
cargo drones 10, 79, 80, 81, 173, 174
CBFM (community-based forest monitoring) 160
Ceballos, Ana 119
Central African Republic see CAR
Chabot, D. et al. (2014) 159
Chad 47, 50
Chandler, David 30, 32

Chaotic Unmanned Personal Intercept
    Drone *see* CUPID
China 54, 89
Cho, Yeonmin 119
Choi-Fitzpatrick, A. 7
Chow, Jack 79
Chow, Rey 143
civil airspace: access to 111–13; blurring
    of boundaries 7; control of post
    9/11 11; deregulation of 8; as global
    commons 16
"civil security" 30
civilian casualties: Geneva Convention
    67, 68; mitigation by precision 26, 27,
    34–5
civilians, protection of *see* PoC
    (protection of civilians)
CLOSEYE project 102
Coll, S. 35
collateral damage *see* civilian casualties
collision warning and avoidance 118
Colombia 89, 144, 145
combat drones 33, 34–6, 37, 66, 71–2,
    73, 176
commercial sector and air space 16, 17
"Common Pre-Frontier Intelligence
    Picture" *see* CPIP
community-based forest monitoring *see*
    CBFM
complexity theory 31
connectivity 27, 29, 30–3, 36
conservation use 153–63; anti-poaching
    160; automatic object recognition 158,
    159; hacking of system 162; and illegal
    activities 162–3; local participation
    161; marine environments 158; privacy
    issues 161
constructivism 5
control hacking 162
cost-benefit advantage 8, 12
cost-effectiveness 13, 49, 95, 155
counter-insurgency 32
CPIP ("Common Pre-Frontier
    Intelligence Picture") 94, 95
Crang, Mike and Graham, Stephen 6,
    121
crashes 14, 47, 118, 119, 156
crime, cross-border 89, 93, 94, 95, 96, 99
criminal potential 120–1, 122
critical infrastructures 30, 31
critical security studies 27, 92, 169
cross-applicability, civilian and military
    143
crowd control 110, 116

Culver, Kathleen B. 116
CUPID (Chaotic Unmanned Personal
    Intercept Drone) 117, 118
cybersecurity 6, 14

Daberkow, Stan and McBride, William
    140, 141
Darfur 70
data collection: algorithmic analysis 177,
    178; and natural disasters 79; non-UN
    contractors 57; and social sorting 98;
    storage period 57
data protection 112, 180, 181; *see also*
    data collection; data protection
    Act 1998 UK; EU Data protection
    Directive
Data Protection Act 1998 UK 162
de Lint, Willem 116
De Shaw Rae, J. 182
decision-making 182–3
demining 3, 79, 80
Democratic Forces for the Liberation of
    Rwanda *see* FDLR
Democratic Republic of Congo *see* DRC
Department of Homeland Security
    Report 2015 99
deterrent effect 49, 74, 76, 77, 80, 83
deterritorialization 36
displaced people 49, 69, 73, 78, 80
Doering, C. 144
Dorn, W.A. 59n7
double-tap strikes 13
DRC (Democratic Republic of Congo)
    17, 45–9, 51–6, 58, 75
"drone antisociality" 14
drone utopianism 6, 20n4
drone warfare: characteristics 13, 14;
    politico-military rationale 6, 7
drones, use of term 3, 15, 16
Duffield, Mark 8, 9, 74, 81
Dufresne, B. 15, 16

ECtHR (European Court of Human
    Rights) 94, 95
Ecuador 89
effectiveness 12
efficiency 8, 12
emergency management 20, 168–86; and
    the body 184–5; and data collection
    176, 177–8; and reasoning 182–3;
    regulatory discourse 179, 180–2
Emmerson, Ben 27
Eng, P.C. et al. (2009) 182
Ernst, Cornelia 102

EU (European Union) 89–103; and
access-to-airspace 109, 110, 111;
border control 18, 19, 89, 92, 93;
intelligence surveillance 94; maritime
borders 94; public order 121, 122
see also EUROSUR; Mare Nostrum
operation
EU Data protection Directive 98
EUFOR 47
European Charter of Fundamental
Rights 181
European Commission, civil drone use
regulation 180
European Court of Human Rights *see*
ECtHR
European Union *see* EU
EUROSUR (European Border
Surveillance System) 90, 91, 92, 93,
101, 102
explosive remnants 80

FAA (Federal Aviation Administration)
112, 119, 120, 132, 133, 180
Falco drones 48
Faria, Viviane 131–2
fatalities in employment, avoidance of
12
FDC (Fox Drone Catcher) 121
FDLR (Democratic Forces for the
Liberation of Rwanda) 53
Federal Aviation Administration *see* FAA
Federal Republic of Yugoslavia 81, 82
Ferguson, J. 9
Ferris, E.G. 84
Finn, R.L. et al. (2013) 181
first responders 13, 115, 170
force, threshold of use 13
Foucault, Michel 28, 31, 141
Fox, E. 145
Fox Drone Catcher *see* FDC
France 54, 137
French National Research Agency 120,
121
Friedenzohn, Daniel and Mirot,
Alexander 112
Frontex 89, 93, 94, 95, 96, 102

Galloway, A.R. and Thacker, E. 33
Gberie, L. 53
Geneva Convention 1949 26, 67, 98
Genocide Intervention Network 26, 76
"geofencing" 16
georobotics 137
Germany 180, 181

Getzin, S. et al. (2012) 159
Global Hawk drones 70, 130, 170
global north 143, 170
global regulatory system 9
global south 147, 170, 180
Gnat drones 69, 130
Gogarty, B. and Hagger, M. 179, 180,
187n2
Goglia, John 133
Goma 49
"good" drones, characteristics of 9,
10–11
Graham, Steve 113, 114, 117
Greece: migration safety 90; public order
use 116; "push-back operations" 95;
selling of public land 144
Gregory, D. 9
Gulf War 135
Gunneflo, Markus 32, 39n23

hacking 120, 121, 162
Hadjimichalis, Costis 144
Haiti earthquake 79
HALE (high altitude long endurance)
drones 70
Hamas 70
handheld microdrones 70, 109
Harvey, David 144
Harwood, M. 32
Hayes, B., Jones, C. and Töpfer, E. 93,
96, 121
Hayes, B. and Vermeulen, M. 93
HCG (Hellenic Coast Guard) 97
Heidegger, Martin 143
helicopters 47, 48, 49, 59n7, 115, 154
Hellfire missiles 4, 15
Henn, S. 142
Heron drones 70
Herwitz, S.R. et al. (2004) 137
high altitude long endurance drones *see*
HALE drones
Hildyard, N. et al. (2012) 144
Hirsi Jamaa and others v Italy 2012 94
hobbyist drones 10, 14, 15, 16, 110, 118,
119–20
human–human relationships 186
human rights violations, documentation
of 26
humanitarian PoC 12, 20, 66, 78–82, 83

ICC (International Criminal Court) 74,
76
ICRC (International Committee of the
Red Cross) 26, 68

IHL (international humanitarian law) 11, 26, 67, 69, 70, 72, 78
India 54, 89
institutional power 5
insurance 13, 120
intelligence, pre-frontier 100
intelligence, surveillance and reconnaissance *see* ISR
intelligence, Western control of 57
International Civil Aviation Organization 16
International Committee of the Red Cross *see* ICRC
International Criminal Court *see* ICC
international humanitarian law *see* IHL
IOM (International Organization for Migration) 89
IPI (International Peace Institute) 95
Isaacs, Gerald 136
ISR (intelligence, surveillance and reconnaissance) 69–70, 71, 72
Israel 4, 70, 89, 145
Italy 89, 94, 95, 114, 115 *see also* Mare Nostrum operation
Ito, Nobutaka 136
Ituri 52

Japan 4, 135, 136, 137
Joachim, Jutta and Schneiker, Andrea 65
Joronen, Mikko 142
Jünger, Ernst, *The Glass Bees* 183

Kahn, P.W. 35
Karlsrud, J. and Rosén, F. 74
Kawamura, Noburu 136
Kawamura, Noburu and Namikawa, Kiyoshi 135, 136
Kennedy, C. and Rogers, J. 75, 77, 78, 82, 84
Kenya 89, 158
kill lists 13
Kisangani massacre 52
Koh, Harald 9
Koski, W.R. et al. (2009) 158
Kosovo 135
Kreps, S. and Kaag, J. 72

Ladsous, Hervé 45, 48, 53, 57
Laitinen, Ilka 95, 100
Lake Kivu, DRC 56
Lampedusa 90
land-cover classifications 159
land grabs 143, 144–6, 147
Landolt, Gilbert 130

Latour, Bruno 38n12
Law, John and Urry, John 38n11
Lazzarato, M. 141
legality 13, 27, 29, 36
legitimacy 13, 27, 33, 36, 69, 78, 109
Lemberg-Pedersen, M. 93
lethal miniature aerial munitions system *see* LMAMS 10
Libya 68, 81, 82, 94, 95
licensing 132, 180
Lie, Jon Harald Sande 65
LMAMS (lethal miniature aerial munitions system) 10
long-endurance platforms 10, 11
Lösing, Sabine 102

Maire, F. et al. (2013) 158
MALE (medium altitude and long endurance) drones 69, 70, 96, 122n3
Mali 17, 45–6, 50, 53, 56, 75
Mare Nostrum operation 89, 90, 95, 100, 101, 102, 103
marketing 111
Maroni, Roberto 90
matter and materiality 28, 29, 30
Matternet 79
Maurer, Peter 26, 27, 37n5
McBratney, A. et al. (2005) 140
McClure, W.F. 136, 137, 139
McMurry, Andrew 146
media: and first responder use 115; and land acquisition 146; and new information 3; and potential 138; social media 31; and UN use of drones 51; use in agriculture 132, 133; use in law enforcement 113; use of terms 15
Médecins Sans Frontières *see* MSF
Mediterranean Sea 89, 90
medium altitude and long endurance drones *see* MALE drones
Mégret, Frederic 69
Mendel, J. 33
Mexico 99
Migrant Offshore Aid Station *see* MOAS
migration: safety 89, 90; deaths 90 *see also* Mare Nostrum operation; SAR (search and rescue)
miniaturization 10
MINURCAT 47
MINUSCA 46
MINUSMA 17, 45–6, 49, 50, 53, 54, 55, 59
MOAS (Migrant Offshore Aid Station) 90

Modernization and Reform Act 2012
FAA 112
"modular" drones 135
Monahan, T. and Mokos, J.T. 6, 121
MONUC 47, 52
MONUSCO 17, 45–6, 47, 48–50, 52,
53–9, 66
MSF (Médecins Sans Frontières) 79, 90
Mueller, M. 6
Muenkler, Herfried 33, 34
Mulero-Pázmány, M. et al. (2013) 158
Mulero-Pázmány, M. et al. (2014) 158, 160
multispectral images 131

nanodrones 122n3
NASA (National Aeronautics and Space
Administration) 137
National Oceanic and Atmospheric
Administration *see* NOAA
NATO Research and Technology
Organization 134
natural disasters, and humanitarian PoC
78, 79, 115, 170, 171, 180
near misses 119
neoliberalism 12, 93, 141
network centric warfare 28
Neyroud, P. and Vassilas, P. 99
Nicas, J. 100
Nielsen, N. 102
Nigeria 82
9/11 terrorist attacks 11, 16, 36, 133
Nkunda, Laurent 52
NOAA (National Oceanic and
Atmospheric Administration) 159
non-refoulement of refugees 94, 98
normalization 113, 118, 130, 134–8, 139,
142
Northern Ireland 116

Obama, Barack 37, 81
OCHA (Office for the Coordination of
Humanitarian Affairs): Aide Memoire
68, 73; and emergency drone use 182;
To Stay and Deliver 81
O'Grady, Nathaniel 31
Omeje, K. 144
Operation Barkhane 50, 53
Opération Serval 49

Pakistan 39n19, 54, 112
Pandolfi, M. 9
Papua New Guinea 79
Paris 14, 120
Pathfinder Plus drone 137

peace enforcement, UN 45, 53, 58, 77–8
peacekeeping, UN 17, 18, 45–59,
73–8; economic concerns 51; and
humanitarian sector 55–6, 57;
member states division on 53, 54–5;
poor technology 50; and surveillance
concerns 50, 51; as unarmed 51
PED (processing, exploitation, and
dissemination) cells 11
Pennic, F. 179
PERSEUS project 97
personal jammers 16
personality strikes 36
Petraeus, David and Mattis, James 32
PoC (protection of civilians) 65–84;
combatant PoC 69–72, 73, 83; concept
of 67, 68; definition of 68; and
international humanitarian law 67;
and interventionism 84; in military
planning 70; in peacekeeping PoC 47,
73–8, 83 *see also* humanitarian PoC
police use 46, 89, 102, 111, 113–19,
121, 170, 173; paramilitarization of
policing 114–15
politics of the possible 12, 13
precision *see* target precision
Predator drones: agricultural use 130;
dual use 37n4; and Hellfire missiles
4, 15; as image 11; and policing 114,
115, 116; "Predator Empire" 129; and
surveillance 96, 99
preparedness 12, 29, 30, 37
Price, Kevin 133
Prigg, M. 184
processing, exploitation, and
dissemination cells *see* PED
proportionality 26, 34, 35, 70, 71, 72
protections against misuse, built-in 12
PSCs (private security companies) 93
public attitude 101, 111, 112
public order use 109–22; criminology
and surveillance studies 110; and
disadvantaged groups 117; and
disciplinary effect 109; in emergencies
13; non-lethal agents 117, 118; and
weaponization 116–18; zonal banning
117
Pugliese, J. 36
push-back operations 94, 102

Qube 115

Rajkovic, N.M. 29
Reaper drones 13, 50, 53, 115, 116

reconnaissance 4, 47, 69, 70, 83, 135, 138
  see also ISR (intelligence, surveillance
  and reconnaissance)
refugees, protection of 47, 78, 94, 95,
  98, 100
registration, proposed 16
Remotely Piloted Aircraft Systems
  (RPAS) *see* drones
Remotely Piloted Airplane (RPA) *see*
  drones
remoteness 4
renaming and public acceptance 112
resilience 29, 30–2, 37
"Responsibility to Protect", NATO *see*
  RtoP
Rieland, Randy 115
risk and security management 81
Ronell, Avital 142
Rosén, F. 70
RPAs (Remotely Piloted Airplanes) *see*
  drones
RPAS (Remotely Piloted Aircraft
  Systems) *see* drones
RPVs (remotely piloted vehicles) *see*
  drones
RtoP ("Responsibility to Protect"),
  NATO 68, 81, 82, 84n3
Runge, C.F. et al. (1990) 139, 140
Russia 54, 76
Rwanda 54, 65
Ryan, Missy 13

safe landing systems 118
Safety of Life at Sea Conventions *see*
  SOLAS
Sandvik, K.B. et al. (2014) 81
SAR (search and rescue) 12, 79, 90–1,
  100–2, 170, 177, 179, 185
satellites 69, 90, 94, 96, 99, 156, 159, 160
Sauer, F. and Schörnig, N. 27
Schengen area 92
Sea Shepherd charity 160
search and rescue *see* SAR
securitization 5, 6, 27, 28–9, 30–2,
  120–1, 122
Seiffarth, O. 94
Selex 48, 51, 57
self-defence principle 36
ShadowHawk drones 113, 117
Shaw, D. 171, 174
signature strikes 13, 27, 28, 36, 37, 71, 72
Skunk Riot Control Copter 118
Sloterdijk, Peter 139, 142
"smart bombs" 34

Smith, D. 118
Sniderman, Andrew and Hanis, Mark
  26, 76
social body, protection of 28, 31
Sofaer, Abraham 39n23
SOLAS (Safety of Life at Sea
  Conventions) 102
South Africa 118, 160, 162–3
South Korea 135
South Sudan 75, 76
sovereignty 36, 51, 57
Spain, Guardia Civil 90
spying 14
Sudan 70
Sumatra 155, 159, 160
SUNNY project 102
surgical strikes 32, 66, 71
surveillance drones: capabilities 97;
  cost-efficiency 95, 96; deterrent effect
  74; documentation of atrocities and
  war crimes 73, 74; information to
  humanitarian organisations 80, 81;
  local reaction to 55; maritime 91,
  92, 94, 99–102; as most used 69; and
  neutral evidence 76; new uses for 96;
  and peacekeeping 73; replacement of
  staff 80; sorting, control and order
  97–100; UN peacekeeping 17, 45–59;
  used to attack civilians supporting
  enemy 70; wide-area surveillance 11
Syria 70, 76, 90
Szantoi, Z. et al. (in review) 159

Tams, Christian 39n21
targeted killing 26–37; legitimacy of 27,
  34, 36; and peace enforcement 77–8
targets: discrimination of 34, 35;
  identification of 70; precision 12, 26,
  27, 29, 32, 33, 34–5, 71–2, 73; selection
  of 69
TCCs (troop contributing countries) 58,
  59
technological determinism 5
technological fantasies 5, 6, 121
technological optimism 5, 6
terrorism: and changing warfare 8, 9;
  maritime surveillance 99; networks
  27, 29, 32–4, 36; potential 120–1, 122;
  transnationality of 33
Tesar, Delbert 137
Thacker, E. 31
thermal imaging, airborne 79
time lapsed images 131
transparency 57

triage in emergency management 185
Triton operation 101
troop contributing countries *see* TCCs
Tucker- Lowe, N. 183
Typhoon Hayan 79

UAVs (Unarmed Aerial Vehicles) *see* drones
UK (United Kingdom) 50, 51, 54, 116, 117
Ukraine 14
UN Convention on the Law of the Sea 102
UN Convention Relating to the Status of Refugees 1951 94, 98
UN FIB (Force Intervention Brigade) 3, 17, 45, 52, 53, 55, 58
UN Humanitarian Country Team 55
UN Security Council mandates 17, 47, 48, 54
unmanned airplanes, historical 4
UNMISS mission South Sudan 75, 76
US (United States): access-to-airspace 109, 110, 111; agricultural drones 136, 137; army 4; border surveillance 89, 99, 100; civil drone regulation 180; exports of drones 72, 73; hobbyist drones 119; pioneer of drone warfare 50, 51; and policing 114, 115; surveillance and criminal activity law 162; war on drugs 99
US Customs and Border Protection (CBP) 96
US Department of Homeland Security 114
US Federal Aviation Administration 12
USDA Forest Service 159
utopianism 12

van Blyenburgh, Peter 134, 135, 138, 142
video collection ability 10
Vietnam War 4

Wall, T. and Monahan, T. 99
Walters, W. 38n13
war crimes, evidence of 57, 74
"War on Terror" 8, 9, 11, 66, 69, 77, 78, 82, 114
Waterfield, Bruno 121, 122
weather warnings 172
Weber, Samuel 34
Weissensteiner, M.H. et al. (2015) 157
Whetham, David 76, 80
White, B. et al. (2012) 144
White House, amateur drone crash 14, 120
Whittle, R. 15
wildlife protection 19, 20
Willis, A. 145
World Food Program 79
WWF (World Wildlife Fund) 160

Yemen 112
Yom Kippur War 148n6

Zehfuss, Maja 34
Zhang, C. and Kovacs, J.M. 134